FROM
GAS
STREET
TO THE
GANGES

FROM GAS STREET TO THE GANGES

EXPLORING BIRMINGHAM'S HISTORICAL LINKS WITH THE COMMONWEALTH

SIMON WILCOX

For Fiona

First published 2021

The History Press
97 St George's Place,
Cheltenham,
Gloucestershire,
GL50 3QB
www.thehistorypress.co.uk

British Library Cataloguing in Publication Data.
A catalogue record for this book is available from the British Library.

ISBN 978 0 7509 9334 0

Typesetting and origination by Typo•glyphix, Burton-on-Trent
Printed and bound by TJ Books Limited, Padstow, Cornwall

ABOUT THE AUTHOR

After growing up in Birmingham in the 1960s and '70s, Simon Wilcox graduated from the University of Liverpool with a BA Honours in Modern History. Afterwards, he moved down to London and worked as a journalist on magazines and newspapers before moving to the business pages of a national newspaper in Singapore. On returning to Britain he worked as a reporter for BBC local radio and as a website editor for an NGO in London. More recently, he has written a travel book, *Mudlark River* – the story of a trip he made along the River Thames in 2013.

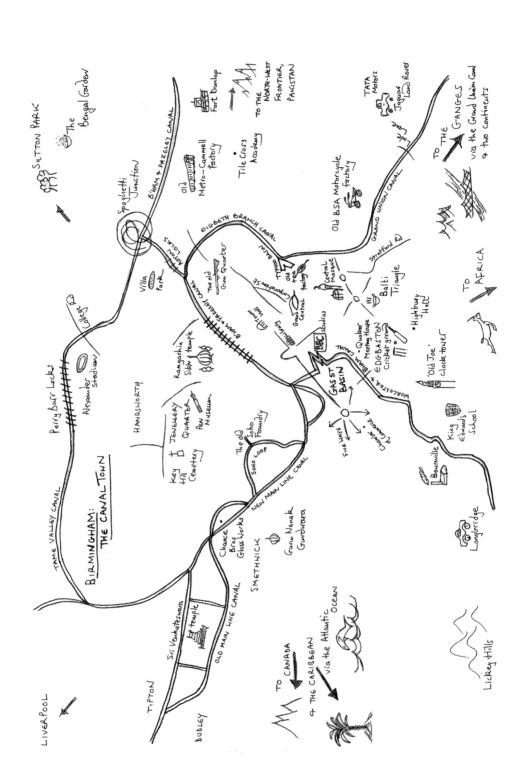

CONTENTS

PREAMBLE: CANAL TOWN

Funnily enough, I had always wanted to go back to Birmingham. Often derided as a city of dreary post-war ring roads and industrial warehouses, not to mention a strange local accent, the city had often been dismissed by the many who had never visited it as an ugly sort of place. Yet it was the place where I was born, and where I grew up. It had just been a matter of time really before I returned.

So, in the dying embers of 2017, the week before Christmas to be more precise, I caught a train to New Street Station to have a look around again. It was the first of a couple of days wandering around town, ambling here and there, for old times' sake.

An escalator took me up from the platform and into Birmingham's iconic Grand Central shopping centre. Opened to great fanfare in 2015, I had never seen it before; and now here I was, looking up at a vaulted glass ceiling held up by swooping columns of white steelwork. All around the concourse were hundreds of shoppers. Young Muslim women from Sparkbrook chatting together in Punjabi; men of Jamaican descent from Sutton Coldfield whose grandparents had been part of the Windrush generation; an elderly Chinese couple who had arrived from Hong Kong fifty years ago emerging from John Lewis: just a small microcosm of a modern multicultural city where many communities have made their home.

Asians and Caribbeans from the Commonwealth, formerly the British Empire, started arriving in the city in the 1950s to work in the metalworking factories and put cars together in the boom years of the Midlands automobile industry. The Chinese community began to emerge during the First World War, the Welsh in the inter-war years; while Irish, Italian and Jewish families can trace their origins in the city further back still.[1]

The one thing that the city could always offer these émigrés was work. No trip to Birmingham, it has to be said, can be undertaken without taking account of its commercial heritage. After leaving Grand Central, therefore, I headed off to where it all began – the Jewellery Quarter in Hockley, where goldsmiths and silversmiths have been plying their trade for more than 200 years.

These craftspeople began to congregate in small workshops in this area just north of the city centre from 1760 onwards. Birmingham had always made small metal trinkets such as buckles and buttons. From there it was a short hop into precious metalworking.

In fact, slit it, roll it; whatever you could do with a sheet of metal by the eighteenth century, Birmingham did it. Foundries were sprouting up all over the city. Most famous of all was the Soho factory in Handsworth, which was the world's first purpose-built factory for making metal goods when it was set up in 1762 by industrialist Matthew Boulton. Over the next few decades, all manner of carriage fittings, candlesticks and teapot spouts clattered out of its doors.

To go back to precious metalworking, though, if there was one particular craft that would write the city into the history books over the nineteenth century it was pen-making. In 1790 local entrepreneur Samuel Harrison came up with a handmade steel writing tool. By the 1830s, a number of pen manufacturers had moved into Hockley, among them Hinks, Wells & Co. and Brandauer. At its height, three-quarters of everything written down in the world was written with a Birmingham pen.[2]

This calligraphic alchemy was conjured up in typical red-brick buildings such as the Albert Works on Frederick Street, which is now home to the Pen Museum. A red door underneath an archway of alternating blue and terracotta brick invited me in on a cold December day, and ushered me into a long, dark workshop illuminated half-heartedly by a row of arched windows.

In the fragile light, I could make out several glass display cases. They were filled with pens of all shapes and sizes – gold ones, wooden ones, even glass ones. Either side of them, and in between them, were clusters of notebooks, diaries, almanacs, all illustrating in one way or another the pens' handiwork.

At the far end of the room, meanwhile, there was a willowy man sitting at a desk filled with old stamping presses and ink stands, inspecting nibs. He would take one out of a tin box, inspect it with a magnifying glass and then, after being satisfied by something or other, he would place it in another box. He seemed deep in his work. He looked up and smiled as I came in, but thereafter barely seemed to notice me.

As soon as I stepped out of the workshop and into the adjoining gift shop, however, he was there behind the counter. We got talking. He had been working at the Pen Museum for nine years, along with other volunteers. He loved it.

'It's like being part of one big happy family, all of us,' he said in that syrupy Brummie accent I knew so well, slightly curdled at the edges, yet still bubbling up into melodic high points as he told me his life story.

It told me about something else too, I realised as I stood listening to him.

Glutinous and treacly, his accent spoke to me about my roots, my childhood and the great commercial city where I grew up.

◦◦

But how did Birmingham make the step from a handful of workshops making trinkets to being a fledgling industrial powerhouse? The answer lay in my next destination.

My route now took me past the duck-egg blue of the Ramgarhia Sikh Temple and down Newhall Street towards Birmingham city centre. Christmas lights were flickering into life on a few buildings; the African-Caribbean pupils of the City Academy were spilling out onto the street; and a group of men were smoking on the pavement underneath the ruddy chimney stacks of the Queen's Arms.

Where the street dips down before rising again for its final ascent into the centre, there was a plaque commemorating the Elkington Works, where the process of electroplating on a large scale was pioneered. However, it was the sight next door to it that I had come to see. A stepladder of lock gates leading uphill towards Gas Street Basin – a key feature of the Birmingham and Fazeley Canal, built in 1789.

Canals – or 'cuts' as they were known locally – drove the early days of Birmingham's industrial expansion, as a small band of Midland visionaries embraced the new mode of transport. Matthew Boulton, along with pottery manufacturer Josiah Wedgwood and others such as doctor and poet Erasmus Darwin, all played a part in setting up the new inland waterways, while engineer James Watt built the steam contraptions that would line their banks.

It was a diverse group of men, but they were all good friends, all members of a famous club. Every so often, on or near the night of a full moon to be precise, they used to meet at each other's houses to drink and laugh and swap ideas. In short, they were the self-proclaimed 'Lunaticks' and 'conjurers' of the Lunar Society of Birmingham. And whether or not the strange forces of the moon ever had a hand in what they did next, one thing is certain: between them they set in motion the wheels of Britain's Industrial Revolution.[3]

Insofar as coal and steam were the main drivers of that revolution, then the partnership between Boulton and Watt was pivotal. Restless entrepreneur as he was, Boulton encouraged the young Scottish engineer in 1774 to move down to the Midlands and develop the experimental steam engine he had patented north of the border. Within a few years, there were Watt engines at work in local blast furnaces, on the canals and at Boulton's Soho factory.

But other Lunaticks were hard at work too – Josiah Wedgewood calculating the ideal furnace temperature for firing clays and glazes, James Keir building a pioneering chemical works in Tipton in the Black Country, and Joseph Priestley discovering the chemical element of oxygen.[4]

And making it all possible were the canals. With the unveiling of a small stretch of canal linking the Black Country coalfields to Paradise Street in 1769, a local poet called John Freeth wrote an ode called 'Inland Navigation' on how it would open up a world of trade.

'From the Tagus to the Ganges', should the demand for a variety of goods arise, 'in what kingdom, on what shore, lies the place that can supply?' he asked.[5]

The answer was, of course, Birmingham.

Nor was his gushing optimism, in the long run, unfounded. The barges started shuffling into the sooty wharves of Birmingham laden with rough metals from the Pennines and elsewhere: and here in the smoke-belching factories that nestled up against the jetties these raw materials would be turned into something else: brass fittings, perhaps, or buttons or guns. Soon, Birmingham was being called the 'city of a thousand trades'.

The trend continued with the coming of the railways. By that time, Birmingham companies were exporting all over the world. Osler chandeliers glittered in Indian palaces; Metro Cammell railway carriages slipped out of the Saltley works near the Grand Union Canal on their way to Jamaica; Cadbury's began to send chocolate bars to Australia.

And even though the canals were steadily eclipsed by the railways as a way of transporting goods, they still had a significant role to play. For a while, the canal network linking London and other English ports with Birmingham was the network taking a weekly shipment of tea chests from Sri Lanka to the Bordesley Street depot of Typhoo.

The Gas Street Basin lies at the heart of a canal network that in the late eighteenth and early nineteenth centuries opened up a world of trade for Birmingham. (Photograph by Madrugada Verde, Shutterstock.com)

However much the railways were gaining the upper hand, the canals weaving around Birmingham – from the Bird's custard factory in Digbeth to the Edwardian gables of Bournville Village – still lay at the heart of a manufacturing powerhouse extending its reach across the globe.

At the centre of this network was Gas Street Basin. In the icy stranglehold of a midwinter's day, this was where I was heading next. The path alongside the stepladder of locks was pointing the way.

It was dark when I arrived at the Basin. Strings of lights belonging to barges moored up alongside the bankside shone out in the night, tethered securely, and yet also floating in an incandescence of soft illumination, mixing with lamps on the crumbling warehouse walls on the opposite side of the water, jostling with the bright smudge of Broad Street up on the bridge.

Two hundred years ago, this whole area would have been slung with chains and cables, and clanking with the noise of cargoes being loaded and unloaded at the wharves. I could just make out the shape of one of these old warehouses in the darkness. Up there on the jetty, there would have been a strong reek of smoke and slime, and also perhaps an earthy hint of tea.

And was there a whiff of sadness about the long lost years of my youth in the air? I couldn't tell. Strolling on, I spotted a gap in the brick wall next to the canal path. A few moments later, I was up on Gas Street.

⸿

If you know a little bit about the history of Birmingham, then to visit its city centre without encountering a sense of Joseph Chamberlain would be like visiting Stratford-upon-Avon without realising that William Shakespeare had anything to do with the place.

This charismatic businessman became mayor of the town in 1873, determined to carry out the late Victorian gospel of civic duty: the idea that through grand municipal works you could improve the lot of the people, and build 'a new Jerusalem' on earth. Once in office, he immediately set about taking back control of the local gas and water supplies from private firms. The results were dramatic, with thousands of new street lamps being erected in a few years. Moreover, large profits had now been released for the local authority to plough into slum clearance in the central districts. This last scheme also involved the building of a 'great street' up to Old Square.

Corporation Street, or 'Rue Chamberlain', as the Birmingham politician's detractors dubbed it, was my first port of call on my second day walking around Birmingham. Despite the fact that some of the properties had been destroyed in the German bombings of the Second World War, most of the sturdy Victorian buildings were still there, as gabled, gilded and confident as any Paris boulevard.

'High Victorian Birmingham really did bear some resemblance to a promised land, a holy city,' wrote local historian Victor Skipp and this was the thing,[6] I suppose, about the Midlands city in the nineteenth century: it really did exemplify the Protestant doctrine of 'Progress'. It was no coincidence that it was in this era when the city adopted a new motto for its coat of arms that said it all. The motto was: 'Forward'.

And forward Birmingham went.

Everything went forward, as a matter of fact. Soon the car factory at Longbridge was launching the four-seater Austin Seven; and then the war came along and the Luftwaffe were dropping bombs in the black night, and my mother was picking her way to King Edward's School for Girls between the uprooted tramlines.

Afterwards, city engineer Herbert Manzoni was rebuilding the flattened Victorian metropolis as a city of high rise and ring road; and Abdul Aziz was

⸿

opening up Birmingham's first curry house, the Darjeeling, on Steelhouse Lane.

Around the same time, my father arrived in town as the industrial correspondent of the *Birmingham Gazette*. He didn't know it yet, but before long he would be meeting my mother at the local Liberal Club, and in a year or so they would be married. A first child would come along, a girl; and then a second, a boy.

And then, in 1973, the boy was sitting with his father in a shadowy cove of crushed burgundy wallpaper and piped Raga music. It was a new restaurant up the road called the Bengal Garden. Barely 11 years old, it was the first Indian restaurant the boy had ever been to. There he was, at a table lit up only by candlelight and a pervasive sense of mystery, with his father, who always smelt of pipe smoke and Pears soap, wondering what was going to happen next.

What happened next was a rickety food trolley laden with large crisp wafers they called papadums and various silver dishes of chicken and mutton marinated in brown pungent gravy. Whatever Bengal was, the boy was instantly smitten.

'What is Bengal?' I finally asked my father.

'It's a place,' he said. 'It's where the River Ganges flows into the sea.'

◈

However, things weren't going well for Birmingham in the 1970s. By now, it was showing all the signs of a city that had fallen on hard times. There were the dwindling fortunes of its bellwether car industry, there were the bitter industrial disputes, there was the football hooliganism.

As I walked on now, taking a circular route off Corporation Street, up Bull Street and onto Colmore Row, I recollected those times. I remembered cowering in the corner of the bus station as opposing groups of football fans, some carrying knives, clashed on its concourse. I saw a boy fall to the ground.

I remembered being tugged by my mother around the dismal Bull Ring Shopping Centre, with its thin veneer of 1960s sparkle, and I recalled my fears about being out in town after that November night in 1974 when IRA bombs killed twenty-one people in two city centre pubs.

By this time, too, my father was retreating into poor health, and retreating further still into his memories of being in the RAF in Ghana during the war. He had a large album of all the photographs he took there. It was wedged inside a wooden bookcase next to all my mother's books. A compilation of essays by Francis Bacon, *A Passage to India*, *Rebecca* – she always loved reading.

Things weren't right. I just wanted to leave. Had I been born in another age, I suppose, I might have felt differently; but, for me, Birmingham was never the promised land, still less a holy city. For me, as young person with a typical yearning for adventure, it was just a sweep of dreary ring roads and industrial units, not to mention the strange local accent – all piled up on a bleak plateau in the Midlands.

In contrast, I craved jumbles of irregularity: jagged rooftops and narrow alleyways; white Regency porticos and cafes open all night; and a big rolling brown river. After an interlude at Liverpool University studying and then graduating in Modern History, there was only one answer: London.

Later on, after years of working in London in editorial jobs, I took to travel and kept a diary, following the advice laid down in Francis Bacon's essay, *Of Travel*. Go searching for 'havens and harbours, antiquities and ruins',[7] the Renaissance writer, statesman and philosopher had urged, and this is, more or less, what I did. What followed, in fact, was years of intermittent working and travelling in Asia, taking it all in.

I ate cuttlefish curry in Singapore when I was working there as a journalist on its main daily newspaper, saw the last vestiges of evening sunlight on the Jama Masjid mosque in Delhi while travelling around northern India, and caught a train weaving its way through deep gorges and high tunnels up to the tea plantations of Sri Lanka. Eventually, I even went to Bengal and found its garden: legions of fluttering palm trees spilling out of Kolkata and down to the Ganges delta.

As far as I was concerned, that was that. I had drawn a line around it. Birmingham was a distant memory.

෬෯

But now I was back home. Near the end of my second day tramping around, I found myself in Chamberlain Square, just outside the museum and art gallery, famous for its paintings of the Pre-Raphaelite Brotherhood, and one of their leading lights, Edward Burne-Jones, who had always been my mother's favourite artist.

The city was in a Christmas mood. The annual German market was in town, and I could hear the sounds of it nearby: the fizzle and spit of sausages on hot grills, the discordant notes of a barrel organ, the chatter and laughter of people in a beer tent. Although an amber winter sun was already hanging low, the square was alive with noise and smells.

Bars in the city centre would be starting to fill up now; and across town, the central mosque would be preparing for evening prayer, a band might be rehearsing in a basement somewhere in downtown Handsworth, and the Balti curry houses on Stoney Lane and Ladypool Road would be opening up their doors to their first customers of the night. Birmingham was a town where South Asian and Caribbean energies – Commonwealth energies, you could say – mingled actively with those once seen as traditionally from the Midlands.

This was also still Joseph Chamberlain's town. It still thought big. It was a place of constant reinvention. In the 1990s, it had broken the stranglehold of the inner ring road and thrown a pedestrian bridge over Paradise Circus to Centenary Square, where it would build a new Symphony Hall for the city's increasingly famous orchestra under the conductorship of Simon Rattle. It had also revamped the canal network and the Jewellery Quarter, and a little later on, for good measure, built a new library that looked like a collection of party hat boxes stacked up on top of one another.

In the past month, furthermore, the council had been targeting Asian investors at an international property summit. The pitch was that Birmingham was a dynamic proposition: not least because of its youthful population.[8]

Like the canals that once opened up so many rivulets of global trade, Birmingham was reaching out again. Moving forward.

And the city was about to make another giant leap. Down the road from Chamberlain Square, in New Street, I bought a *Birmingham Mail.* The front page 'splash story' was a tragic one about a local taxi driver who had died in a road accident in the city centre.[9] Such was the poignancy of the story and the photographs of the father of six that it was difficult to take notice of anything else. Nevertheless, if you looked closely enough, there it was in tiny letters above the masthead, telling us that the newspaper was an official backer of the bid.

The news came through a couple of days later. It was confirmed. Birmingham would be hosting the 2022 Commonwealth Games.

☙

There was one more place I wanted to visit. Why I should really want to return was anyone's guess, but as I turned into Gate Lane in Birmingham's north-easterly suburb of Sutton Coldfield and saw the warm glow of its lamps peering out behind its louvred blinds, I felt glad that I had. Moments later, I had stepped over the threshold, and into the crushed burgundy of the Bengal Garden.

The restaurant hadn't changed all that much. The wallpaper wasn't quite so crushed, so flock, as it had been in the 1970s, and the piped music was more Lionel Ritchie than Raga; but beyond that there was still that pervasive sense of Oriental mystery, and in the accents of the families and couples sitting at nearby tables a prevailing sense of familiarity.

I was here. I had returned home. This was a phenomenon that had exercised poets throughout the centuries – from Homer right through to T.S. Eliot. In *Four Quartets*, Eliot had written that at the end of all life's wanderings we would arrive where we began and 'know the place for the first time'.[10] And I must admit that I had half an idea that by returning home, I would shed some light on my memories of it.

Frankly, though, I wasn't sure that I really had.

But in the Bengal Garden's flickering light, there was something. In fact, the more the warm spices of my curry – the turmeric, the cumin, the garam masala – took hold, the more a new realisation began to spring into existence: the realisation that however hard I had tried, I had never really escaped Birmingham. It had always been there with me.

First and foremost, there was the influence of my parents: it was my mother's bookcase that first got me reading, got me into novels and poetry and histories; and it was my father's scrapbook of newspaper cuttings that he often showed to me that pushed me towards a career in journalism when I went down to London.

In addition, there was the influence of the city itself. This was where people of varying faiths from all over the Commonwealth and the world – Hindu, Sikh, Muslim, Christian, Buddhist – had made their home, their communities taking root in places like Handsworth and Sparkhill. This was where my love of curry was born, and my curiosity awoken. Many years later, I went travelling and working overseas, finding gurdwaras and mosques, different ways of life and different manners, and, incidentally, some very good curry. I even made it to Bengal.

This was it. Like the moon that had held a strange fascination for the men of the Lunar Society in the eighteenth century, so too had Birmingham held sway over my life. Like the moon that pushes a tide up the beach.

In the late eighteenth century, members of the Lunar Society of Birmingham used to meet on nights of a full moon to drink and laugh and swap ideas. (Illustration from *Les Marveilles de la Science* published 1870, Alamy Stock Photo)

At the same time, the city had continued to change. It had come a long way from the rain-spattered desolation of my youth, and since then more new settlers had arrived, making the city more diverse, and more global than ever. Now it was going to stage the Commonwealth Games.

And in that very fact, I could feel Birmingham beginning to wield its influence again as I sat in the cosy environs of the Bengal Garden. As one of the waiters arrived to clear my dishes, the picture was becoming clearer. The city was about to send me on another journey. I could sense it.

Not to London this time, though, or even to Bengal; but into libraries and dusty archive rooms to find out more about my home town's links with the Commonwealth – past and present. During the city's bid for the Games, some statistics had been quoted by a local newspaper. One in ten people in the city had been born in an overseas Commonwealth country, and many more had family in member nations such as India, Jamaica, Pakistan, Australia, Canada and Nigeria.[11] With those sort of numbers, I knew the connections had to be strong.

The simple fact was that I wanted to know. Given that Birmingham was going to host teams from seventy-one Commonwealth countries and overseas territories at a major sporting event, how far did its connections with these places go back?[12] How deep were its relationships with places like Pakistan, India or Jamaica, given that many residents of Birmingham can trace their roots back to these places?

Furthermore, what was the nature of Birmingham's dealings with the Commonwealth? With the growth of Birmingham as an industrial powerhouse in the eighteenth and nineteenth centuries, dealings early on were clearly all about trade; but did they span out in subsequent years into something more, spilling out perhaps into the political and cultural spheres?

And perhaps most important of all, what were the individual stories behind these networks? Who went where, when, and why? What were the impressions of John Sumner, the founder of Typhoo Tea, when he first travelled to Ceylon in 1909 to speak to tea growers? By the same token, what were the experiences of Jamaicans arriving in Birmingham in the 1950s to seek work in the booming car town?

The more I thought about it, the more I wanted to know.

'Would you like a coffee, sir?' the waiter was asking.

I said I would. Then I sat back in my chair, and peered through one of the restaurant windows at the night sky outside: dark, but illuminated in part by a full moon.

The moon was there. It was in place. It was just a matter of time now for the city of my youth to cast its spell once more.

But like a wave in the moonlight, approaching a distant shore, the question was: where exactly would I wash up?

Notes

1   The story of Birmingham's early settlers is covered by Chris Upton in *A History of Birmingham* (Stroud: Phillimore & Co./The History Press, 2011), pp.100–06.

2   More information can be found in *Tales from the Pen Room: an account of the pen-making process* by Robert Stanyard – an interesting little pamphlet available to buy in the Pen Museum in Birmingham's Jewellery Quarter.

3   The story of the Lunar Society of Birmingham is told by Jenny Uglow in *The Lunar Men: The Friends who Made the Future* (London: Faber & Faber, 2002).

4   The Black Country is the area to the north and west of the city of Birmingham, which earned its name due to the acrid smoke that billowed from the thousands of ironworking foundries and forges in the area during the nineteenth century as well as from the dust produced by the local coal mines. Centred around Dudley, Sandwell, Walsall and Wolverhampton, the area played a major part in the Midlands' Industrial Revolution, and thus the story of Birmingham itself.

5   John Freeth, 'Inland Navigation: An Ode', p.5, in *The Political Songster, or A Touch on the times, on various subjects, and adapted to common tunes. The sixth edition, with additions* (Birmingham: The Author, 1790).

6   Victor Skipp, *The Making of Victorian Birmingham* (Studley, Warwickshire: Brewin Books, 1996), p.187.

7   Richard Wilson (ed.), *Essays and other writings of Francis Bacon* (Letchworth: The Temple Press, 1943), p.69.

8   Birmingham City Council news release [Online], *Birmingham looks to Asia for post-Brexit investment*, 29 November 2017. www.birmingham.gov.uk/news The council claims that the city is the youngest in Europe, with under-25s accounting for nearly 40 per cent of the population. www.birmingham.gov.uk

9   Front page story: 'Last Call Home', *Birmingham Mail*, Various reporters, Tuesday, 19 December 2017.

10 T.S. Eliot, *Collected Poems 1909–1962* (London: Faber & Faber, 1963). Quote from 'Little Gidding', p.222 (1974 edition).

11 Neil Elkes, 'One in ten Brummies was born in an overseas Commonwealth country – the 2022 Games will be made welcome here: Census reveals that Birmingham truly is a Commonwealth city and will give games a warm welcome', *Birmingham Mail*, 12 July 2017.

12 There will now be seventy-two teams after the readmission of the Maldives into the Commonwealth in February 2020, bringing the total number of nations in the global organisation to fifty-four. The Maldives had quit 'the club' in 2016 after being threatened with suspension over its human rights record. An election in the Indian Ocean archipelago in 2018 returned a new reformist government, which swiftly committed itself to re-joining the Commonwealth.

CHAPTER ONE

GIBRALTAR

Stand at one of Gibraltar's highest viewing points – the eighth-century Moorish castle on Willis's Road that winds up eventually to the lofty peak of this famous Rock clinging to the edge of Spain – and you are rewarded with one of the world's great views. A town of tenement blocks and sturdy stone houses sporting brightly coloured Genoese-style window shutters – scarlet reds, insouciant greens, fierce yellows – all built on terraced rows spilling down to the waterfront. Just below you is a synagogue and below that, Main Street, the city's principal thoroughfare. To your right, you can see the marina and cruise terminal; and to your left, the palms and hibiscus trees of the Botanic Garden; and then, beyond all that, the azure blue waters of the Strait of Gibraltar, sparkling in the Iberian Peninsula's almost ever-present sunshine. Such a tranquil and serene view would be hard to come by almost anywhere else in the world.

But appearances can be deceptive. The Strait of Gibraltar is, in fact, a very choppy waterway. The intermingling of the Atlantic Ocean with the Mediterranean Sea here makes for a turbulent channel. As water flows in and out of the Mediterranean, two currents are formed, amounting to an upper layer of Atlantic water heading eastward into the European sea, flowing over a lower layer of saltier and heavier water flooding out into the ocean. A sudden rise in the sea floor at this point also serves to complicate matters, causing the two currents to clash against each other, generating rough, rolling waves.

Add to that a number of counter-tides, particularly near the African side of the Strait, often whipped up by strong winds, and shipping can be difficult, especially when the weather truly turns and the sedate palms of Gibraltar's Botanic Gardens are sent snapping and flailing in the lashing rain.

Yet it is shipping that has been the lifeblood for this precarious British enclave hanging onto the side of Europe ever since Admiral Sir George Rooke occupied it in 1704 during the War of Spanish Succession and it was ceded by Spain to Britain in the Treaty of Utrecht in 1713. The safe passage of vessels in and out of Gibraltar – when it was a British crown colony, and now as a

British Overseas Territory in the Commonwealth – has always been of paramount importance, and this is where, in the nineteenth century, a Birmingham engineering firm played a crucial role.

☙

Almost as soon as Spain ceded 'the Rock' to Britain in 1713, it set about winning it back again, bombarding it during three conflicts in the eighteenth century, culminating in the Great Siege of 1779 to 1783 when its forces, with the help of the French, tried to sever all links the British military base had with the outside world. A Spanish army also gathered at the line of fortifications that it had built half a century before – called the Spanish Lines – effectively blockading the British garrison town by land.

British troops held out until a major naval relief force arrived in 1783 and the siege was called off; but the whole affair highlighted how dependent Gibraltar was on the safe passage of food and supplies by sea.

Precarious as its early existence was, however, the British colony was now growing into a significant community with several waves of immigrants joining the British military forces cooped up in their garrison. First there were the seafarers of Genoese and Ligurian descent, then there were the Maltese and Portuguese labourers and shipwrights, then the Sephardic Jews who turned up from their long-term Moroccan exile from Spain to become shopkeepers and lawyers. And there were others too: Spanish merchants from the mainland; Moroccans; and last, but by no means least, Hindu merchants from Hyderabad in India who came to take advantage of opportunities at the other end of the British Empire.[1]

And what were these opportunities for these communities who still make up the population of Gibraltar today? Well, by the early nineteenth century, Great Britain was the world's pre-eminent mercantile power, controlling half of the world's trade; and after the loss of the American colonies in 1776, a lot of this trade was refocused on India and the East Indies (as Southeast Asia was known in those days).

The tales of the East Indies brought back originally by sixteenth- and seventeenth-century sailors such as Sir Francis Drake, James Lancaster and William Keeling to the taverns of foggy London had now been rolled out like some great sail into colonial dominion over most of India, and a string of ports, starting with Gibraltar and Malta, threading their way towards it. Gibraltar was

☙

the first port of call along a route that took ships – before the opening of Suez Canal in 1869 – to Alexandra on the Egyptian coast, where passengers and cargo were offloaded for a rather rough trip across the desert to Suez, where another ship would be waiting to continue the journey on to Aden, Bombay and beyond. After the opening of the canal, the journey was made much easier, with the waterway linking Britain with its Asian dominions in one seamless, unbroken sea journey. As a result, tiny Gibraltar hanging onto the edge of Spain became increasingly a major trading port and, as steamships began to replace sailing vessels, a major coal refuelling station.

British cargo steamers stopped over in large numbers, carrying in their holds an eclectic mix of manufacturing: from stainless steel knives and forks from Sheffield, and sauces from Reading, to brass fittings from Birmingham. In addition, there was the mail boat of the Peninsular & Oriental Steam Navigation Company (P&O), chugging round the bay carrying its twice-monthly consignment of parcels to British Empire ports in Asia. On board too were people travelling out to these ports, carrying letters of employment in their pockets.[2]

But all this depended on safe navigation as these ships entered the narrow and treacherous strait between North Africa and the Spanish peninsula, passing the African port of Tangier on their right before falling under the shadow of the African mountain Jebel Musa, one of the fabled Pillars of Hercules squaring up to the other on the opposite side of the water – the Rock of Gibraltar.

Seafarers had traditionally relied on a paltry light being emitted from an oil lamp at the top of a Roman Catholic chapel called the Shrine of our Lady of Europe, sitting on a flat promontory at the end of the Rock. But as the volume of traffic rose rapidly in the nineteenth century the authorities decided that what Gibraltar needed was a lighthouse to guide ships safely into port, or through the straits if they were continuing their journey.

So, eventually, it got one.

The Europa Point lighthouse, built on the same promontory as the Shrine of our Lady of Europe and containing a single-wick lamp far more powerful than the shrine could ever muster, was inaugurated on 1 August 1841. In 1843, the lighting was upgraded to improve visibility from Sandy Bay on the eastern Mediterranean coast of Gibraltar, and by 1854 the lighthouse was visible within a span of about 16 miles.

Whether or not the passengers of the P&O mail steamers on their way to far-flung corners of the Empire fully appreciated the work Europa Point was doing to keep them safe is a matter of debate, but many of them certainly waxed lyrical about their arrival in the crown colony of Gibraltar. 'We skirted along the dark, savage mountains of the African coast, and came to the Rock just before gunfire,' novelist William Makepeace Thackeray wrote during a journey out to Cairo around 1846. 'It is the very image of an enormous lion, crouched between the Atlantic and the Mediterranean and set there to guard the passage for its British mistress.'[3]

A decade or so later, another P&O passenger, a Mr F.R. Kendall, said of the experience: 'As the ship was steaming into the bay we had a good view of the fortifications, dockyards etc, guns peeping out of all sorts of impossible places at a tremendous height. It reminded me altogether of a giant's castle in a fairy tale.'[4]

The fairy tale was still in danger of being spoilt, however. About 6 miles away from the safety of the Gibraltar quaysides – on the western side of the entrance to Gibraltar Bay – was a dangerous clutch of stone stacks collectively known as 'Pearl Rock'. On this reef, many a vessel had foundered. The arcs of light emanating from Europa Point did not penetrate this treacherous piece of water. This was a problem that needed to be solved.

Enter the Chance Brothers, a glassmaking company from Birmingham.

☙

The Chance family business had its roots in England's housing boom in the early decades of the nineteenth century, which had created the need for glass windows to be produced on an industrial scale. Out went the old-fashioned craftsmanship of glass-making and in came bulk melting furnaces, casting tables, and grinding and polishing machinery. Riding the wave of this development was a London glass merchant called Lucas Chance, who, realising he needed a steady source of glassware products, looked to Birmingham to provide it, buying up a factory in Spon Lane in Smethwick, a warehouse in Snow Hill, and bringing in experts from all over the country to build his newly formed Midlands business into one of the market leaders in glass technology. What Josiah Wedgewood had done for pottery in Stoke-on-Trent, Lucas wanted to do for the world of glassware.

Joining him in this endeavour were his brothers William, who contributed much needed capital in the difficult years of the late 1820s, and George, who looked after the New York side of the business, finding a growing demand in the US for his company's products.

But perhaps the most important figure in this family drama would be Lucas's nephew, James Timmins Chance. Born in London in 1814, James studied Theology at Cambridge University before becoming an optical scientist. He was delivering lectures on light when the family company was just beginning to experiment with the manufacture of optical glass. His admission as a partner in the Chance Brothers business in 1840 became a perfect opportunity to apply science to a burgeoning business.

A journalist visiting the Spon Lane Works in 1862 waxed lyrical in the *Illustrated Times* about the Chance Bros factory in general, which now employed around 2,000 people, and James Chance in particular: 'I am in a long spacious building, crowded with what seems an inextricable mass of machinery – wheels, shafts, bands, rubbers, "radial arms" – whirring, rolling, hissing, rumbling, vibrating – a very chaos of animated iron, and, as it were, a torture chamber of art,' the excited reporter wrote. 'For, bound upon great circular tables, whirred around with unerring and inevitable sweep, like the stroke of fate or the dreadful circle of condemned lovers in the Dantean Inferno, lie the zones of glass being slowly and surely ground into perfect accuracy of form and polished into perfect transparency of surface ...'[5]

This excruciating hyperbole was then extended to James Chance. 'I go on to the scientific obscurities of the "dark shed" or chamber, where Mr James Chance pores over the final adjustment of the optics of the finished lenses and prisms, ascertaining their optical quality, a delicate and most important duty.'

It was in this 'dark shed' presumably where the cerebral James drew up the technical plans for the company's first lighthouse lens, to be exhibited at the 1851 Great Exhibition at Crystal Palace, which itself was adorned with 950,000ft of rolled-plate glass produced and shipped by his company via canal to London.

In 1854, Trinity House, Britain's general lighthouse authority, invited Chance Bros to tender for a contract for Bardsey Island off the north-western tip of Wales. The Birmingham firm was successful, and more lighthouse apparatus contracts soon followed, one for the lighthouse on Lundy Island, another for Whitby lighthouse, and then one further afield, in Vancouver, Canada.

Over the next few years, the company manufactured about sixty lenses for Trinity House and other lighthouse authorities spanning the globe, from Port of Spain in Trinidad to Trincomalee in Sri Lanka and Victoria in Australia.

By now, James was becoming a leading authority on optical technologies, and was receiving encouragement in his work from the famous scientist

Michael Faraday. Chance's work on lights that could account for a dip on the horizon, and also on the dioptric mirror, a lens that could not only throw out a spectrum of light rays but would also reflect light back into a desired direction, was bringing him scientific recognition.

This was only to be cemented by what happened next. In the early 1860s, a Trinity House contract to replace the existing light at Gibraltar's Europa Point came the way of the Chance Bros. As we know, the original installation had been a single-wick oil lamp, which, although it was aided by mirrors and a fixed lens to refract the emanating light, was not sufficient to illuminate some particularly hazardous stretches of water such as the one around the infamous Pearl Rock. James Chance set to work.

The result was a wide-ranging solution. The Birmingham engineer replaced the single-wick lamp with a four-wick burner with a new lens and a red beam to be thrown over in an arc to Pearl Rock, while an additional 265-degree beam of white light was thrown over the coastline adjoining the point. The lantern that was erected in November 1864 also featured a complex array of vertical and horizontal prisms that further helped to illuminate the whole area, even in poor weather conditions.

Optical glass engineered by the Chance Brothers factory in the 1860s enabled the Europa Point lighthouse to illuminate a particularly hazardous stretch of water in the Gibraltar Strait for the first time. (iStock.com/Michael Rayment)

Chance explained his innovations in an 1867 paper for the Institute of Civil Engineers, and this know-how helped to secure his company a leading place in optical engineering. From then on, the Chance Bros firm was heavily involved in the design of the lighthouses now springing up all over the British Empire: from Burma and Borneo in the east to the Gold Coast (Ghana) and Jamaica in the west.

James retired in 1872 and bought himself a large house just north of Birmingham, in the area of Four Oaks in Sutton Coldfield, later to become a suburb of the city. He had a house in Kensington in London too, until he finally settled in Hove, near Brighton. He never quite forgot the city that had made his name, however, and in 1900 he endowed Birmingham University with £50,000 in order to establish an engineering school.

∞

Despite the retirement of James Chance, the business he had done so much to develop carried on prospering. After supplying so much of the rolled-plate glass for the Crystal Palace emporium of 1851, the firm went on to glaze other major buildings with a new method of 'double-rolling' glass in 1887. Another innovation was the creation of something the company branded as 'Flemish' style – a smooth, undulating artistic flourish said to be inspired by the rippling waters of the Birmingham canals, that was soon adorning bathroom windows the world over. Nor did sacred architecture miss out on the Chance touch – the glassblowers of Spon Lane were often employed to mould something more coloured and ornamental for British church windows.

Besides architecture, the company was also branching out into other spheres. By the 1930s, it had got round to producing tableware and collaborating with John Logie Baird to create some of the first cathode-ray tubes for televisions. The following decade it opened a new plant to produce glass for specialist scientific equipment such as penicillin flasks and medical syringes.

Meanwhile, the firm's optical and lighting expertise that had started with James Chance and his work on lighthouses in the nineteenth century was put to good use in the great challenges that Britain would face in the following century. Chance factory lenses were fitted to the thousands of British gunsights, range finders and periscopes used in the Second World War, and when in 1949 everyone in the country was granted free healthcare, Chance lenses were rolled out for use in NHS spectacles.

Glass blowers at Chance's Works on Spon Lane making glass for the 1851 Great Exhibition at Crystal Palace. The same craftsmanship of using pipes to inflate molten glass was still being used by the firm a hundred years later. (Chronicle/Alamy Stock Photo)

It seemed fitting, therefore, that a Chance Bros optical beacon would soon play a major part in the Festival of Britain, the festival arranged to showcase British manufacturing prowess 100 years on from the Great Exhibition at Crystal Palace. The light was fitted to the top of the Shot Tower standing on the South Bank in London and shone out throughout that summer of 1951 as the country tried to shrug off its post-war blues in the merriments of the festival.

The company produced a commemorative booklet to mark the occasion – a rather groovy affair designed and written by a London ad agency called Cecil D. Notley Advertising, which, with the help of some glossy yet minimalist graphics sporting a thoroughly modern 1950s look, waxed lyrical about the achievements of the Birmingham firm. 'The men and women who work for Chances' of Smethwick for the most part belong to Smethwick – many, indeed to Spon Lane – and that through generations,' it gushed. 'These are the Black Country folk … their voices are distinct, their traditions permanent, their loyalties obstinate and their sense of humour very much their own.'[6]

Later, it added smoothly: 'Exports now total more than 25 per cent of the company's turnover … Add to this the value of Chances' indirect exports … in cameras and optical instruments, headlight lenses, Crookes glasses for spectacles, industrial components and so on … and the grand total becomes impressive.'[7]

However, despite the buoyant fortunes of the Chance export department that was now operating through a network of agents in more than seventy-five markets, divided up into three distinct regions – the British Commonwealth, the Western Hemisphere, and Europe and the Rest – it appears that the glass the 1951 booklet was looking through was definitely rose-tinted. In 1952, rival company Pilkington bought up Chance Brothers in a takeover that may well have appeared a positive move at the time, but in hindsight spelt the beginning of a slow decline in fortunes: a decline that all too closely mirrored the fortunes of small- to medium-scale British manufacturing as a whole in the post-war period.

Within a year or two, Pilkington had sold off Chance's lighthouse division as it sought to focus everything around its own core business of rolled-plate glass. At first, this seemed to benefit the Chance Brothers, and by 1960 there were three furnaces at Spon Lane churning out rolled-plate glass. However, over the course of the 1960s Pilkington gradually moved all its rolled-plate capabilities to its plant in St Helens, and in 1976 stopped rolled-plate production altogether at the Chance factory.

It was the beginning of the end. The Spon Lane factory stumbled on for a few years, producing fluorescent tubing for electrical devices, as well as vases and bowls for a tableware division that, having fully embraced the garishness of 1960s design, were probably even more fluorescent.[8]

The end, when it arrived, came amid the savage recession of 1981 in Britain. It was then that the glassworks finally closed down, with a loss of 500 jobs.

The factory still stands, however. A ruin of crumbling dark red brick and broken windows sitting forlornly on the banks of Birmingham's Main Line Canal in Smethwick. Here and there, a wall has come away to reveal the peeling amber plasterwork behind the brick, and high up on the main façade there are five gold letters holding onto the brickwork – almost half-heartedly, it seems. They spell out the word 'Glass', the only reminder that this building once housed the largest glass-making company in Britain, a building once glowing from the heat of its vast melting furnaces, and all the glass being blown, pressed, poured and rolled underneath its high, Victorian roof.

In stark contrast, the Europa Point lighthouse still perches proudly on a cliff top high above the Strait of Gibraltar. With the distinctive red band around its middle to help mariners pick it out against the formidable limestone of the Rock behind, it saw a series of modernisations after the innovations pioneered by James Chance in 1864, and in the late twentieth century it became fully automated – controlled and monitored from Trinity House's centre in Essex.[9] In local circles, it is regarded very much as both a historic landmark and a tourist attraction.

Notes

1   The very distinct character of the Gibraltarian community is analysed in E.G. Archer, *Gibraltar, Identity and Empire* (Abingdon, Oxfordshire: Routledge, 2006).

2   The shipping company came to represent the British Empire at sea, as Ruth Artmonsky demonstrates in *P&O: A History* (Oxford: Shire Publications, 2012).

3   Ruth Artmonsky, Susie Cox, *P&O: Across the Oceans, Across the Years: a Pictorial Voyage* (Woodbridge: the Antique Collectors' Club 2012), p.58.

4   Ibid., p.57.

5   *Illustrated Times*, 21 June 1862 cited in Toby Chance & Peter Williams, *Lighthouses: The Race to Illuminate the World* (London: New Holland Publishers, 2008), p.143. The book goes on to chart the pioneering lighthouse work of James Chance.

6   Chance Bros Ltd, *Mirror for Chance* (Smethwick, 1951), p.13.

7   Ibid., p.15.

8   Some of them are pictured in David P. Encill, *Chance Expressions: The History of Domestic Glassware by Chance Brothers* (Bromsgrove: Cortex Design, 2007). The 'Fiestaware' patterns were particularly cheerful, as displayed in Chapter 4, matched only by the rather psychedelic vases and bowls exhibited in Chapter 6.

9   Trinity House has all the details on its website, www.trinityhouse.co.uk.

CHAPTER TWO

SRI LANKA

Sailing into the mercurial Strait of Gibraltar one autumn day in 1909 would have been the *Moldavia*, a P&O mail ship heading out east. One of the 245 passengers on board was a grocer from Birmingham called John Sumner.

Whether or not the Midlands businessman noticed 'the dark, savage mountains of the African coast' on the starboard side as the novelist Thackeray had done is open to conjecture, but one thing is certain: this was a man, now in his 50s, on a serious mission to build a business empire.

Sumner was the inheritor of a family grocery store on the High Street situated near all the market stalls of Birmingham's well-known Bull Ring area. Founded in 1820 by his grandfather, William Sumner, the grocery was one of many small enterprises in the city doing good, if not spectacular business; and would have remained just that it had not been for 'a fortuitous circumstance', as outlined in a little book published in 1926.

In fact, 'a great business actually arose out of a simple domestic incident,'[1] explained journalist S.J. Renmus in *The Story of Typhoo: once an idea, now a great business*, before going on to tell the story that would become the famous tea company's founding mythology. According to Renmus, a lady in Birmingham had been suffering regularly from indigestion, and on hearing about her ailment, a friend sent her a packet of 'very special tea' that, she was assured, would cure it. The tea was in tiny particles, unusual in those days when practically all tea was of the large leaf variety; nevertheless, the lady tried it, and to her surprise, found relief from it. She passed some of the tea on to her gardener and other fellow sufferers from indigestion, and they all, so the story goes, found benefit.

Coincidentally, as the Typhoo-sponsored book would have it, the lady was John Sumner's sister, and one day she suggested to her brother that he start selling the beverage in his store. Sumner had long sought some sort of speciality that might help him expand his business. This tea with unusual healing properties got him thinking.

So he bought thirty chests of the tea to try it out, and even though a friend warned that this type of tea was called dust, consisting of the tiny remnants of tea leaves after they have gone through the sorting and crushing process and of lower quality than the full-leaf teas, Sumner went ahead and splashed out £200 on advertising his new find.

Next, he needed a name, and perhaps this is where Sumner showed a real genius for marketing. Convinced of the tea's medicinal qualities, he chanced upon an English approximation of the Chinese word for 'doctor';[2] and in a single sleight of hand had given his new brew not only a healthy feel but also an Oriental one. Typhoo was born, and very soon was selling so well in his grocery store that the Birmingham entrepreneur also made it available on a wholesale basis through a network of agents. Within a year or so, he had sold his grocery business and had moved into the top two floors of a place just round the corner from the old shop, together with a small team of tea-packers – ten in all – and there, with a typewriter, a duplicating machine, a telephone and 1,661 agent stamps, built up a new business.

But it would not be until 1909, six years or so after launching Typhoo, that Sumner made the momentous decision that would transform a small enterprise into a global conglomerate. By then he was feeling that his company was on a firm enough financial footing for him to take some time out of work, and do what he needed to do: visit the place where his tea came from. That place was Ceylon, the Indian Ocean island we now call Sri Lanka.

On 23 September that year he left the Port of London on the *Moldavia*, a 5,000-tonne P&O ship[3] bound ultimately for Sydney, but stopping off at all the major ports along the way. One of those ports was Colombo, the capital of Ceylon.

☙

So what was the journey like? Well, as we know, the Birmingham businessman was following a well-worn route of travellers on the P&O mail steamer, mostly British, heading out to the various outposts of the British Empire in Asia – India, Ceylon, Singapore, Hong Kong and Australia. Not only would these have included smartly dressed men poised to join the army or the colonial civil service in India, but also Indian university students returning home after three years at Oxford or Cambridge, rubber planters destined for a lonely hillside in Malaysia, or doctors with a letter of appointment for a hospital in Singapore.

Launched in 1903, the *Moldavia* operated on P&O's England to Australia route via the Suez Canal. (Reproduced with the kind permission of the P&O Heritage Collection)

The music room on board the *Moldavia* where Typhoo founder John Sumner is likely to have spent some of his evenings during the long sea journey out to Sri Lanka (then called Ceylon). (Reproduced with the kind permission of the P&O Heritage Collection)

Like P&O passenger Fred Reynolds, who observed an eclectic mix of people on his way to India in 1896, including Indian 'Parsees', 'Mohammedans' and 'Hindus', as well as youths 'going to fight for fame or fortune' and 'fair maidens speeding at the call of love'[4], John Sumner may well have encountered enormous diversity in the 'army of globetrotters'[5] travelling on board the *Moldavia*.

So let us imagine the Typhoo founder – one of a significant group of passengers travelling alone – standing at the Victoria Docks in London's East End, porters milling around him, while waiting to board the ship and be shown the way to his cabin. Once on board, perhaps he stood on the top deck and waved farewell to family and friends on the quayside as the great vessel slowly pulled out of its berth and into the River Thames.

By dusk, the two mighty funnels in the middle of the 530ft-long ship would be belching smoke into the fading light in the English Channel as the engine boys far below stoked the furnaces in the boiler room. In contrast, Sumner would be sitting in one of *Moldavia's* ornate, floral-patterned saloons listening to a pianist, glass of whisky in hand, wondering what lay ahead.

What lay ahead may well have been lashing winds and rolling waves in a stormy Bay of Biscay until eventually – a day or so later – the steamer would be rounding Portugal's capricious Cape St Vincent, and chugging along the southern coast of the Iberian Peninsula towards Gibraltar.

At first light, it would appear. Peering out of the low grey cloud. The green line of Mediterranean buckthorn, olive and vine climbing sharply to a summit, on the other side of which was the formidable cliff that formed the east face, plunging 1,400ft into the sea, its rivulets of limestone running wild and white into the abyss. The Rock.

Gibraltar would have been the *Moldavia's* first refuelling stop, and a chance for its passengers to spend a day on shore before the evening sailing. Perhaps John Sumner had grasped at the opportunity to look around the British colony, climbing up to the Moorish Castle or simply ambling around the busy streets of the town before making his way back to the boat.

It was probably dark when the *Moldavia* pulled out of the harbour but the water would be full of lights: some hanging like diamond necklaces on the harbour moles, others burning brightly out of ship cabins, and over on the other side of the bay, the street lamps of Algeciras would be coming on. Once out of the bay, the *Moldavia* would be turning eastwards into the Mediterranean. The next leg of its journey would take it on to Malta.

Arriving in Valletta, the capital of the British colony of Malta, in the early 1850s, P&O passenger W.H. Bartlett was clearly impressed: 'To a stranger there can hardly be a more brilliant spectacle than the Grand Harbour,' he wrote in a travelogue called *Gleanings, Pictorial and Antiquarian on the Overland Route*:

> When his vessel casts anchor, he gazes with admiration upon the ponderous tiers of batteries, and lofty terraces of flat-roofed and green-balconied houses, which, apparently carved out of, rather than built in, the brilliantly white stone, everywhere rise out of the blue of the harbour below, tracing their outline with almost dazzling distinctness upon the blue of the sky above.[6]

He noted the busy activity of the harbour itself too: 'among the crowd of merchant vessels, boats are plying incessantly across the harbour, or clustering around some newly arrived steamer or ship of the line ...'[7]

Half a century later, when John Sumner passed through, the harbour would have been even busier because of all the commercial vessels using Malta as a stopover point and coaling depot as they headed east towards the Suez Canal, the great shipping highway that had transformed world trade in the previous four decades. The town too was perhaps an even greater spectacle due to all the additions the British had made to their fortress city in the Mediterranean since the 1850s. The Royal Opera House had been erected in 1861, a covered market fashioned almost entirely out of iron girders built, and numerous well-lit roads laid out.[8] In other words, Valletta now bore all the hallmarks of a classic Edwardian city: as prosperous, handsome and well-lit as a Glasgow or a Birmingham.

But, arguably, even greater sights lay ahead for the Birmingham businessman on his four-week journey to Sri Lanka. There was the strategic line of water cut through the desert by the Suez Canal Company in Egypt, the rugged cliffs of the Red Sea, as well as the minarets and markets of the British Protectorate of Aden; and, then, after drifting for three or four days in the blue radiance of the Arabian Sea, there was Bombay.

Presuming he stepped ashore to look around, it was probably this city on India's western seaboard that provided the most eye-opening experience of his journey, because here was not only astonishing splendour but also the most harrowing desolation. As the P&O ship approached Wellington Pier, where in a few years' time the magnificent Gateway of India would be built, the

Midlands businessman might have spied the spires and gabled roofs of British India. He might have glimpsed in the grey smudge of dawn the giant dormer windows of the High Court, the immense clock tower at the university, or the turrets and onion domes of the Western Railway Headquarters where a Gothic architectural style reminiscent of London's St Pancras Station had been fused with the florid craftsmanship of an Indian palace.[9] On disembarkation, however, he would also have witnessed the other side of the city: the beggars and wild dogs on the street corners, cows sitting down at road junctions, the colourful vegetable markets and the chai wallah stalls, all jostling together in the bright, confusing, impoverished land that was India.

By all accounts, though, the British Empire in India was at its zenith when Sumner arrived in the autumn of 1909. There was no greater reminder of this than the luxurious Taj Mahal Palace Hotel on the waterfront, which had first opened its doors in 1903. Perhaps the Midlands entrepreneur and his fellow travellers had stepped inside, looking for respite from the hot, sticky air of the city, and had been ushered to a table among the lush palms of the hotel gardens to take tea and tiffin. Who knows?

But now it was time to return to the P&O ship waiting at the pier. It had delivered its India mail, offloaded its passengers bound for India, and would soon be ready to leave, taking with it all the passengers and mail destined for all points beyond.

Sumner was one of them. Having visited three important destinations in the British Empire, later to become members of the Commonwealth – Gibraltar, Malta and India – he had one more to go. His final destination.

The lights were coming on all across Bombay now as the *Moldavia* prepared for its departure. Slowly the steamship pulled away from the quayside. Out to sea the lamps of tug boats and ferries were beginning to twinkle, offering guidance and comfort to a harbour now surrendering to the inevitable. Each manifestation of the gathering dusk was now that little bit darker; each interchange of shade, each shimmer, each spectral flush a little bit weaker than the last until, finally, the P&O mail boat slid into the deep blackness of the night.

Two more days at sea, and Sumner would arrive in Sri Lanka.

☙

In the early hours perhaps of a late October morning in 1909, the *Moldavia* would have been ushered into the Port of Colombo by a flashing light on top of the clock tower in the Fort area of the city. Three short sharp flashes at intervals of thirty seconds and visible from 18 miles out, the lantern was the handiwork of the Birmingham glass company, the Chance Brothers.

Shortly afterwards, the ship would have puffed into harbour, flanked on its starboard side by what *A Handbook for Travellers in India, Burma and Ceylon,* published that year by John Murray of London, described as 'a magnificent breakwater … completed in 1885 at a cost of about £700,000. It is 4,210 feet long, and is formed of concrete blocks of 16 to 32 tons each, capped by a solid concrete mass which rises to a height of 12 feet above low water level …'[10]

After a few days at sea since Bombay, it is debatable whether Sumner really noticed it, or if, after clearing the customs house on the landing jetty, he, like many other weary travellers, made for the first watering hole, which in this case was the Grand Oriental Hotel. This magnificent building decked out in white stucco like some Regency house in Chelsea or Belgravia had first opened its doors in 1875, and billed itself as the 'first modern hotel in the East', according to an advert in the back of the *Handbook*, fully equipped with 'electric light, lift and fans in all public rooms and bedrooms'.

The problem with the Grand Oriental, however, was that it was right in the chaos of things. Not far away were the crowded bazaars of Pettah, where in congested streets filled with rickshaws, Tamil and Muslim traders in tiny shops haggled and hawked their wares. Closer still was the busy commercial district orbiting around the clock tower and Cargills department store, and even though Typhoo would soon set up its agency office in Queen Street nearby, perhaps Sumner took the *Handbook's* advice and found a base in Colombo's quieter neighbourhoods. 'The traveller who intends to stop a day or two may prefer to drive on,' the *Handbook* urged, 'a little more than a mile, to the Galle Face Hotel.'

Sumner was going to be in Ceylon for a few weeks or more, so perhaps he took up residence in one of the rambling rooms of the Galle Face overlooking the waves of the Indian Ocean breaking softly on the seafront. Who knows?

What we do know is that before long he was heading up into the Hill Country. It would have been on this journey – quite possibly by train – that he first witnessed the breathtaking natural beauty of the island that the British East India Company had seized in 1794.[11]

This journey into the central highlands by the railway built in the 1880s by British engineers would have taken Sumner right into the heart of Sri Lanka's tea-producing country – deeper into valleys coated with the bright green of tea bushes and onwards into uplands dotted with wild waterfalls.

In fact, winding upwards around dale and hill, Sumner would have been plunged into deepening contrasts. On the one hand, there were – and still are today – the regimented rows of tea trees criss-crossed by a geometric pattern of intersecting pathways stretching out across the landscape like surveyor lines. At the end of a pathway here and there would have been an isolated tea estate bungalow with its low gables and sturdy chimneys, encircled by manicured lawns. On the other hand, almost incongruously, there were ragged hills and rocky outcrops, some cut through with cascading waterfalls, others entangled, first with banana trees and jungle bramble, and then as the train reached the higher elevations, slashed and speared by forests of pine and eucalyptus.

His train would have struggled on, rattling across bridges suspended over fast-flowing rivers, tilting over the sides of ravines, clinging onto the sides of cliffs, trundling into wide vistas of shade and sunlight flickering across the mountains, until finally it would have creaked and clattered into a railway station fitted out with all the adornments of civilisation – wooden seats and timetables, a couple of engine sheds and a tea shop, looking for all the world like a suburban stop in Surrey if it had not been for the remains of a heavy monsoon rain shower sloshing out of the roof guttering.

The chances are that this was Hatton Station, which, according to *The Handbook for Travellers*, was 'the point from which the great tea districts of Dickoya and Dimbula may be most conveniently visited'.[12]

The tea country in Sri Lanka is a mixture of rugged mountainous beauty and tea plantations laid out in fierce geometric lines. (Commonwealth Secretariat photo by Kevin Nellies)

Into this picture, Sumner was about to make a big step. At the station, a rickshaw sent out by a local tea planter would have been waiting for him, ready to take him to the place where he would learn a lot more about the tea industry in general, and the type of tea in particular that would soon make Typhoo into a household name. 'It may be of interest to record,' the Birmingham tea merchant wrote in an afterword to *The Story of Typhoo*, 'that when visiting Ceylon in 1909, a large tea planter in the mountains, at whose bungalow I stayed, in reply to my enquiry, stated that there was no market for this portion of the leaf [the leaf-edge tea fannings now being sold under the Typhoo brand] until comparatively recently' but 'today it is worth more than the whole-leaf portion of the tea from which it comes because it is the better part.'[13]

We don't know how long John Sumner stayed at the tea planter's bungalow or even who the tea planter was but perhaps this is where the Birmingham entrepreneur, sitting on the veranda of the bungalow one evening, watching the sinking sun casting a mellow light over the valleys of the Hill Country, finally hatched his plan.

∾

The plan was that Typhoo, in contrast to many other British tea companies who bought up their consignments in the tea auctions of London's Mincing Lane, would establish a tea buying and blending agency in Sri Lanka itself – in Queen Street in Colombo to be precise – where 'beneath electric punkahs or fans, cooling the tropical heat'[14] tea buyers would taste samples of leaf-edge tea from the various private tea estates on the island, and once ensuring the right standards for the Typhoo brand, make their purchases on the weekly Colombo market or privately from the estates. From then on, the tea would be transported to dedicated Typhoo warehouses at Colpetty just south of the Galle Face Hotel, where the tea would be blended, packed into Typhoo-branded chests, and loaded onto bullock carts for transit to the Colombo docks. Here, a ship would be waiting to transport the consignments on the 7,000-mile journey back to one of four major ports in England – London, Liverpool, Manchester or Avonmouth – and, from there, carried on by canal to the Typhoo packing factory in Birmingham.

On John Sumner's return from his trip to Ceylon, the company set up the new system.

It was a huge commercial success, and soon Sumner and his fellow company directors were scouting around for larger premises in Birmingham. They found it in 1923 at an old industrial facility in Bordesley, just to the east of the city centre, which they transformed into a private bonded warehouse and a state-of-the-art works. The 'private bonded warehouse' bit was important, because now the directors had come to an innovative arrangement with the UK customs authorities whereby their Ceylon tea shipments would bypass customs at port. Instead, customs clearance would be carried out inland at the new Typhoo factory in Bordesley.

A shipment of up to 3,000 chests of tea arrived at the Bordesley depot via a relay of canal boats every week, each boat carrying between 250 and 400 chests. Whether they were coming from the north or the south, each barge would make their way into the Digbeth Branch Canal, which slips underneath the Fazeley Street Bridge and disappears into the bowels of the Typhoo building. Once inside a covered shed there, the chests were unloaded from the barges onto an electric conveyor belt rolling into a customs office, and then after clearance, into the warehouse itself. Once inside, the chests were put into a lift and taken to the packing works on the floor above.

The handling only really started upstairs on the Birmingham packing floor, when a row of Typhoo workers – they were almost always women – opened up the chests of tea. Loose tea was then tipped into a sifter, and transported via a series of bucket elevators and conveyor belts and weighing machines to another team. These workers were responsible for the final packing of the loose tea into Typhoo's trademark quarter-pound and half-pound packets – the final stage in a process that had seen consignments of tea travel all the way from Sri Lanka to Birmingham with hardly any handling involved.

It was a system to be proud of if reading *The Story of Typhoo* is anything to go by, not only because of the seamless link forged with Typhoo's source of supply – Ceylon – but also because of the model works the firm had put together in Birmingham, featuring as it did not only the most advanced equipment of its day but also a large canteen, and mess and recreation rooms for its staff.

It was a system that enabled the firm to take Ceylon tea fannings – the sort of leaf residue that is now regularly sold in teabags the world over – and turn them into a 1920s success story.

❦

At the beginning of the 1930s, however, things took a turn for the worse. The first sign that something was wrong was when Typhoo's tea consultants in

London, Holborns, who occasionally tested samples of the company's consignments from Ceylon, reported that one of the shipments had a peculiar flavour, and another had been affected by damp or mould. It was clear that the usual quality of the tea was not being maintained. Then, in December 1930, came the bombshell. A letter to Birmingham from a concerned employee of Typhoo's Ceylon agent spoke of a conspiracy to the effect that the agency's directors were buying large quantities of inferior teas privately at a low price, and mixing them with the genuine fannings to disguise the deceit. The following spring, director Alfred Tustain and J.R. Hugh Sumner, the son of the Typhoo founder, were dispatched to Ceylon, only to be met on arrival in Colombo by 'two grim-faced directors' from the agency who informed them that their MD, Mr Burns, 'had killed himself'.[15]

That was the end of that for Typhoo's first agents in Sri Lanka, but luckily not the end for the fruitful trading relationship between Birmingham and the Indian Ocean island. In January 1933, the firm appointed new Colombo agents, Carson & Co. Ltd, who took over the responsibility for buying and blending the Hill Country teas, and ships departing from Colombo, most notably those of the carrier Bibby Line, continued to make the 7,000-nautical-mile journey back to Britain with their holds stuffed full of Typhoo chests. Thereafter, canal barges, full to the gunwales, still took the consignment onwards, slipping each week into the quayside at the Bordesley Street warehouse.

A few changes were made, however. The company now diversified its tea purchases to include buying on the London market, and also installed a new blending plant at the Birmingham Works to reduce its reliance on blending in Ceylon. Over time too, especially as the company's fortunes soared after the end of the Second World War, it looked around for additional sources of supply, mostly in the tea estates of India. By the 1960s, Typhoo was packing more than 80 million lb of tea every year, and exporting to more than forty countries around the world.

This was despite the big hit that the Birmingham Works took in the German air raids of the Second World War. In the early hours of 10 April 1941, two bombs fell on the Bordesley plant, one relatively harmlessly at the rear of the building, but the other a direct hit through the main canteen roof. The resulting explosion ripped through the building, causing a huge fire that swept through the factory, almost completely destroying it. The next day, the pavement outside the factory was swirling with a mixture of water and tea, 'rushing along the gutter in a brown slurry to disappear down the drains'.[16]

Fortunately, the tea firm was able to construct temporary warehouses alongside the southern arms of the Digbeth cut with access from Pickford Street, and with some of its machines brought back into use, production was continued.

Nonetheless, it was not long before the Birmingham canals would bow out of the Typhoo story. As more haulage moved to the roads in the 1950s and '60s, the company ceased all transport by canal barge.

The huge plant in Bordesley would soon follow suit. In 1974, Typhoo's new owners, Cadbury Schweppes, installed a tea plant on Merseyside – it was the first time in history that Typhoo tea had been packed outside Birmingham – and, in November 1978, all operations were moved north. Production at Bordesley Street finally came to an end.

Typhoo tea continues to thrive today under the guidance of a new parent company – the Indian conglomerate Apeejay Surrendra Group – and the Typhoo story will doubtless continue.[17] Sadly for some, though, it is no longer a story belonging to Birmingham.

☙

The Bordesley Street factory is still standing, however – a haunting brown brick presence near a long railway viaduct carrying trains out of Moor Street Station on their way to London. Recently, a portion of it became home to a warehouse store owned by a family business called Latifs – started by a Pakistani immigrant to the Midlands in the 1950s – and on a larger scale there has been talk of it one day becoming a 'creative innovation centre' for Birmingham City University. Nonetheless, for the most part it is derelict, as derelict as the day it was abandoned by Typhoo in 1978. Where a proud art-deco-style entranceway on Bordesley Street once stood, now there are only smashed windows. Where upper floors in towers once looked down imperiously on the city streets, there is now only graffiti and sheets of tarpaulin.

Surprisingly, though, it still dominates the landscape, mainly due to its sheer size. It stretches across a whole urban block, taking you from the front entrance on Bordesley Street, around the sides on New Canal Street and Pickford Street, and then round the back on Fazeley Street.

It is at the back – on Fazeley Street – that you first spot it. A grubby, coal-stained bridge with stagnant green water sitting slimily underneath it. But scan the stretch of that water, and you will notice that very soon it disappears

A Birmingham tram, around 1953 or earlier, carries a Typhoo advertising pitch along Fazeley Street – the street that runs behind the old tea factory. (Simon Webster/Alamy Stock Photo)

mysteriously behind some green bushes and then into the great Typhoo factory itself. It is at this point that you realise. You realise that this is the canal upon which barge after barge once travelled, laden with tea chests from Ceylon, bound for the unloading dock inside the Packing Works.

Linger there for a while longer, and you can begin to imagine it. The canal barge that has picked up its consignment from the Liverpool docks at Ellesmere Port on the River Mersey for the journey south through Cheshire and Shropshire to the industrial heartlands of the Midlands. A journey on canals that scythe through the countryside, dividing fields and marooning one farmstead from another. A line that slices straight through hills and rips through cliffs. A line of industry that re-engineers the land.

Then slowly, as the high banks and the deep cuttings of the shires begin to give way to factories and warehouses, the line carves through brick and cement, setting the boundaries between one business and another, forcing apart one workshop from another, circumscribing the areas where workers can pour molten glass out of a furnace or bash brass into ornament, and where they cannot.

And then the lead barge in the Typhoo convoy is descending the flight of locks between Brindley Place and Water Street on the Birmingham and Fazeley Canal, dropping more than 100ft, before furrowing under the Livery Street Bridge, as the line of the cut forces its way between low warehouse windows and the sooty walls of factory yards.

Notwithstanding the industrial precision of the waterway, the line is always half-hidden. Unless you are a cargo handler at a local wharf, the channel of water is always below this window line or that stone walkway. The ravine that feeds the city with rough metal for its forges, sand for its glass works and tea for its cafe-goers always lurks in the half shadows of the city, far away from the civic squares, the busy thoroughfares, and hotel foyers: unloved, unseen and yet vitally necessary.

I can see it now. As the lead barge in the Typhoo convoy slips along the gully severing the Victorian tenements of Gosta Green from the bingo halls and breweries of Aston, and into the Digbeth Cut, a November fog begins to unfurl over the water. Very little can be seen or heard now as the barge-man's hand tightens over the tiller. Accompanied only by ghostly shapes on the towpath, the dripping water in the gloom of the Curzon Street Tunnel, and the flickering lights of the banana warehouse at the junction with the Grand Union Canal, the boat now enters the Typhoo Basin and under the Fazeley Street Bridge. Moments later, it is slipping into the long-lost secret wharf of the Typhoo Packing Factory.

NOTES

1   S.J. Renmus and others, *The Story of Typhoo: once an idea, now a great business.* (Birmingham: Sumner's Typhoo Tea Ltd, 1926), p.18.

2   *The Story of Typhoo* offers the explanation that the Chinese Pinyin word for 'doctor' is 'daifu', with the 'd' sounding like 't' to the English ear. Pinyin is the system for writing out Chinese words in the Roman alphabet.

3   Ship Passenger lists held by The National Archives and made available on Findmypast.co.uk.

4   Fred Reynolds (1896) cited in Ruth Artmonsky, Susie Cox, *P&O: Across the Oceans, Across the Years: a Pictorial Voyage* (Woodbridge: the Antique Collectors' Club, 2012), p.157.

5   Ibid., p.157.

6   W.H. Bartlett, *Gleanings, Pictorial and Antiquarian on the Overland Route* (London: 1851), p.6.

7   Ibid., p.23.

8   Descriptions of Valletta's British architecture can be found in Malcolm Borg, *British Colonial Architecture, Malta: 1800–1900* (San Swann, Malta: PEG, 2001).

9   Descriptions of Britain's colonial architecture in Mumbai can be found in Christopher W. London, *Bombay Gothic* (Mumbai: India Book House, 2003).

10   Herbert Charles Fanshawe, *A Handbook for Travellers in India, Burma and Ceylon* (London: John Murray, 1909), p.473. Other descriptions of Sri Lanka in this chapter have been gleaned from the author's own travels around the Indian Ocean island.

11   This had been ostensibly to stop a Dutch territory being seized by a post-revolutionary France on the warpath, though the British decided to keep the island in the Anglo-Dutch Treaty of 1814. It was probably no coincidence that the island happened to possess a much-coveted harbour in the form of Trincomalee, extensive forests containing cinnamon bark and a local sea bed crammed full of pearls, as historian Martin Kitchen notes in *The British Empire and Commonwealth: a short history* (London: Macmillan Press, 1996), p.12.

12   Fanshawe, p.480.

13   John Sumner in S.J. Renmus and others, *The Story of Typhoo: once an idea, now a great business* (Birmingham: Sumner's Typhoo Tea Ltd, 1926), p.43.

14   Alfred Tustain in S.J. Renmus, p.53.

15   Kenneth Williams, *The Story of Ty-phoo and the Birmingham Tea Industry* (London: Quiller Press, 1990), p.89.

16   Ibid., p.98.

17   The reader can find more information on typhoo.co.uk.

CHAPTER THREE

THE INDIAN SUBCONTINENT

I. EARLY CONTACTS

If you were to hop on a narrow boat in the Typhoo Basin, and then take a trip around the Birmingham canals, you would soon find yourself making a journey around a city heavily influenced by a place a very long way away, but which has, nonetheless, played an important role in the city's history; first as a trading post in Britain's once huge commercial empire, then as a source of inspiration, and finally, as the source of new communities setting up home in the Midlands. That place is the Indian subcontinent.

In fact, steer your canal barge in any direction, and you are travelling through numerous districts touched by the land that unfurls itself across a vast plateau south of the Himalayas. Head in a south-easterly direction, navigating yourself through the Camp Hill Locks on the Grand Union Canal, and you will be skirting the districts of Sparkbrook and Sparkhill, home to a large Muslim community originally hailing from Pakistan and Bangladesh, and also the birthplace of Birmingham's famous curry dish, the Balti. Head northwards again, on a loop through the Ashted tunnel before the Digbeth Cut joins the Birmingham and Fazeley Canal at the Aston Locks, and you will not be very far away from Steelhouse Lane, where Birmingham's first Indian restaurant – The Darjeeling – opened up in the 1950s.

Turn left here, and the canal will transport you up the stepladder of lock gates to the Old Turn Junction by some old brewery buildings that now house the Malt House pub; and if you keep right here, on to the Birmingham Main Line Canal, you will be led westwards to Smethwick, the home of Birmingham's sizeable Sikh community, originating from the Punjab, the fertile plain forged by five rivers running down from the Himalayas. On your way, you will pass

∽

through the site of the old Soho foundry, founded by Matthew Boulton and James Watt, which in the early nineteenth century was busy exporting steam engines to India.

Retrace your steps now, back to the city centre, on the cut flowing underneath Broad Street where once furniture maker Osler crafted beautiful pieces of glass decoration for Indian palaces, and on to the Gas Street Basin. This presages the beginning of the Worcester & Birmingham Canal that, on its 30-mile journey to the River Severn in the south-west, will first take your barge to the leafy suburb of Edgbaston and its famous boys school, King Edward's, which among its alumni includes architect Laurie Baker, who spent all his working life in India, and Charles Freer Andrews, campaigner for Indian independence and confidant of Mahatma Gandhi.

In case you thought that dreams of India were a strictly male affair, however, you would be wrong: there were also Birmingham women inspired by the subcontinent. Intrepid Victorian adventurer Helen Caddick would have enjoyed memories of Darjeeling in her Edgbaston drawing room after visiting the British hill station in the Himalayan foothills during an 1893 expedition, and Elizabeth Cadbury, philanthropist and part of the chocolate dynasty based at Bournville, a mile or so downstream, toured India in 1936 as head of a British delegation to an international women's conference in Calcutta.

By the time Dame Cadbury was standing up to speak at the Calcutta conference, the British Raj was little more than a decade away from packing up its bags and quitting India; but let's start our story about Birmingham's relationship with the subcontinent in the early days of the Raj, at the beginning of the nineteenth century. If ever there was a moment, this was the moment when the British East India Company made the transition from being an operator of a handful of trading enclaves around the coast to supreme rulers of India. In the half-century since Captain Robert Clive's 1757 conquest of Bengal, the Company had appointed the first governor-general for its Indian territories, Warren Hastings, and across India had seen off several local Mughal rulers such as Tipu Sultan of Mysore making their final stands against its military might. But it was during the first two decades of the nineteenth century that it really finished the job. This was when the British Redcoats, and the rank and file Indian army in their employ, went on to conquer most of the subcontinent, taking Delhi as early as 1803, mopping up with Gujarat and Maharashtra in 1818, and making the East India Company masters of all India in the process. Only the Sikhs of the Punjab held out, until they too finally succumbed to British power in 1849.[1]

∽

But what had all this empire building in a faraway land to do with a city in the English Midlands? The answer is quite a lot. Unpalatably perhaps for the twenty-first-century reader, British military aggression in India now paved the way for a new breed of British industrialists back home to exploit the opportunities, not least the export-oriented factory owners sitting alongside the canals of Birmingham, eager to expand their influence around the world. As John Freeth's poem had predicted in 1769, all the way 'to the Ganges'.[2]

The Soho foundry, founded by Boulton and Watt in 1796, was particularly active. Matthew Boulton's act of faith in bringing Scottish inventor James Watt down to the Midlands to build industrial steam engines had laid the foundation for the partners' respective sons, Matthew Robinson Boulton and James Watt Jr, to build on the business in the early 1800s, and if drawings held at the Birmingham Library are anything to go by, particularly in the export trade. Extensive drawings held at the Wolfson Archive Centre show, among other things, the firm's plans for the Calcutta and Bombay Mints in the 1820s. The charts portray a welter of engines, as well as all manner of cranks and shafts, pulleys and lashes, for use in the engine houses and pump rooms that accompanied the copper and silver melting houses, the coining rooms and the rolling mills.[3] Like the Soho foundry in Birmingham, the Mints were huge industrial complexes.

But what could work for 'dark satanic mills' could also work for majestic homes. Between 1813 and 1814, the company was busy drawing up plans to pump water around the grounds of a royal palace in Lucknow in northern India. Belonging to the Nabob Vizier of Oude, a local Indian prince, the palace would receive a steam engine and a couple of boilers, a network of tunnels and pumps leading to and from the local river, as well as a new iron bridge spanning the river. In a memorandum to a Mr Hugh Thompson, probably the project manager, on 12 March 1814, James Watt Jr wrote:

The Engine, of 14 Horse Power, is intended to be erected at Lucknow upon the banks of the River Goomty and to be applied in the first instance to the working of pumps for supplying the cofferdams to lay the foundations of a new Ironbridge being constructed by Mr Rennie who will send out the pumps for that purpose as well as the shafts of machinery for connecting them with the engine and will also supply the company drawings and instructions. The Engine will have to be erected somewhere near the bridge and not far distant from His Highness's Palace and Gardens in the situation in which it is intended to remain after the completion of the foundations of the bridge.[4]

It was then planned that the engine house would be applied to the double purpose of supplying a large reservoir in the Nabob's garden and pumping water to the palace itself. Watt also provided comprehensive details as to how the engine would work via a working beam carrying a water stream from which would descend 'a rod which works the great pump'.[5] Despite the high technology being installed, however, the engine house itself was designed in the traditional Mughal style as would befit a Muslim prince. A half-coloured drawing of the engine house façade from 1814 shows a building complete with arched doors decorated with swirling arabesque patterns, shuttered windows and turrets crowned with onion domes.[6]

Candelabras made by Broad Street glassware firm F. & C. Osler were nothing if not ostentatious. (Jeff Morgan 14/Alamy Stock Photo)

What was true for local Indian princes in the early years of the nineteenth century was also true for their successors later on that century. By the look of their palaces, it appeared that the thing they wanted most was style and ostentation, and when it came to finding it there was no need to look any further than another Birmingham enterprise, F. & C. Osler. From modest beginnings as a maker of glass trinkets, the Broad Street firm suddenly popped up in India in the early 1840s, opening a showroom right in the heart of Calcutta, in Dalhousie Square, to sell an extensive range of chandeliers, candelabras and other lighting devices.[7]

The ploy soon paid off. Soon Osler chandeliers – mostly colourful affairs of ruby red, green, gold or opal – started to turn up in the grand residences of Indian maharajahs. A green chandelier was erected in the durbar hall in the fort of Qila Mubarak in the Punjab, an opal chandelier was installed in the Jai Vilas Palace in Gwalior as well as an opulent glass fountain, and the lake palace at Udaipur received a glass settee.

If you were a wealthy Indian, it seemed, and you were in need of a crystalline dinner service or a clock in a crystal case, or even a glass Ottoman that you could then upholster in crimson velvet, then the Osler showroom in Calcutta was the place for you. Particularly popular was the 'punkah lamp' invented by the firm with India in mind. 'The Punkah lamp is an especial favourite in India with all who have seen it,' Osler's Calcutta agent, James Bowerman, wrote to Follett Osler back in Birmingham in April 1854. 'Everyone says it is perfect and there can be no higher praise than that.'[8]

If anything, the problem with the lamp and its accompanying dish was just keeping up with demand. Many of Bowerman's letters to head office – letters now held in Birmingham's Wolfson Archive Centre – seem to be urgent pleas for more stock to be sent as soon as possible. '… I must say the quantity both of dishes and lamps is nothing like what we should dispose of if we had them,' he wrote to Follet Osler on 4 April. 'To sum up the matter I would say you cannot send <u>too much</u> of anything.'[9]

◈

As Bowerman was writing, preparations were well under way for the opening of Calcutta's first railway line, and on 15 August the same year the first steam locomotive pulled out of Howrah Station, taking passengers 20 miles up the track to the town of Hooghly. Over the next decade, the East Indian Railway Company would extend the line along the Ganges plain all the way to Delhi, complementing all the other lines now being built across the subcontinent by British engineers in India's great railway revolution. From now on, firms such as Osler would find it easier to meet orders all over the country. From the Himalayas in the north to the backwaters of Kerala in the south, Victorian industry had now truly arrived.

What had also arrived by then, for better or for worse, was imperial idealism. Some of this was in the form of a political arrogance – honed on the anvil of empire – that saw it as Britain's historic mission to bring the 'benefits' of British law, education and administration to the old and corrupt 'Orient'. If it could do this, thought liberal thinkers such as Thomas Babington

Macaulay, then it could put places such as India on the road to political liberty and progress, just as the Magna Carta had put the English on the same course centuries before.[10]

The second form, which sometimes went hand in hand with the first, was a religious evangelism – the zeal of British missionaries to convert Indians to Christianity. This second form is where Birmingham came in once again.

This may have been due to the particular religious character of the place. A Puritan and Parliamentary stronghold in the English Civil War of the 1640s, as fiercely anti-Royalist as, say, Oxford University was Royalist, Birmingham by the seventeenth century already had a reputation for nonconformity. Some have mooted that this was because, lacking city status, Birmingham was not subject to particular restrictions placed on nonconformist worship, unlike Oxford, which had been 'incorporated' by the Crown, and therefore bound by the strictures of successive pieces of legislation, which curtailed dissenters' ability to practise their religion within 5 miles of the city.[11] Whatever the reason, as Birmingham grew rapidly in the following centuries, it became a place to which followers of non-Anglican creeds – Baptists, Quakers and so forth – tended to migrate. As Baptist churches opened their doors in Cannon Street and Lombard Street, Quakers established a meeting house in Bull Street, Methodists set up camp in Coleshill Street, and Unitarians gained a foothold in Moor Street and Philip Street,[12] so too did religious activism grow.

The implications for the wider world very soon become apparent. Hard-wired into the nonconformist DNA was a strong evangelising fervour coupled with a deep yearning to better the world, both at home and abroad. As we will see later in this book, Midlands nonconformists played a major part in the anti-slavery movement. It was inevitable that India would also fall under their gaze.

Arriving in Birmingham in 1828 as the minister of the Cannon Street Baptist Church was a man who, in fact, had spent some time in India. The Rev. Thomas Swan had previously been a professor of theology at a college in India run by the Baptist Missionary Society. The Society had established its first overseas mission in 1800 at Serampore, a town on the Hooghly River just north of Calcutta, and it was there that it set about spreading the gospel, printing translations of the scriptures into Bengali, campaigning against injustices such as sati – the Hindu practice whereby a widow would be burnt alive on her late husband's funeral pyre – and founding schools. It also established the institution where Swan taught – Serampore College, the first university in India for Indians, which is still in existence today, affiliated now to the University of Kolkata.

Back in Britain, in Birmingham, Swan carried on his work for the Society by becoming the secretary of its Birmingham Auxiliary, compiling annual reports and detailing the work of the Baptist missions in India, which had now spread beyond Serampore. In Calcutta, he wrote in the 1835 annual report, 'the gospel is regularly preached, not only by Baptist missionaries, but also by those of other denominations. Young natives of talent, who have abandoned idolatry, and are members of churches, receive theological instruction from the missionaries, preparatory to their becoming efficient preachers of the gospel to their countrymen.'[13]

He also reported that Christian boarding schools had been set up for local children where they 'are carefully instructed in the doctrines and duties of Christianity' and that missionary stations had also been formed in the outlying villages, not far from Calcutta, 'where churches are planted, public worship regularly conducted and heathens, from time to time, converted to the faith of Christianity'.[14]

Not content to stop at Calcutta, though, the missionary society also took its efforts to Allahabad, venerated by Hindus as a place of pilgrimage and as the venue for an annual Hindu mela. 'Allahabad has been visited at the time of its great annual fairs when the gospel was preached to the assembled thousands,' Swan wrote in the 1836 report.[15]

The following year, he sounded an even more triumphant note. 'In the city of Calcutta alone, more than two thousand Hindoos are receiving a Christian education,' and being 'called forth by the interesting facts of modern science and the impressive verities of the Christian faith.'[16]

Although there is no doubting the credentials of Swan as a reformer – he was also a vocal campaigner for the abolition of slavery in the Caribbean – these words, echoing down the ages, to the modern ear undoubtedly smack of evangelising arrogance and racism – two contributing factors, arguably, to what was very soon to happen in British India.

The Indian Mutiny of May 1857, historians say, was triggered by a particularly insidious piece of cultural insensitivity when a rifle was introduced to the Bengal Army that required native soldiers to bite off the end of the cartridge, 'widely reputed to have been greased with pig or cow fat, polluting to both Hindus and Muslims'.[17] Almost overnight the Indian sepoys rose up in revolt, massacred the English residents of Meerut in north India, and began to march on Delhi. Within weeks, they had been joined by disaffected groups in the countryside – 'landlords and peasants, princes and merchants' who each 'for their own reasons, took up arms'.[18] Christian missionaries were often singled out for attack, but these were by no means isolated incidents. By the time the Indian summer rains were in full flow, vast swathes of northern India were in open rebellion against British rule.[19]

James Bowerman of the Osler glassware company felt the repercussions in Calcutta. 'I regret to have to tell you of the almost entire stoppage of trade in this city,' he informed Follet Osler in a letter back to Birmingham on 1 August 1857. This was owing 'to the Delhi revolt and now the general rising of the Native troops who are ravaging the country, plundering, murdering everyone they can'.[20]

A few weeks later, things were looking even more serious. 'We are threatened in Calcutta during the next eight days with a rise among the Moslems,' he wrote. 'Blood is hot on both sides, it will take little to make the Christians strike.' If there was a clash between the communities, he added, 'a battle is inevitable'.[21]

Help, however, was not far away. Somewhat surprisingly, given they had not so long ago been vanquished themselves by the Redcoats, the East India Company's Sikh and Bombay regiments remained loyal to the British and

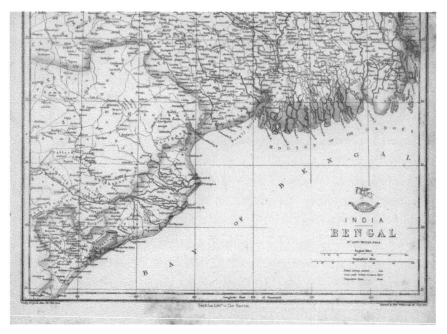

Trade came to an abrupt halt for the Osler showroom in Calcutta during the 1857 Indian Mutiny, but by the time this map of British Bengal was drawn up it was back to business as usual. (Map by London cartographer Edward Weller for the *Dispatch Atlas*, 1863)

within months, the tide began to turn against the rebels. With help too from loyal local magnates, the uprising would soon be quashed.

Certainly, the incorrigibly optimistic Bowerman, who had always spent a lot of words in his letters telling his Birmingham employers about the excellent health he was enjoying in India, was in a better frame of mind towards the end of the year. 'There can be no doubt that our business is as healthy … as any in Calcutta,' he wrote in October. 'Our name stands A1 and name is everything in India.'[22]

It was back to business as usual, it seemed.

NOTES

1   The story of the British conquest and rule of India is ably told in a number of histories, including B.D. Metcalf and T.R. Metcalf, *A Concise History of Modern India* (Cambridge: Cambridge University Press, 2006), and Burton Stein, *A History of India* (Chichester: Wiley-Blackwell, 2010).

2   John Freeth (1790) cited in the preamble to this book. Also cited in Chris Upton, *A History of Birmingham* (Stroud: The History Press, 2011), p.88.

3   Drawings and notes in the *Boulton & Watt and Matthew Boulton archives* [MS3147 & MS3782] at the Wolfson Centre for Archival Research, Library of Birmingham.

4   Memo by James Watt Jr, 12 March 1814 in the *Boulton & Watt and Matthew Boulton archives* [MS3147 & MS3782] at the Wolfson Centre for Archival Research, Library of Birmingham.

5   Ibid.

6   'Engine House for his Highness the Nabob Vizier of Oude. Front entrance elevation.' February 1814 in the *Boulton & Watt and Matthew Boulton archives* [MS3147 & MS3782] at the Wolfson Centre for Archival Research, Library of Birmingham.

7   A good source of information about the history of F. & C. Osler is the website of crystal chandelier specialist Wilkinson Ltd, which took over the remnants of the defunct Birmingham firm, together with the Faraday lighting company in the 1980s. wilkinson-ltd.com/osler-faraday. An even more comprehensive history of the firm is told on the website of the Corning Museum of Glass, based in New York State, US. www.cmog.org/article/f-c-osler.

8   Letter from James Bowerman to Follet Osler, Calcutta, 4 April 1854. In *F. & C. Osler papers* [MS6] at the Wolfson Centre for Archival Research, Library of Birmingham.

9   Ibid.

10 Historian Simon Schama is very good at explaining the liberal creed that underpinned the British Empire in a chapter 'The Empire of Good Intentions: Investments' in the third part of his *A History of Britain* (London: BBC Worldwide Ltd, 2003). Macaulay's idea – idealistic and extremely condescending in equal measure – was that old, corrupt, superstitious India had fallen under the trusteeship of the British Empire, which would give it a good shaking through good government until India became modern and liberal enough to outgrow the system.

11   Birmingham Museum & Art Gallery has an ongoing exhibition called *Birmingham Revolutions – Power to the People*. On an information board about Birmingham's response to the French Revolution of 1789, the text reads that: 'At the time, Birmingham had no civic status and was neither a town nor a borough, making it a melting pot for different religions and political ideas … As an unofficial town, Birmingham was a centre for Dissenters including Quakers and Unitarians. Dissenters were unable to practise their religion within five miles of an official town and were not allowed jobs in civic or military offices under the Test Act (1673) or Corporation Act (1661).' The National Archives website takes up the nonconformist story of Birmingham, www.nationalarchives.gov.uk/pathways/citizenship/ rise_parliament/birmingham.htm. Could the city's dissenting traditions have fuelled the 'Birmingham Enlightenment' in the eighteenth century when members of the Lunar Society were leading new thinking in science, politics and economics?

12   Chris Upton, *A History of Birmingham* (Stroud: The History Press, 2011), p.50.

13   The Rev. Thomas Swan, 1835 annual report of the Baptist Missionary Society, *The Rev. Thomas Swan papers* [MS1675] held at the Wolfson Centre for Archival Research, Library of Birmingham.

14   Ibid.

15   The Rev. Thomas Swan, 1836 annual report of the Baptist Missionary Society, *The Rev. Thomas Swan papers* [MS1675] held at the Wolfson Centre for Archival Research, Library of Birmingham.

16   The Rev. Thomas Swan, 1837 annual report of the Baptist Missionary Society, *The Rev. Thomas Swan papers* [MS1675] held at the Wolfson Centre for Archival Research, Library of Birmingham.

17   B.D. Metcalf and T.R. Metcalf, p.101.

18   Ibid.

19   Burton Stein, *A History of India* (Chichester: Wiley-Blackwell, 2010), p.222.

20   Letter from James Bowerman to Follet Osler, Calcutta, 1 August 1857. In *F. & C. Osler papers* [MS6] at the Wolfson Centre for Archival Research, Library of Birmingham.

21   Letter from James Bowerman to Follet Osler, Calcutta, 22 August 1857. In *F. & C. Osler papers* [MS6] at the Wolfson Centre for Archival Research, Library of Birmingham.

22   Letter from James Bowerman to Follet Osler, Calcutta, 22 October 1857. In *F. & C. Osler papers* [MS6] at the Wolfson Centre for Archival Research, Library of Birmingham.

II. TRAVELLERS AND VISIONARIES

If the Rev. Thomas Swan went to India in the 1820s to convert it, then Birmingham traveller Helen Caddick went to India in the 1890s to appreciate it.

Born in 1845, Caddick lived first in West Bromwich, a very typical working town in the Black Country, and then later on in a fairly ordinary, well-to-do street in Edgbaston. York Road was just one of many streets in this middle-class suburb that were filled with sturdy red-brick Victorian villas with bay windows and a room in the attic.

But there was nothing particularly typical or ordinary about this particular woman. First of all, she was a nonconformist (a Unitarian of the Church of the Messiah on Broad Street), who took an active role in local educational institutions. She was the first woman member of the West Bromwich Education Committee and also one of the first governors of Birmingham University.

Secondly, and perhaps most importantly, her interest in travel and anthropology led her, in 1889, to embark on a series of travels that over the next quarter of the century would take her to the furthest corners of the globe – from Japan and Java in the east to Panama and Peru in the west. In these solo wanderings, she became one of a very select band of Victorian women – including Mary Kingsley, who waded through the swamps of West Africa; Gertrude Bell, who was only really happy when she was in a tent in the Arabian desert; and Isabella Bird, who travelled through the jungles of Malaysia in search of a mythical antique land called 'the Golden Chersonese' – that defied the conventions of the time and went out into the world in search of adventure.

She recorded her experiences in one book, *A White Woman in Central Africa*, and many volumes of diaries, many of them hundreds of pages long, which not only record her impressions of the people she met and places she saw but also include photographs that she took or collected on her travels. She was also a collector of ethnographical artefacts, which are now housed at Sandwell Museum in the Black Country.

In 1893, her diaries covered a journey across India, in which her fascination for different cultures is apparent. Disembarking from her ship in Bombay at the beginning of January, on Tuesday the 10th she was attending a wedding ceremony in the local Parsi community, a community that after fleeing religious persecution in Persia (now Iran) centuries beforehand had ended up in Bombay, where the British had decreed complete religious tolerance after they had taken control of the city in 1688.

In her diary entry, Caddick describes alternating between two houses on either side of an outside space prettily lit with oil lamps. The first port of call was the bridegroom's house, in which there was a large room full of 'ladies in lovely "sawries" and splendid jewellery. The shades of crepe and silk were lovely, and beautiful borders of rich velvet worked with gold and silver. The Bride came in and salaamed to her Mother-in-law and various relations.'

All the wedding guests were then summoned over to the bride's house on the other side of the open space.

'There, seats were arranged all round and in the centre a carpet was spread and on it two chairs placed. Presently the girls went to fetch the Bridegroom, he was met at the door by the Bride's mother who put a garland round his neck, waved dishes over his head and various performances we did not understand. But just before this, the Bride came in and was presented to various relations ...'

The bride and bridegroom then sat down on the two chairs, and the wedding ceremony performed by two priests began. 'The priests repeated endless exhortations and prayers in Sanscrit,' Caddick observed. They then, 'took handfuls of rice etc and every few moments threw some at the couple who remained seated'.

The ceremony lasted about half an hour, and then after bride and groom had made 'profound bows', the bride went off to prepare for the big wedding dinner. Caddick described the dinner:

... long tables were arranged down the room with chairs on one side, plantain leaves for plates, a tumbler but no forks etc. When all were seated (about 600) the cooks came round with huge dishes and spooned a dab onto each leaf – first fish, then potato chips, then sorts of pies, sweet stuff, fried fish, cakes etc till each leaf was nearly covered. We watched the children eating – they took everything in their fingers, but so neatly, only using one hand, and ate of each thing![1]

In contrast, a walk out to the sacred Hindu village of Walkeshwar up on Malabar Hill a few days later was a much more rustic affair. 'Temples all round,' Caddick jotted down, 'with curious roofs, figures of oxen all decorated, very holy men with hair long and matted, their faces covered with paint and grease, no clothing, squatting before a small altar set out with "toys" which they were decorating with flowers and leaves ...'[2]

After leaving Bombay, she took a traditional route across India, northwards to the 'pink city' of Jaipur, where she witnessed a Hindu wedding procession with the 'Bride veiled and seated on an elephant, gorgeously got up',[3] and then on to the old Moghul city of Delhi; and finally Agra, home to the ethereally beautiful Taj Mahal.

Although these were clearly visits in pursuit of the picturesque, Caddick also made time for the gruesome, going on to visit Cawnpore, the site of a terrible massacre of 400 British women and children during the Indian Mutiny, many of their remains thrown down a nearby well. 'The site of the house where the massacre was is marked by a stone and is close to the well,' she wrote. 'Little graves abound and the Memorial Church is full of tablets.'[4]

Sitting on India's most famous river, Cawnpore (now Kanpur) was at the beginning of a route she now took across the Ganges plain, taking in the holy city of Benares (now Varanasi) before she turned north-east and towards the place she probably would have dreamt of going to most in her residence back home in Birmingham.

She arrived on the British-built miniature railway winding its way up into the Himalayan foothills on Saturday, 4 March. 'Reached Darjeeling at 4.25,' she wrote. 'Stopped on the way at Clarendon Hotel for tiffin. Splendid journey, through woods for the first part. The train line runs along the road way, twists and turns about at the edge of precipices in several places, makes loops and crosses going under and over bridges and in four places goes up zigzags, shunting and going forward.'[5]

With her anthropological hat on she soon noticed the ethnic change in Darjeeling. 'The hill people very different from those in the plains, more like Chinese, short, strong and healthy and merry looking,' she scribbled down in her diary. They 'wear pigtails and quantities of silver and gold and turquoise ornaments and huge necklaces of rupees. Use prayer wheels, which they twist round in their hands.'[6]

But with the highest mountains in the world sitting on the horizon, the picturesque was always going to top observations of local humanity. On the Monday after her arrival, Caddick went for a long walk in the hills. Her trek yielded 'beautiful views of Kinchinjunga, covered with snow and the hills all round, pretty blue light on them'.[7]

☙

As Caddick took in the view of the snowy peaks of the third highest mountain in the world, another Birmingham luminary, or certainly someone who was going to become so, was penning an essay on the 'Mutual Influences of Mohammedans and Hindus in India' in his cloistered room at Trinity College, Cambridge.

Frederick William Thomas had come up to Cambridge after being a star pupil at Birmingham's King Edward's School, established by royal charter in 1552 and widely regarded as the best school in town. There, Thomas had begun to study the ancient Indian language of Sanskrit, which took him to

Cambridge to read classics and Indian languages. He graduated with a First in the Indian Languages Tripos in 1890, and was elected fellow of Trinity College in 1892.

Had his father not died he may well have stayed there, but soon afterwards he returned to live again with his family in Birmingham. In what was probably a difficult time for the young man, he went back to his old school as a head-master's assistant, and immersed himself again in life at the lavish Victorian institution on New Street in the centre of town – a neo-Gothic building that had produced some brilliant pupils in the previous decades, including the Pre-Raphaelite painter Edward Burne-Jones, and would churn out a few more in the following decades.

But even though he was deeply involved in school life, Thomas did not abandon his interest in India, and by 1897, with the help of Cambridge professor of Sanskrit Edward Byles Cowell, he had translated an epic Sanskrit biography from the seventh century, the *Harshacharita*, which, written by a court poet called Banabhatta, tells the story of a Buddhist king in northern India.

It must have been off the back of this that the following year he then won an appointment to the institution that would employ him for the rest of his career – the India Office Library in London – first as assistant librarian, then very soon afterwards as librarian.

Obtained during the high noon years of the Raj,[8] this was a prestigious position in 'the colonial information order',[9] which over the decades had invested much time and effort into knowing more about Britain's foremost overseas possession. This was built on the early work of the Asiatic Society of Bengal, founded in 1784, which had dedicated itself to the study of India's ancient Hindu and Buddhist kingdoms, together with the Great Trigonometrical Survey, begun in 1818, that had divided the subcontinent into neat triangles so that it could map every contour, every flood plain, of this vast country. By the time of Thomas, it had moved on to a whole indus-try of gazetteers, almanacs and censuses including the well-respected *The Imperial Gazetteer of India*, dedicated to detailing every aspect of Indian life past and present.

To this ever-expanding canon of knowledge, F.W. Thomas added an impor-tant contribution. One of his first tasks was imposing order on all the East India Company papers relating to India, from the 1600s when the company first started trading along the coastline to its dismantling in 1858 after the Indian Mutiny.

Throughout his tenure, the librarian was closely associated with the Royal Asiatic Society, cataloguing many of its Sanskrit manuscripts, and regularly contributing scholarly articles to the Society's journal. As a British 'orientalist' – an old-fashioned term now for those who studied the history and culture of Asian societies – his academic interests were focused on the ancient languages of India and its borderlands as unearthed in historical manuscripts (philology). He contributed three chapters to the first volume of the *Cambridge History of India*, concerning the ancient Indian fiefdom of Maurya and its famous Buddhist emperor Ashoka; and was the editor of *Epigraphia Indica*, the official publication of the Archaeological Survey of India, from 1916 to 1922.

During 1920 and 1921, he took some time out to spend eight months on the subcontinent, travelling widely, mostly by train, in Nepal, Tibet and India, and delivering public lectures at the universities of Mysore, Calcutta and Bombay.

He was to recall this trip years later in 1937 when he was in India again, this time at a conference in the south. By then he had retired from the India Office Library, and had for ten years been the Boden Professor of Sanskrit at Oxford University. In his presidential address to the Ninth All-Indian Oriental Conference at Trivandrum in Kerala, the ageing academic now opened up a bit about his love for India.

Remembering his previous visit there December 1920, he spoke of 'the entrancing vision of moonlit forest glades when at night I drew my curtain in the train; the flourishing paysage inclined towards the radiant Indian Ocean which the first daylight revealed ...'[10]

৭৩

Attending another conference in India just the year before, in 1935, had been another shining light of Birmingham, albeit someone who had married into the city rather than being born or brought up there. 'Dame Elizabeth Cadbury, with three other prominent members of the National Council of Women of Great Britain are leaving London today by *Rawalpindi* [a ship] for Calcutta to attend the international conference of women organised by the National Council for Women in India,' the *Manchester Guardian* reported on 3 January 1936. 'Among the subjects to be discussed will be peace and the League of Nations, education, public health, legal disabilities of women, traffic in women and girls, the cinema, broadcasting, and women and the press.'[11]

Although she was now nearly 80, it was no surprise that Elizabeth Cadbury, or Elsie as she was affectionately known, was heading up the British delegation to the International Council of Women's meeting. In line with the council's objectives, she had dedicated her whole life to social reform and international peace. Born into a London family with strong Quaker commitments to bettering the world, she had spent much of her childhood visiting workhouses with her mother and volunteering in children's hospitals. The chances were, therefore, that when she married fellow Quaker George Cadbury in 1888, some years after his first wife had died, and moved to Birmingham, that these good works would certainly continue, if not accelerate.

She threw herself into philanthropy, in fact, as well as finding time to bear George six children. George, of course, as his name suggests, was one of the founding partners of Birmingham's famous chocolate firm, and Elsie was soon involved in developing the Bournville estate, the model village providing company workers and others with good housing, schools and leisure facilities that her husband had established alongside the factory he had opened next to the Birmingham & Worcester Canal in 1879. By 1900, the village had expanded to 370 cottages, all built in the distinctive Arts and Crafts style, but available at affordable rents.

The 'tall, dignified, impressive' woman of a 'kindly and generous nature'[12] also joined her husband in his commitment to adult education, working to improve part-time and night class education for workers and their wives. In addition, she campaigned for medical inspections in children's schools and chaired the Birmingham School Inspection Committee.

It was not long, too, before she was casting her net wider, providing support for Belgian refugees in England during the First World War, and when the League of Nations was set up in the aftermath of that conflict, becoming its local representative and campaigning for international disarmament.

The net was cast even wider with the Calcutta conference of 1936. Village development, education and health – Elizabeth Cadbury's strong preoccupations – were all themes picked up by the conference, as the *Manchester Guardian* predicted. 'The opening session was held under the presidency of the Maharani of Baroda, who spoke of the need of greater education among Indian women,' the *Sunday Times* correspondent, very probably Elued Lewis, who accompanied Dame Cadbury to India, wrote. 'Among the subjects discussed during the week have been village schools (it is worth noting that 90 per cent of the population of India are village dwellers) …'[13]

Elsie herself was struck by the 'very stiff battles' Indian women were fighting with the British authorities in India to get 'the grants for medical inspection', which 'had been cut in the Budgets', restored.[14]

This engagement with the issue of medical provision also manifested itself in a visit to a Quaker mission in central India before the Calcutta summit. Here, at the Friends Mission in Itarsi, Cadbury made a donation towards the purchase of a mobile medical dispensary.

On her return to Britain, William Tandy of the Friends Hospital in Itarsi wrote a letter of thanks:

The Travelling Dispensary and Ambulance which you so kindly gave to the Hospital has now arrived ... [It] is very satisfactory. There is room for over a dozen people in it. It is fitted up with shelves for bottles, and has cupboards and shelves for dressings and instruments, and can transport seriously ill patients ... It is going to prove of immense value to this district. None of the large villages around here have any medical aid of any sort, and the regular visit of a doctor complete with Dispensary will make a tremendous difference in their lives. I took it out for the first time last Tuesday, and I should like you to have seen the looks on people's faces when I told them that it would be visiting them every week ...'[15]

☙

What William Tandy didn't tell Dame Cadbury was that he was increasingly concerned about the situation in India. He saved that for a letter later that year to a Paul Sturge of the British Friends Service Council, a Quaker organisation in London committed to foreign humanitarian work. Beginning the letter with comments about the deteriorating political situation in Europe, especially the civil war in Spain, he went on to write:

India is also seething with unrest. Serious communal riots in Bombay with 60 deaths ... Nehru disturbed and fretful about the whole social structure, and yet recoiling in horror at the thought of violence, but not knowing any alternative in order to rebuild it ... Nehru attracts me because he quite sincerely loves and is concerned about the ordinary Indian peasant whose lot is a sorry one. I know because I am just beginning to learn a little about the villagers for myself. I'm wondering where it is all going to lead; and, both in India and in Europe, where Christ comes in, in all the turmoil.[16]

The turmoil in India described by Tandy can be traced back to 1919. Disquiet with the British Raj and calls by nationalists for *swaraj*, or self-rule for India, had been growing for decades, and the British had responded with gradual reforms to bring more Indians into legislative assemblies and democratic institutions. It was 1919 that, in the face of growing social unrest caused by post-war economic hardships, saw first the repressive Rowlatt Acts, which extended police powers of detention without trial, and then on 13 April, the terrible catastrophe of the Amritsar massacre. This was the fateful day when local commander Reginald Dyer ordered British troops to fire on a crowd of peaceful protesters gathered in the Jallianwalla Bagh gardens, killing at least 400 people. Despite the Government of India Act of the same year, which set in train a process towards self-government for the country,[17] it was this massacre, in particular, which proved, in the view of many historians, to be the tipping point for British India. It was the event, writes historian Michael Wood, 'from which the Indian perception of British fair play, goodwill and justice never quite recovered'.[18]

It was this perception that led to a political movement against British rule known as 'non-violent non-co-operation' led by a charismatic new leader, Mohandas K. Gandhi, who had recently returned from twenty years in South Africa, and thereafter a campaign of civil disobedience led by Gandhi and other nationalist leaders such as Jawaharlal Nehru. Against a background of ongoing 'communal riots' between the Muslim and Hindu communities described by Tandy, the authority of the Raj was being increasingly challenged.

Amid the turmoil, though, there was one British man, in particular, working hard to bring the opposing sides together. He had a hand in bringing Gandhi to Britain in 1931 for the Round Table Conference between the British government and Indian leaders, and he also had a hand in the drafting of the India Act of 1935, which greatly extended the Indian electorate and brought the Indian National Congress Party led by Gandhi and Nehru into government in several provinces across the subcontinent. His name was Charles Freer Andrews, and he was educated at Birmingham's King Edward's School. He is famous in India to this day. In his own country he is almost unknown.

C.F. Andrews grew up in Birmingham with a father who was a great believer in the British Empire. 'The vast Empire in India was, in my father's opinion, the most glorious achievement of the Anglo-Saxon race,' Andrews wrote in a book in 1932. He continued:

> Tales of British heroism in India fixed my own imagination and I said to my mother: 'when I grow up I am going to live in India'. Not one word was told me of the evils and weaknesses involved in the British imperial system. My father simply could not believe that this country had done anything that was unfair or ungenerous to others. These same patriotic convictions were so strongly in-wrought in my own character that it was long before I could be induced even by my own experience to believe that there was 'another side of the medal'.[19]

A minister in the Catholic Apostolic Church in Birmingham, Andrews' father was thrown into financial misfortune due to the duplicity of a friend, and had it not been for a scholarship to King Edward's, Charles' education might have been cut short. His was a brilliant school career, although not without its difficulties. 'At a rapid pace, I was pushed up the school from one class to another,' Andrews wrote. 'This process left me always the youngest boy in the class and an easy victim for the stronger boys to bully.'[20]

Despite this issue and the mental torture it almost certainly would have brought, the King Edward's boy won a scholarship to Pembroke College, Cambridge, to read Classics and Theology in 1890 – the same year as fellow Edwardian F.W. Thomas graduated from Cambridge. Over the following five years, he moved his allegiance from the church of his father to the Church of England, perhaps under the influence of Brooke Foss Westcott, who was the regius professor of divinity at Cambridge at the time, as well as being the Bishop of Durham.

A deepening awareness of social injustice then took this idealistic young man, now with a First Class Honours degree under his belt, to the Pembroke College Mission in south London to get involved in the issues of slum housing and unemployment that beset the poor communities there, and it was during this time that he became ordained as a Church of England minister.

A subsequent breakdown in health, however, took him back to Cambridge University as a staff member for a few years. But then came the news that, given his childhood dream, seemed almost pre-ordained: his friend Basil Westcott (the son of Bishop Westcott) had died of cholera in Delhi. It was tragic news, certainly, but it served to open a new chapter for Andrews. In March 1904, he arrived in India to take his old friend's place as a teacher at a Delhi college founded by Cambridge dons, St Stephen's.

Now that he was in India he began to see 'the other side to the medal', seeing for himself the racial prejudice that some in the British Raj dealt out to the native Indian population. Then, a few years later, came the moment of truth. Acting temporarily as a chaplain at Sanawar in the British hill station of Shimla, he discovered that the attitude of one of his British colleagues meant that an Indian friend from St Stephen's, Sushil Kumar Rudra, would not be able to stay there as his guest. The insult 'to his friend, and to India, made Andrews burn with shame'.[21]

The incident coincided with a letter published in a Lahore newspaper that abused Indian political leaders. 'With a heart full of indignation and sorrow', Andrews sat down and wrote back, defending the Indian politicians and signing the letter with his full name, address and official rank: military chaplain.[22]

The letter was a turning point. Overnight, Andrews had become 'a rebel':[23] a rebel against the racial arrogance of the British Raj, and a rebel against his own middle-class security. Members of the Indian National Congress began to seek him out, and his writings began to appear in Indian journals.

A rebel with an artistic temperament, Andrews loved drama, poetry and music; he had a gift for painting and drawing; and he was a skilled writer. Here he is describing the 'Bengal renaissance', the intellectual and artistic movement that swept through Calcutta at the turn of the century:

There is a day in the east never to be forgotten, the day of the coming of the monsoon rains after the long dusty drought. The dead parched ground seems to put on a new verdure in a single night, and the new tender grass appears upon the barren soil … so it has been in the last few years in India … new ideas are visible on every side. They produce whirling eddies in the rising flood of waters. The onward tide is like one of those great Indian rivers after the monsoon rains.[24]

வ

It was a chance meeting with one of the leading lights of the Bengal renaissance, the poet Rabindranath Tagore, which would turn Andrews, the rebel, into Andrews, the activist; and, in turn, make him lifelong friends with not only Tagore but also Tagore's comrade, Mahatma Gandhi. Back in England on leave in 1912, Andrews went along to a private reading being held by the Bengal poet at a house in London. He was instantly enchanted by both the poetry and the poet himself.

The feeling was mutual, and the two soon entered into correspondence, a correspondence that soon included Gandhi as well. The three would carry on sending letters to each other until the first of them, Andrews, died in 1940.

Inspired by Tagore and Gandhi, Andrews left his teaching role at St Stephen's, and after a spell at Tagore's ashram at Shantiniketan in West Bengal, spent the next decade or so helping poor communities in India, and also Indian communities in Fiji and South Africa. In India, he reported on the plight of villagers in Orissa left homeless by floods and the 'untouchables' of Kerala, and also inspired the opening of Christian ashrams – spiritual centres established in the spirit of St Francis of Assisi. In Fiji, where he came known as Deenabandhu, or 'friend of the poor', he collected evidence on the living standards of plantation workers. In South Africa, he met Gandhi for the first time, bending and touching the Mahatma's feet in an Indian gesture of respect in front of astounded white colonialists; and was instrumental, some say, in the Indian lawyer's decision to return to India to take up the civil rights struggle.

When the time came, therefore, it was C.F. Andrews, as his trusted confidant, that Gandhi turned to when he needed a mediator between him and the colonial establishment. Between 1928 and 1937, Andrews was not often in India, but instead became India's unofficial ambassador in Britain. It was the King Edward's boy who prepared the ground for Gandhi's twelve-week visit to Britain in 1931 when the frail-looking Indian leader, wearing the simple loincloth of the Hindu holyman, met

Mahatma Gandhi shares a joke with Charles Freer Andrews at an ashram in central India in 1939. The Indian freedom fighter and the former Birmingham schoolboy were close friends and confidants. (Dinodia Photos/Alamy Stock Photo)

religious leaders and Lancashire mill workers, as well as politicians at the Round Table conference in London. It was the King Edward's boy who wrote two books about Gandhi's ideas and his work to coincide with the visit, and worked hard to interpret India to those in the British government responsible for drafting the India Act of 1935. 'I am trying hard to make my countrymen realise the immediate necessity of granting Dominion Status to India,' he had written in a letter to Gandhi in 1929.[25]

Dominion status would have given India the same self-governing institutions as those already enjoyed by the 'white-settler' dominions of Canada, Australia and New Zealand. Whatever political freedoms C.F. Andrews and his two comrades in Gandhi and Tagore sought, though, they would not be realised for many years. It would take a world war to precipitate the final demise of British India.

Andrews died during the first flurries of that war. He had returned to India – the place of his childhood dreams – in the late 1930s, and passed away during a visit to Calcutta on 5 April 1940. He is buried in the city, in the Lower Circular Road Christian cemetery.

In tribute to his friend, Gandhi wrote: 'There was no distance between us. It was not a friendship between an Englishman and an Indian. It was an unbreakable bond between two seekers and servants.'[26]

Meanwhile, the renowned Indian journalist Ramananda Chatterji wrote: 'Mr Andrews wanted friendship between India and Britain as between equals. This he desired in the interest of Britain as well as of India because he was a great patriot, greater than any British Imperialist. He was one of the heralds of a new age, which is still a dream – an age of international amity, human brotherhood, including Indo-British friendship.'[27]

৩৯

King Edward's School – both the one for boys and the one for girls – went through something of an architectural upheaval in the years running up to the Second World War. Since the nineteenth century, both establishments had been housed in a flamboyant truffle of a building designed by Charles Barry, the architect who went on to draw up the iconic Houses of Parliament still standing at Westminster today. The building on New Street in the centre of town was certainly beautiful. The only problem was the location. With the coming of the railways, the land to the rear of the building was leased to the

London & Birmingham Railway Company, and before too long the screech of the Euston steam train began to reverberate through the hallowed cloisters of the school, while smoke and steam began to cloud the walls. By the early 1930s it was decided – the building was a fire risk, and would have to be demolished, while the school itself would move out to a leafy new site in Edgbaston. Although there continued to be teething architectural problems, two adjacent schools in Edgbaston – one for boys, the other for girls – were officially inaugurated in 1936, and Birmingham's cleverest children were now educated in smart red-brick buildings, which, in a nod to the institution's Tudor origins, included wide stone doorways and oriel-style windows on the outside and timber beams on the inside. My mother, Joy Perkins, studied there in the 1940s, and the schools have been there ever since, producing some of Britain's brightest and best – for instance, the writer Jonathan Coe and BBC broadcaster Reeta Chakrabarti, who is from an Indian Bengali family.[28]

One of the last pupils of the old building in New Street, though, one of the final few drowned out by the whistle of the steam trains when trying to recite Shakespeare, was a boy called Laurie Baker, who would go on to become one of India's most renowned architects.

Whether the school's neo-Gothic exterior or the hallowed church-like corridors of the interior designed by Gothic revivalist Augustus Welby Pugin inspired him or not, on leaving school Baker enrolled at the Birmingham School of Architecture. He graduated in 1937 at the age of 20, and started his professional apprenticeship only for it to be stopped in its tracks by the outbreak of war.

As a Quaker and therefore a conscientious objector, Baker (1917–2007) was sent out to southern China as a trained paramedic with the Friends Ambulance Unit. Close to the Burmese theatre of war where fellow Old Edwardian Field Marshall William Slim was trying to repel the Japanese advance into British India, he was involved in tending to severely wounded victims, and later worked at a leprosy hospital.

The hardships of this life eventually took their toll on the young Birmingham man's health, and in 1943 he was told to return home to recover. But it was then that a chance encounter laid the foundations of the very different kind of path that Baker would soon take. Staying in Bombay with a Quaker family who happened to know Gandhi, waiting for the ship to take him home, he happened to meet the Indian guru. Smitten now by India, Baker told the Mahatma about his urge to return to work there 'even though the British were being urged to get out'. In response, Gandhi encouraged him 'to return to India'.[29]

Back in Birmingham nearing the end of the war, Baker was now witness to the huge devastation that the Luftwaffe had wrought on his city. The air raid sirens had fallen silent, but in their wake Birmingham had been reduced to rubble. From Bennetts Hill to John Bright Street, from Yardley to Ward End, people picked their way through the fallen masonry. My mother crossed the uprooted tramlines on the way to her teacher training undergraduate course at Birmingham University, arm-in-arm with her new boyfriend, a languages student called John Andrews. But Laurie Baker would ultimately turn away.

'Obviously, there was going to be a major requirement of architects once the war came to an end,' he wrote later. 'Even so, the housing needs of many of the millions of people in India seemed to be far greater and their chances of getting people to help them build extensively far lesser than those in Britain. So within a few months, I found myself on board a ship bound for India.'[30]

Given his experience in China in a leprosy hospital and his architectural training, Baker was plunged into work back in India, converting old buildings into modern leprosy hospitals, and very soon too was to meet the woman who would become his wife – an Indian doctor called Elizabeth Jacob.

The couple – married in the late 1940s despite some opposition to such a mixed union from family and friends – settled down in the Himalayan town of Pithoragarh, and here Baker was soon involved in building schools, hospitals and community centres. It was a huge learning curve for the architect, because he was having to adapt all the theory he had learnt at a school of architecture in an industrial city thousands of miles away to a mountain terrain where the building materials consisted only of what could be found locally: rock, mud, cow dung and wood. He was now putting up dwellings on steep slopes, overlooking terraced fields, which had to be able to cope with all the extremities of the Himalayan climate: from heavy snow and bitter winds in the winter, to violent rainstorms and blistering heat in the summer. As a result, his architectural style began to take on the quality of being rooted in the local environment.

But it was in Trivandrum in the southern state of Kerala, where the couple moved some years later, that Laurie Baker's architecture truly came of age. It was here, according to Indian architect Gautam Bhatia, where the ideals of self-sufficiency and local craftsmanship expounded by the guru Baker had met by chance during the war – Mahatma Gandhi – and his own deep Quaker beliefs in 'simplicity and austerity'[31] came together to produce a very distinctive idiom.

Unlike the bloated modernist buildings of glass and concrete that dominate many Indian cities today, argues Bhatia, the Baker-constructed buildings scattered across Trivandrum blend into the local landscape. In other words, the vocabulary of sloping tile roofs, overhanging eaves and open plan courtyards fit perfectly into the tropical climate of Kerala, where the orientalist F. W. Thomas had once seen his 'enchanting vision of moonlit forest glades'.

In buildings such as the Centre for Development Studies, Baker adapted a traditional Indian technique to produce his own 'jali walls' – brick walls perforated with tiny regular openings that not only served as windows and ventilation shafts, but also created intricate patterns of light and shadow.

In others, he used discarded remnants of old architecture that he found in local junkyards. It was a rare find of 'the portico of a temple demolished in one part of Trivandrum which became the formal entrance to the Chitralekha Studio Complex because of its ornamental woodwork'.[32] This would have chimed well with his Quaker inclinations towards careful conservation and keeping costs down.

One of Baker's most famous buildings was St John's Cathedral in Tiruvalla, deep in the Keralan countryside. Inside, this place of worship is set out like a

The Centre for Development Studies in Trivandrum features the trademark 'jali walls' of architect Laurie Baker. (Dinodia Photos/Alamy Stock Photo)

Greek cross, with a square central mass and four arms of equal length. Outside, it looks like a Hindu temple, with a steeply pitched roof covered with traditional terracotta fish tiles.

This was a church building returned to the local vernacular – where two strong religious traditions, both widely followed in Kerala, come together.

Or perhaps Baker's work was always just rooted in a wider religious sensibility born of his Quaker convictions. Gautam Bhatia certainly thought so. Firmly 'anchored to his Quaker beliefs,' he wrote, Baker's architecture 'is ordered by the consideration and circumstances of this ancient ecclesiastical consciousness. To enter a room, a hall, a house built by him is to become immediately aware of this profound connection.'[33]

NOTES

1   Helen Caddick. Diary entry on Tuesday, 10 January 1893. Travel diaries of Helen Caddick [MS908] held at the Wolfson Centre for Archival Research, Library of Birmingham.

2   Ibid., Diary entry on Sunday, 15 January 1893.

3   Ibid., Diary entry on Thursday, 9 February 1893.

4   Ibid., Diary entry on Wednesday, 22 February 1893.

5   Ibid., Diary entry on Saturday, 4 March 1893.

6   Ibid., Diary entry on Monday, 6 March 1893.

7   Ibid., Another diary entry on Monday, 6 March 1893.

8   The Indian Mutiny, or the First War of Independence as many Indians regard it, was by then a distant memory. In the aftermath of 1857, the British authorities had managed to reconsolidate their power by transferring all responsibility for governing India from the East India Company directly to Westminster, and a Secretary of State sitting in Cabinet. On the Indian side of things, educated Indians were very gradually brought into elective councils and the governing structure, including the all-important Indian Civil Service, the administrative elite that ran the country. Economically, India now occupied a central position in Britain's global imperial system: it had the fifth longest railway system in the world, its cities were deeply connected to the mother country by shipping lines and telegraph wires, and commercial activity was expanding apace. This business activity not only benefited British firms for whom India would soon become the chief export market for their machinery, but also for Indian-owned industries such as those owned by the Tata family of Bombay.

9   B.D. Metcalf and T.R. Metcalf, *A Concise History of Modern India* (Cambridge: Cambridge University Press, 2006), p.64.

10   H.N. Randle, *Frederick William Thomas 1867–1956* (London: Oxford University Press, 1959), p.217.

11   'Women delegates to a Calcutta conference', *Manchester Guardian*, 3 January 1936. Press cutting preserved in Elizabeth Cadbury papers [MS466/169] held at the Wolfson Centre for Archival Research, Library of Birmingham.

12   Cited in *Birmingham Mail* report, 17 March 2016. 'Remembered: Dame Elizabeth

Cadbury's tireless work to improve the lives of Birmingham people'. [Online]

13   From our own correspondent. 'Women in Council: Success of Indian conference'. *Sunday Times*, 16 February 1936. Press cutting preserved in Elizabeth Cadbury papers [MS466/169] held at the Wolfson Centre for Archival Research, Library of Birmingham.

14   Report from a 'Special Correspondent' in *Times of India*, 3 April 1936. 'Dame Cadbury's Impressions of India: Indian Women Friendly and Hospitable'. Press cutting preserved in Elizabeth Cadbury papers [MS466/169] held at the Wolfson Centre for Archival Research, Library of Birmingham.

15   Letter from William Tandy, Friends' Hospital, Itarsi, CP, India, to Elizabeth Cadbury, dated 12 July 1936. Letter preserved in Elizabeth Cadbury papers [MS466/169] held at the Wolfson Centre for Archival Research, Library of Birmingham.

16   Letter from William Tandy, Friends' Hospital, Itarsi, CP, India, to Paul Sturge, dated 30 October 1936. Letter preserved in Elizabeth Cadbury papers [MS466/169] held at the Wolfson Centre for Archival Research, Library of Birmingham.

17   Burton Stein, *A History of India* (Chichester: Wiley-Blackwell, 2010), p.293.

18   Michael Wood, *The Story of India* (London: BBC Books, Ebury Publishing, 2008), p.280.

19   C.F. Andrews. *What I Owe to Christ*, cited in S.R. Sharma, *Life and Works of C.F. Andrews* (Jaipur, India: Book Enclave, 2009), p.19.

20   C.F. Andrews, *What I Owe to Christ* (London: Hodder & Stoughton, 1931), p.89.

21   S.R. Sharma, *Life and Works of C.F. Andrews* (Jaipur, India: Book Enclave, 2009), p.6.

22   Ibid., p.6.

23   Ibid., p.7.

24   C.F. Andrews, *What I Owe to Christ*, cited in S.R. Sharma, p.35.

25   Letter from C.F. Andrews to Gandhi, 4 February 1929. Published in *Friendships of 'largeness and freedom': Andrews, Tagore and Gandhi: an epistolary account 1912–1940*, edited by Uma Das Gupta (New Delhi: Oxford University Press, 2018), p.308.

26   Mahatma Gandhi cited in S.R. Sharma, *Life and Works of C.F. Andrews*, p.177.

27   Ramananda Chatterji cited in S.R. Sharma, *Life and Works of C.F. Andrews*, p.188.

28   The story of King Edward's is available from a number of sources – T.W. Hutton, *King Edward's School, Birmingham 1552–1952* (Oxford: Basil Blackwell, 1952); W.I. Candler, Ailsa M. Jaques and B.M.W. Dobbie, *King Edward VI High School for Girls Birmingham* (London: Ernest Benn Ltd, 1971); and the school websites www.kehs.org.uk and www.kes.org.uk.

29   Laurie Baker's writings in Gautam Bhatia, *Laurie Baker, Life, Works, Writings* (New Delhi: Penguin, 1994), p.223.

30   Ibid., p.223.

31   Gautam Bhatia, *Laurie Baker, Life, Works, Writings* (London: Penguin, 1994), p.16.

32   Ibid., p.55.

33   Ibid., p.17.

III. NEW ARRIVALS

When Baker left for India in 1945, never to return, there were about a thousand people from British India living in Birmingham. But exactly how and why and when these people arrived is a little difficult to discern, as if a Jali screen is standing between them and the modern observer, and only the small perforations in that screen occasionally allow us a glimpse of these characters and their lives.

What we do know comprise only brief fragments and images, gleaned from the archives in Birmingham. We know that by the 1860s there were three lodging houses for Asians in the city, one of them run by a Christian convert called Dada Bhai; and we know something about a Birmingham solicitor called George Edalji, the son of an Indian Parsee and an English woman, because he was the victim of an outrageous miscarriage of justice. Wrongly convicted for mutilating a horse in 1903, but released from prison three years later without pardon, apology or explanation, his case was taken up by the famous crime writer Arthur Conan Doyle, who after a long campaign managed to prove his innocence and clear his name.[1]

We also know that Gandhi visited the Quakers in the city and met the Bishop of Birmingham as part of his visit to the UK in 1931, and in 1924 the *Birmingham Mail* carried an advert for Indian eye specialists Jahangir & Sons on Bath Row. But much further beyond these images, the picture is fragmentary and obscure.

Indians celebrated independence in 1947, but the accompanying partition of their country and the terrible suffering it caused would become a major driver behind migration to Birmingham. (Commonwealth Secretariat photo from the archives)

But after the Second World War, it is as if there is a break in the Jali wall and shafts of light now pour in on the history of Indians in Birmingham. There is one overriding reason for this. From that point onwards – certainly from 1948, when Britain's Nationality Act gave British citizenship to citizens of former British colonies – Birmingham would see people from the subcontinent arriving in ever increasing numbers as they became an integral part of the city's post-war reconstruction story.

There were two main drivers behind this large-scale migration: the partition of India and the importance of Birmingham as a manufacturing centre.

To turn to the Partition first of all, we have to return to the final days of the British in India. Britain – as the wreckage of Birmingham's city centre and other cities like Liverpool and London so amply symbolised – lay in ruins. Although it had won the war, Britain was virtually bankrupt and no longer possessed the resources or the will to control an India that was in febrile mood. As the clarion call for independence grew in the aftermath of the war, passions began to run high between India's Muslim and Hindu communities, and it was not long before violence was breaking out between them as it had done before, most recently in the 1930s. This time, the fault lines were mainly in the Punjab and in Bengal, where reinvigorated dreams of an independent Muslim state in those northern states were fuelling catastrophic riots. In five days in Calcutta in August 1946, for instance, 4,000 people from both of India's main communities were killed, and thousands more wounded or made homeless.

As these northern areas descended into chaos, Britain's last viceroy, Lord Mountbatten, sped up the transfer of power from Britain to two new independent states, Pakistan and India, which, despite his best intentions, only served to exacerbate the problem. As the deadline of 15 August 1947 loomed, the violence spread, with the worst of it in the Punjab, where the Sikh community was watching its ancient agricultural land being sliced into two by the new boundary line. In West Punjab, Muslims attacked Hindu and Sikh residents, killing thousands. In return, armed Sikh gangs started roaming the countryside, attacking Muslim majority villages in East Punjab. Meanwhile, trains trying to carry refugees across the border either way started to arrive at their destinations filled with hundreds of dead bodies. By 1948, the dead in the Punjab had reached 180,000.[2]

Generally speaking, many of the Indians who turned up in Birmingham seeking work in the post-war era were from these areas. With long traditions of migration to far-flung posts of the British Empire, Sikhs from farming lands in the Punjab started to arrive. From newly formed West Pakistan, it was Muslims mainly from the district of Mirpur;[3] while from East Pakistan, now Bangladesh, it was Muslims from the Sylhet region and Chittagong. There were Hindus from the state of Gujarat, which now bordered West Pakistan, too.

The thing they all had in their sights was the huge manufacturing sector in the place known as the city of 'a thousand trades'. In 1951, nearly two-thirds of the Birmingham workforce worked in manufacture, almost 400,000 people. Between 1948 and 1966 unemployment was never above 2 per cent and was invariably below 1 per cent, as Birmingham strode like a goliath in the British industrial scene. In the motor sector, there was the huge Longbridge car plant, BSA motor bikes, Lucas and Dunlop; in general engineering there was locomotive maker Metro Cammell and IMI (Imperial Metal Industries); in the food sector there was HP Sauce, Bird's Custard and, of course, Typhoo; and in electrical goods there was Swan Kettles, not to mention the thousands of smaller engineering and metal firms too numerous to mention.

Immigrants who had as children been crammed into the corner of a railway carriage rattling across the Punjab praying that they would reach Lahore without being hijacked by angry mobs, or immigrants whose village in the Mirpur area of Kashmir had been submerged under water as a result of the building of the Mangla Dam in the 1960s, or migrants simply from farms in Gujarat,[4] would answer adverts in local papers, and within months would find themselves in a job in Birmingham. Perhaps this was as an engineer making car light fittings at Lucas, or as a metal caster at a foundry in the Black Country – many migrants had technical skills that they could turn to their advantage in their new life.[5]

Many of them hoped that this new life would be a better life, but in the early days the realities were harsh. Although they were relatively well paid, many of the industrial vacancies the migrants filled, particularly in the Black Country foundries, were in hot, dirty, physically demanding environments.[6] Many of the newcomers also ended up in dilapidated Victorian and Edwardian terraced houses in down-at-heel inner-city areas such as Small Heath, Sparkbrook and Aston as the indigenous population was moved out into municipal 'new towns' in the post-war years and a slum clearance programme struggled to get off the ground.[7]

Finally, there was the racism. Today, Birmingham is one of the most multi-ethnic cities in Europe, with nearly 45 per cent of its population from a migrant background. But, in the 1960s, it looked as if the West Midlands 'could become a cauldron of racial bigotry and violence'.[8]

The issue flared up in one area of the city in particular, Smethwick, when in the general election of 1964 the local Conservative candidate Peter Griffiths sought to exploit smouldering frictions over the local housing shortage by blaming it on an influx of immigrants, many of them Sikhs from the Punjab. While the Labour Party won the election nationally – for the first time in thirteen years – Griffiths won the election locally with a 7 per cent swing from the Labour incumbent. Armed with a loathsomely racist slogan – which this book will not be repeating – his campaign, it seemed, found a ready audience in an area where Indians and Black people were not served in the smoke-rooms of pubs, and where a group of white residents in Marshall Street were petitioning the local Tory council to buy up houses in the street and let them out to white families only. Luckily, the Marshall Street plan was thwarted by Labour's housing minister, Richard Crossman, who refused to lend the council the money to carry out the plan.

Griffiths' squalid campaign shocked Britain, and the new Labour Prime Minister Harold Wilson called on the Tory leader Alec Douglas-Home to withdraw the Whip from the new MP. If he did not, Wilson said in a speech in Parliament, 'Smethwick Conservatives can have the satisfaction … of having sent here as their Member one who, until another General Election restores him to oblivion, will serve his term here as a Parliamentary leper.'[9]

Perhaps more importantly, though, Britain's new communities were ready to fight back. The following year, American civil rights activist Malcolm X visited Smethwick at the invitation of the Indian Workers Association of Great Britain, whose general secretary, Avtar Singh Jouhl, was a Birmingham Sikh. Walking down Marshall Street, Malcolm X was jeered by its white residents, and in the local pub he was told that he had to go to a separate part of the bar to drink his pint of beer. He had come to see the racism for himself, had found it, and was appalled.

Even though Malcolm X himself died only nine days later in a hail of bullets in New York, the moment was a significant one for the anti-racism movement in 1960s Britain, in which Avtar Singh Jouhl, who had been born in the Punjab in 1938 and had arrived in Smethwick in 1958 to work for a local foundry, played a significant part. One of his campaigns with the IWA was to organise pub crawls with white students from Birmingham University, which helped to highlight the colour bar issue in city pubs.[10]

Another local campaigner was Dr Dhani Ram Prem, who, in a book published in 1965, wrote about his early days in Smethwick and of the challenges ahead following the election of Peter Griffiths. Arriving in Smethwick as a locum doctor in 1939, Prem described those first years with fondness – a period when it appears he made many friends locally. 'Never during all those years did I have any indication of prejudice or discrimination', he wrote. 'My admiration for the people of Smethwick grew and grew over the years, and I still visualise that image of Smethwick – friendly and happy.'[11]

At the end of the war, Indian workers and their families were beginning to move into houses in Oxford Road, Cambridge Road and Vicarage Road. 'I used to visit them as their doctor, and always found neighbouring women having tea with the Indian women, or giving them a helping hand in their washing or looking after the children.'[12]

Despite growing frictions over problems such as housing, 'no one had thought to exploit these problems for their personal glory,' he added in an obvious swipe at Griffiths.[13]

Prem was elected as Birmingham's first councillor of Indian origin in 1946, and in 1955 founded the Commonwealth Welfare Council for the West Midlands – a grouping of local authorities, medical officers, employer federations and voluntary organisations looking at issues such as housing, education and recreation that faced recently arrived immigrants from the Commonwealth.

By the 1960s, his area of Smethwick was seeing a growing community of newcomers from the subcontinent, mainly Hindus from Gujarat and Sikhs from the Punjab. He wrote of the Sikhs: 'It is to their credit that they collected several thousand pounds to buy a disused church in Smethwick and turned it into a magnificent Sikh temple.'[14]

But Prem was now increasingly concerned about the parallel growth of racism in the area, and the rise of fascist groups agitating to keep Britain white. Then came the 'squalid campaign'[15] of Peter Griffiths in 1964 which turned Smethwick Tory blue when everywhere else in inner-city Birmingham had turned Labour red.

He ended the book with a warning: 'So long as Mr Griffiths pursues racialist policies, and the people of Smethwick are willing to let him speak in their name and pursue these policies on their behalf, the image of Smethwick will stay tarnished.'[16]

જ

Prem would barely recognise Smethwick today. A lot of water has flowed through the Smethwick canal locks since the 1960s, and now the town sandwiched between Birmingham, West Bromwich and Oldbury is intensely multicultural. According to the last census in 2011, 62 per cent of the local population belongs to ethnic minority groups, with 15 per cent identifying as Sikh and 21 per cent as Muslim, living alongside 40 per cent identifying as Christian. Moreover, as in other parts of Birmingham, according to Jon Bloomfield, these different communities live alongside each other in a spirit of tolerance and 'broad acceptance of Birmingham's multicultural reality'. There has been a 'shift in public mood'[17] in the past few decades, writes the academic, who spent many years working for Birmingham City Council on urban policy. Now, almost overwhelmingly, the people of Birmingham celebrate their cultural diversity rather than recoil from it.

Meanwhile, in Marshall Street itself, which the white residents once petitioned to keep white, a pub that once banned Black people, the Ivy Bush, now has a Sikh landlord and is one of the growing legion of Desi pubs in Birmingham: traditional British pubs with all the usual trappings of beer and darts but serving up Indian food instead of the usual pub fare of fish and chips and so on. The word 'desi', meaning a person of Indian, Pakistani or Bangladeshi origin, is in itself a proud assertion of the diversity of the local neighbourhood.

And on the High Street, the Sikh community has transformed the old congregational chapel, which Prem observed was bought for 'a few thousand pounds', into the largest Sikh temple in Europe. Spanning a total area of about 70,000 sq m, the Guru Nanak Gurdwara is three storeys high and has one of the largest congregations in the UK.

Not far away from the High Street, there is a large warehouse belonging to another Sikh success story. The five Wouhra brothers arrived in the Black Country from India in the late 1960s, and in 1972 started a small store in Wolverhampton supplying lentils, pulses and spices to the burgeoning number of Asian families coming to live in the Midlands. Now, five decades on, East End Foods is a major wholesale business selling to Asian grocery stores all around the UK as well as a number of national supermarket chains. It has even started selling back to India.

Notwithstanding the personal entrepreneurial drive of the Wouhra brothers, East End is actually only part of a much wider success story in Birmingham orbiting around Indian food. It was, in fact, a Bangladeshi migrant, Abdul Aziz, who acquired a restaurant on Steelhouse Lane in the city centre, added curry and rice to the menu, and made it the city's first curry house, The Darjeeling, which opened its doors in 1954. As more and more Bangladeshis arrived in the city over the following decades, settling in areas such as Aston, Lozells, Handsworth and Balsall Heath, a welter of Bangladeshi-run Indian restaurants with names such as Gate of India or The Maharajah opened up all across town. One of the most famous was the Koh-i-Noor established in 1962, but the one best known to me was, of course, the Bengal Garden in Sutton Coldfield, as I mentioned in the introduction to this book.

Bangladeshis in Birmingham are heirs to the Sylheti seamen, who after the Second World War began to desert their merchant ships while in port in the UK in order to find work in the country that once ruled their land. Sylhet is actually a lush, landlocked region in the north-east of Bangladesh covered with tea plantations set up by the British in Victorian times. But its well-travelled river connections with the main market for its agricultural produce, Calcutta, and therefore the global sea routes, meant that when steamships were gradually introduced on the route between London and Calcutta and all the sea ports in between, young Sylheti men began to turn away from the traditional occupation of farming to seek work on the merchant ships. Called 'lascars', these men often worked in very difficult and dangerous conditions as engine crew, particularly during the Second World War, when the Atlantic merchant convoys had to sail through the German blockades.[18]

The tradition of desertion – going into hiding until their ship left port, which began in the post-war period – reached a peak in the late 1950s and early '60s when lots of work was available in British factories and, when under the 1948 Nationality Act, Commonwealth immigrants were automatically granted British citizenship. Like their other Commonwealth immigrants to Birmingham, they tended to gather in inner-city areas where they had to endure poor housing and overcrowding.

But they worked hard and adapted, and when recession hit in the 1980s and the factory jobs went, they turned to different occupations such as the restaurant trade.

It was the community of Pakistani origin, though, that developed the distinctively Brummie curry that has become famous nationwide, and even internationally. During the 1960s and '70s a number of Pakistani cafes had sprung up around the Stratford Road in Sparkhill, serving up the usual rice and curry to industrial workers and their families, many hailing from the Mirpur region of Pakistani Kashmir. But, around 1977, according to Brummie Balti aficionado Andy Munro, a new kind of curry was born: the Balti.[19]

A number of restaurants claim to be the pioneers of Balti, including Al Faisal on Stoney Lane and Imrans on Ladypool Road, but Munro's vote goes to Mohammed Arif of Adil's on Stoney Lane. According to Munro, Arif was searching around for a curry that would appeal both to the local Pakistani community and to Brummies who, he knew, were fast gaining

The Al Faisal restaurant on Stoney Lane was one of the pioneers of Birmingham's famous Balti curry. (Images of Birmingham Premium/Alamy Stock Photo)

a taste for curry. The answer he came up with, after approaching a local Sikh engineer who invented a special type of lightweight metal wok for him, was a dish that was fast cooked in a 'balti' bowl over a high flame, and served up in the balti bowl that it was cooked in. The basic ingredients were the usual staples – tomatoes, onions, turmeric, cumin, garam masala and so forth – but the dish felt lighter than the usual curry because of its fast cooking process.

Balti was born, and although no one is quite sure why it was called that – whether it was because one-pot cooking is popular in northern Pakistan (albeit of the slow variety) and there is an area there called Baltistan, or whether *balti* is simply the Hindi word for 'bucket' denoting a large container to hold food – the phenomenon soon took off.

The 1980s and '90s were the boom years of Balti, with a whole clutch of restaurants opening up in Sparkbrook and Sparkhill and further afield for Birmingham Balti-goers. Now, in addition to the original pioneers, were names such as Khyber Restaurant, Punjab Paradise and Sher Khan to conjure with. Before long, the national newspapers and television stations got in on the act, the small area around the Stratford Road was marketed as the Balti

Triangle, and Balti fever spread, with copycat restaurants opening up across the land. Balti curry houses are still popular today.

ꙮ

Going back to the 1970s, many of those original pioneers followed a traditional route into British life. Adil's owner Arif started off in a textile factory in Bradford, while Mohammed Afzal Butt of Imrans started his life in Britain at a factory in Tyseley. But, mirroring the general trend as the city entered the 1970s and '80s, like all the other local communities, immigrant or otherwise, they had to adapt and change to survive. As the manufacturing prowess of Birmingham, ailing for so much of the 1970s, came to an abrupt end – with the motor and engineering industries, from British Leyland to the Chance Brothers, devastated by the 1980s recession, and the unemployment rate hitting 20 per cent – Birmingham's new communities, like its old ones, had to scout around for different types of jobs.

Some found them in restaurants, retail and corner shops. But later on, as Birmingham reinvented itself and recovered in the 1990s as a business and professional services centre under the dynamic council leadership of Albert Bore, they found them in schools and universities as teachers and academics, or in the media as journalists, or in consultancies as IT specialists, or in the health service as pharmacists and doctors.[20] As History West Midlands, an independent website overseen by historians at Birmingham University, states: 'By the late twentieth century, people of Indian origin entered the middle classes, running shops or firms such as East End Foods or working in the professions and local government. Many moved out of the inner city and settled in suburbs such as Edgbaston, Harborne and Great Barr.'[21]

Birmingham first came of age as an industrial and nonconformist town in the early 1800s that welcomed religious minorities such as the Quakers, who had suffered persecution or discrimination elsewhere. As we have seen in this chapter, the influence of the nonconformists in forging links overseas has been strong.

But now alongside the chapels and meeting houses and churches that sprung up in the nineteenth century, there are mosques, gurdwaras and temples. And around each one of these, communities have grown up and come of age.

The canals can once again be our guide. Navigate yourself through the Camp Hill Locks, for example, and you are on the Grand Union Canal skirting

ꙮ

Sikh women gathering for a religious ceremony at the Guru Nanak Gurdwara in Smethwick. Vibrant communities have grown up around Birmingham's mosques, gurdwaras and temples. (David Bagnall/Alamy Stock Photo)

the very Asian districts of Sparkhill and Sparkbrook. Just a stone's throw away is the main drag, the Stratford Road.

Walking along the Stratford Road from its inauspicious beginnings at a roundabout on the inner ring road is to walk through a history of emigration to Birmingham. The first few shops and cafes you will come across belong to Yemenis, actually the oldest immigrant community in Birmingham, its first settlers having joined British merchant ships at the British port of Aden, sailed the world, and then decided to lay down roots in the Midlands to work in the metal trades.

Soon, though, you will chance upon a store on your left-hand side peeping out from underneath a blue awning, which is the first evidence of a strong Asian presence in the area. This is the Masaka Food Store run by Ugandan Asians, just a small microcosm of a huge diaspora – mainly Gujarati and Punjabis who had settled in what was British East Africa in the early twentieth century and then had to flee the regime of General Idi Amin or the 'Africanisation' policies of Kenya in the early 1970s to find sanctuary in the UK. If you glance inside the shop you might spot crates full of what look like small logs, but are actually the root vegetable that Masaka's is famous for – cassava.

Carry on, and you will reach the junction of Stratford Road with Highgate Road, its tight triangular geometry containing more than fifty Balti restaurants at the last count, their gaudy signs sprouting out from old Edwardian red-brick terraces in the 'Balti Triangle'. Adil's is there. So too are Imrans and Al Faisal.

Beyond the junction, the Stratford Road takes on all the patina of a traditional English High Street, except that practically all the goods on sale have a distinctly Eastern flavour. There is the Indian jewellery shop at Nos 355–357 – DD Jewellers – and further along there is the Bismillah halal cake shop. A few doors down from Bismillah's, there is the Nafees Indian sweet maker.

A tiered cake or a Jalebi snack for a wedding, perhaps? As for the wedding dress for the bride-to-be, there are a number of sari shops on the Stratford Road as well as Midlands Textiles, the Indian fabric store at Nos 517–519. One of the longest-running establishments, meanwhile, is the Gohil Emporium at No. 381, which opened its doors more than forty-five years ago. Started by Nanji Gohil, an Indian Gujarati from Dar-es-Salaam who came to study in England in 1973, the shop, now run by his daughter-in-law, is packed full of all sorts of wedding accessories, from garlands of jasmine to figurines of Hindu deities.

Dive down a side street now, and there is the Shree Ram Mandir, a temple serving the local Hindu community. It used to be the old Waldorf Cinema, which in the 1970s was owned by an Asian called Avtar Randhawa, who showed Bollywood movies there to his compatriots taking time out from their long work shifts. In 2014 and 2015, Randhawa took part in a community heritage project run by local arts organisation Sampad, sharing his memories of the screenings at the Waldorf via audio clip.

Sampad itself has its roots in this sort of grassroots cultural scene. Born in Bengal and moving to Birmingham in 1982, its founder, Piali Ray, was teaching the ancient Indian temple dance of Bharatanatyam at a local dance school when she realised the need for a more formal support structure for all the dancers, poets, painters and musicians from her community who were teaching traditional South Asian art forms in Midlands schools, colleges and adult learning centres. The idea of a venture to combine all their efforts was born, and in 1990, with the help of seed funding from the Barrow and Geraldine S. Cadbury Trust, Sampad, meaning 'cultural treasure', was launched.

Soon finding a home at the Midlands Arts Centre in Cannon Hill Park, the agency quickly became a success story, staging landmark dance performances reflecting the cultural heritage of South Asian immigrants. More recently, it has sought to link the work of artists in Birmingham, Bangladesh and Pakistan in a project called Transforming Narratives, aimed at uncovering the stories of all those who have left the subcontinent to forge a new life in Birmingham.[22]

Indeed, the lives and endeavours of all those who did can be found all across Birmingham's canal network. Head eastwards from the Stratford Road, and on the other side of the Grand Union Canal you will find the strong Muslim community of Small Heath clustered around the Central Jamia Mosque. Then, if we follow the waterway back into the town to the Typhoo Basin, we will be in the Digbeth area, home to Islamic Relief, a global humanitarian agency started up by Dr Hany El-Banna and fellow students from Birmingham University in 1984 in response to the African famine of the time.

And over on the other side of the city centre, not far from the New Main Line Canal, which flirts with Handsworth on its way to Smethwick, is the Soho Road full of sari shops and desi cafes. Here and there, there is also a Sikh gurdwara and a Hindu temple denoting the religious mix of the area.

This mix is replicated as we head further out into the Black Country. Smethwick, as we know, is home to Europe's largest Sikh temple. Further out still in Tividale, sandwiched between four canals – the old and new Main Lines, and the Gower and Tunnel branches – there is the extensive Sri Venkateswara Temple, completed in the last decade, and dedicated to the Hindu god Vishnu.

But it is not just Hindus, or Muslims and Sikhs for that matter. There is also a Parsi presence in Birmingham, albeit of an industrial nature rather than community-based. On the banks of the Grand Union, on the south-east fringes of the city, you will find the Jaguar Land Rover plant at Lode Lane, which in 2008 fell into Indian hands.

The buyers were Tata Motors, part of a business originally founded by a Bombay Parsi called Jamsetji Tata in 1868.

୭୭

This chapter has looked at the journey Birmingham's Asian communities have taken since the Second World War, but what of the young generation? Those still studying at school or university? Where are they heading?

As benchmarks go we could do worse than return to King Edward's School, which, as we have seen, has produced students either greatly inspired by India – alumni such as Charles Freer Andrews – or strongly connected to it – alumni such as Reeta Chakrabarti. The boys' school, as one of the most ethnically diverse independent schools in the country,[23] has a strong record of sending pupils on to Oxbridge, with one of these most recently being a Pakistani student, Ahmad Nawaz, who ended up in Birmingham after being injured in a Taliban terror attack on a school in Peshawar.[24]

Another victim of the Taliban who made it to Birmingham was Nobel Prize winner Malala Yousafzai, who spent many months recuperating in the city's Queen Elizabeth Hospital but then attended Edgbaston High School for Girls.

Her story is a particularly brave one. Growing up in the Swat Valley to the north of Peshawar, in what was once British India's North-West Frontier province, Malala was the clever and ambitious daughter of a school owner. Unfortunately, that was not to the liking of the local Taliban leaders who wielded growing influence in the area, and after Malala started to speak out about girls' rights to education, the die was cast. In 2012, she was ambushed on the bus home from school and shot in the head.

As it happened, a team of doctors from Birmingham led by emergency care consultant Javid Kayani, a British Pakistani, was visiting the country at the time; and as Malala's condition deteriorated the decision was made by both the Pakistani and British medical teams. Her best chances of survival and brain recovery lay at the Queen Elizabeth.[25]

In October 2012 she awoke from a medically induced coma in Birmingham, and began her long road to recovery. But even though she was in a foreign country, surrounded by strangers, her recovery was to be a remarkable one. The following March she attended her first day at school at Edgbaston High, and the following July she was addressing a youth assembly at the UN headquarters.

'One child, one teacher, one book, one pen can change the world,' she said on that day in New York, and as if to prove the point, a few years later she gained a place at Lady Margaret Hall at Oxford. In 2020, she graduated with a degree in Philosophy, Politics and Economics.

It is possible to speculate that had Ahmad and Malala not attended two of Birmingham's most prestigious schools, they might not have won places at the University of Oxford. Having said that, though, it is important to emphasise that these schools do not have a monopoly on links with the Indian subcontinent, or, indeed, academic success.

Over on the other side of town, near the airport, the Tile Cross Academy has had a partnership with a school in northern Pakistan for several years. The link is with the Pakistan Scouts Cadet College, situated near Mansehra, which like the Swat Valley is in the North-West Frontier region, now called Khyber Pahktunkhwa.

Surrounded by mountains and pine forests, the college is an area that couldn't be more different to that of a school in one of Birmingham's most deprived urban areas; but that, after all, is the whole point of the British Council's Connecting Classrooms[26] programme that links up the two establishments. The idea is that pupils from these schools can share ideas with each other on global issues such as sustainable development, gender equality and leadership; and in the process, change perceptions on both sides, and most importantly, forge international friendships. Every year a delegation of staff and students visits Tile Cross from Pakistan, with reciprocal visits regularly made in the other direction.

If a group of 'cadets' from the Pakistan Scouts Cadet College make it over to Birmingham each year, many more students from the Indian subcontinent are choosing the city for higher education. According to a survey in 2016 by the Birmingham Consular Association,[27] young people from the Commonwealth made up 24 per cent of the 10,000 or so overseas students at the city's universities, the three major ones being the University of Birmingham, Aston University and Birmingham City University (BCU). After Nigeria, India was the second biggest source of undergraduates.

Likewise, the presence of local Black and Asian heritage students studying at BCU and Aston is substantial: 45 per cent of BCU students are from Black and ethnic minority communities, while more than a third of the intake at Aston is from an Asian background.[28]

NOTES

1   Papers regarding the case are held at the Wolfson Centre for Archival Research, Library of Birmingham. [ref: 370797/IIR89/ff.163-168] and [ref: 200769 Home Office Parliamentary Report]

2   B.D. Metcalf and T.R. Metcalf, *A Concise History of Modern India* (Cambridge: Cambridge University Press, 2006), pp.217–223, and Burton Stein, *A History of India* (Chichester: Wiley-Blackwell, 2010), pp.348–356.

3   Birmingham has a Treaty of Friendship with Mirpur in Azad Kashmir, Pakistan. See distinctlybirmingham.com/partner-cities

4   Personal stories of Partition based on interviews with immigrants from the Indian subcontinent are told by Jon Bloomfield in *Our City: Migrants and the Making of Modern Birmingham* (London: Unbound, 2019).

5   Ibid.

6   Graham Peet and Emma Purshouse (eds), *Black Country Sikhs: Life in in the Sikh and other Communities of the Black Country* (West Bromwich: Multistory, 2017), pp.68–71.

7   Chris Upton, *A History of Birmingham* (Stroud: The History Press, 2011), p.207.

8   Bloomfield, Introduction xxii.

9   Prime Minister Harold Wilson, Debate on first day of Parliament. Volume 701: debated on Tuesday 3 November 1964, hansard.parliament.uk/Commons/1964-11-03/debates.

10   The private papers of Avtar Jouhl [MS2142] and the papers of the Indian Workers' Association [MS2141] are held at the Wolfson Centre for Archival Research, Library of Birmingham.

11   Dr Dhani R. Prem, *The Parliamentary Leper: Colour and British Politics* (Aligarh: Metric, 1965, and Birmingham, 1966), p.5.

12   Ibid., p.8.

13   Ibid., p.8.

14   Ibid, p.44.

15   Ibid., p.94.

16   Ibid., p.1.

17   Bloomfield, p.143.

18   Yousef Choudhury and Peter Drake, *From Bangladesh to Birmingham*, 2001.

19   Andy Munro, *Going for a Balti: The Story of Birmingham's Signature Dish* (Studley, Warwickshire: Brewin Books, 2015).

20   The evidence can be found from a number of sources including: *Black Country Sikhs: Life in in the Sikh and other Communities of the Black Country* (West Bromwich: Multistory, 2017), which also tells the story of the Wouhra Brothers; and in Chapter 3 of *Our City: Migrants and the Making of Modern Birmingham* (London: Unbound, 2019).

21   Malcolm Dick, *Indian Experiences*, www.historywm.com

22   More information on Sampad can be found online at www.sampad.org.uk and in Tesawar Bashir (ed.), *The Sampad Story: A Twenty Year Retrospective* (Birmingham: Sampad South Asian Arts, 2010).

23   John Claughton, 'Why the King Edward's schools are so important to Birmingham', www.business-live.co.uk/economic-development/john-claughton-king-edwards-schools [Online].

24   *Birmingham Mail*, 'Taliban attack survivor wins place at Oxford', 14 August 2020.

25   Malala's story has been covered extensively by the BBC, www.bbc.co.uk.

26   The Connecting Classrooms programme is a British Council initiative, connecting-classrooms.britishcouncil.org

27   More information can be found at www.birminghamconsularassociation.org.uk/consulates_in_the_midlands.htm.

28   Bloomfield, *Our City: Migrants and the Making of Modern Birmingham* (London: Unbound, 2019), pp.92–94.

CHAPTER FOUR

THE CARIBBEAN

1. 'AM I NOT A SISTER?'

It is just a short walk from the futuristic neon shimmer of Birmingham City University's glass-fronted campus at Millennium Point or the brutalist 1950s tower block that lies at the core of Aston University's campus to the network of thoroughfares – from Steelhouse Lane to Shadwell Street – where for centuries gun-makers bashed metal on anvils and looked down barrels, perfecting a craft that had been forged in the genius of the city's foundry-driven know-how. Gun-making was a peculiarly Birmingham craft that played a crucial role in supplying British troops in the Napoleonic Wars and the two world wars of the twentieth century. Unfortunately, however, this trade also, for a while, forged links with the evils of the transatlantic slave trade.

Britain had first become involved in this infamous trade pioneered by Portuguese and Spanish colonialists when, in the 1600s, its Caribbean colony of Barbados began to convert from an English style of agriculture with small farms growing crops, cotton and tobacco to large-scale sugar production. The growing and harvesting of sugar cane required large numbers of labourers, and soon the plantation owners were looking to slaves imported from West Africa to meet the need. Ships now began to slip out of English ports to join the triangular trading pattern that saw vessels from Europe filled with arms, textiles and wine sail to the west coast of Africa. There, as the European ships hovered off the coast between the Senegal and Niger Rivers, these goods would be traded, over weeks and months, for slaves captured somewhere in the interior by African traders. The African intermediaries would have raided settlements inland, capturing young and healthy men and women, and marching them, shackled together, to the waiting ships.

Once full, the European merchant's ship would depart for the Americas or the Caribbean on the notorious Middle Passage, in which hundreds of African slaves were crammed tightly together in the ship's hold for the 5,000 nautical mile voyage, typically chained together in fetid and stinking conditions, unable to sit upright due to the low ceilings. Up to a quarter of them did not survive the trip, but those that did were then sold on to the plantations, and the ships returned to Europe, their holds bursting now not with human cargo this time, but with sugar, rum, tobacco and other 'luxury' items. While well-to-do society in the drawing rooms of London, Amsterdam or Lisbon took spoonfuls of sugar in their tea, thousands of Africans were being chained and beaten into the holds of vessels anchored off the African coast. Britain soon became the worst offender, with the French and the Portuguese not far behind, enslaving nearly 500,000 people in the British colonies by the 1790s and transporting 3 million Africans across the Atlantic by the beginning of the nineteenth century.

Had Birmingham not been a city filled with foundries and workshops by the eighteenth century, making all sorts of metal objects, including guns, perhaps it would never have had any involvement in this trade; and the notoriety would have belonged solely to the slave ship ports of Liverpool and Bristol. But it was, and by the early eighteenth century its wrought-iron products – nails, hoes, bills, scythes and so forth – were making their way by the chest-load to the sugar plantations of the British West Indies. In fact, exports almost trebled between 1710 and 1735. Not only that, but Brummie workshops were also making fetters, collars and padlocks for the slave ships.

At the same time, the city's thriving gun-making community, which had established itself in the alleyways in between Birmingham and Fazeley Canal and Steelhouse Lane, were, by now, supplying large quantities of arms to slave merchants in Liverpool and Bristol, who would trade in these arms for slaves once their ships arrived on the West African coast. By 1766, more than 150,000 Birmingham-made guns were being sent annually to Africa. Prominent in this trade was Galton and Farmer, based on Steelhouse Lane. Surviving company letters from 1751 to 1757 held in the Birmingham Archives reveal a buoyant relationship with merchants dealing with West Africa, one of them a careful estimate of the expenses of the ship *Perseverance* on a voyage 'from Liverpool to Africa, thence to the West Indies and back to England with a cargo of goods and 527 slaves'.[1]

It was obviously a lucrative trade, but what was so surprising about the firm's involvement was that one of the partners, Samuel Galton, was from a Quaker family. And the Quakers (known formally as the Religious Society of Friends) in Birmingham were about to play a leading role in the anti-slavery movement.

As we saw in the first part of Chapter Three, Birmingham had over the years become a hotbed of nonconformist creeds. So when, in the 1770s and 1780s, Britain went through 'a great flowering of dissenting faiths and Churches in which the Bible was read ... as a proclamation of the doctrine of common humanity',[2] it was perhaps only natural that the city would be at the forefront of the movement.

For Midlands men like Joseph Priestley, one of the founding fathers of the nonconformist Church of Unitarianism, 'Jesus was no longer to be thought of as the son of God but as the first of the reformers' who had 'preached the indissoluble bonds of obligation tying the more fortunate to those less so'.[3] For fellow Unitarian Josiah Wedgwood, the campaign for the abolition of slavery led by the Quaker movement was a cause to which he would devote the final years of his life.

As it happens, both Dr Priestley, better known to us as one of the discoverers of oxygen, and the Staffordshire potter Wedgwood, were also members of that exclusive Birmingham dining club, the Lunar Society, and soon both would be throwing their weight behind the abolitionist movement.

As early as 1761, the Quakers had come to view abolition as a Christian duty, and all members of the Society of Friends were barred from owning slaves. Thereafter, the abolition movement gradually gained traction, with the real tipping point coming with the horrifying scandal of the slave ship *Zong* in 1781, in which 132 sick slaves were thrown overboard so that the owner could claim the insurance. Riding the huge wave of sympathy for the appalling plight of African slaves that followed, the Quakers presented a petition against the slave trade to Parliament, and four years later, with support from some quarters of the Anglican Church, formed the Society of the Suppression of the Slave Trade.

Wedgwood became a committee member, helping to draw up petitions. But perhaps his most famous contribution to the cause was the creation of his earthenware anti-slavery medallion for the Society, portraying a kneeling Black slave raising his hands in supplication. Above him was inscribed the plea: 'Am I not a man and a brother?'[4]

Like the caps and T-shirts of the Black Lives Matter or Me Too movements of today, Wedgwood's medallions became popular symbols – men displayed them as coat buttons, women carried them as bracelets or ornamental hairpins – and very soon they were everywhere, a new fashion promoting justice and

Lunar Society member Josiah Wedgwood turned his famous pottery business to a good cause with the production of the 'Am I not a man and a brother' anti-slavery medallion. (CPA Media Pte Ltd/Alamy Stock Photo)

humanity. Very soon, they were joined by a female version of the emblem: 'Am I not a Woman and A Sister'.[5]

Dr Joseph Priestley, meanwhile, had become a leading member of Birmingham's newly formed Anti-Slavery Committee, petitioning Parliament over the issue and raising money for the national movement.

But the Birmingham business community remained divided over the issue. Like the Galtons, many merchants, manufacturers and gun-makers depended heavily on the slave trade. Moreover, many Midlands families actually owned estates in the West Indies – families such as the Ward family (the Earls of Dudley) which had a plantation in Clarendon, Jamaica – and some of these, no doubt, employed Boulton & Watt engines for their sugar mills. According to the 'Soho papers' held at the Library of Birmingham,[6] more than 100 Boulton & Watt machines were ordered by Caribbean planters between 1778 and 1825.

Despite his business interests in the Caribbean, though, Matthew Boulton himself joined other Lunar Society members to welcome former slave and abolition campaigner Olaudah Equiano[7] when he came to speak in Birmingham in 1789. Also part of the deputation was Samuel Galton Jnr, who had joined his father's gun-making business in the 1770s and joined the Lunar Society the following decade. Interested in the areas of optic, light and colour, Galton Jnr was an active member of this quasi-scientific society.

All this, however, was not enough to impress the Society of Friends, who had begun to question the Galton interests in the slave trade. When Galton Snr left the business to his son in 1795, Galton Jnr was asked to defend the position of the company. The following year, the Society declined to 'receive any further collection from Galton'.[8] Nevertheless, when the Lunar Society member died in 1832, he was still buried in Quaker grounds.

In the meantime, the contradictions within the Birmingham business community had continued, never more so than within the Boulton and Watt matrix, which on the one hand saw Matthew Boulton and James Watt manufacturing engines for sugar mills in the West Indies and, on the other hand, minting coins for the Sierra Leone Company, which was involved in starting a new colony for freed slaves in West Africa. In 1807 Boulton & Watt's Soho Mint struck a commemorative coin for a Sierra Leone trading company with the inscription, 'We are all brethren. Slave trade abolished by Great Britain in 1807.'[9]

It was, of course, referring to the victory of William Wilberforce and his allies in their fight to abolish the trading in slaves between Africa and the Americas.

But the battle had only just begun to abolish slavery altogether. That mantle would be passed on to a large extent to the next generation.

࿐

Like the area of West Bromwich bounded to the south by the trench line of the Birmingham Canal and to the north by the high embankments of the Tame Valley Canal, fixed lines circumscribed the life of women in the nineteenth century, increasingly so as the century wore on. Their sphere was that of the home and the hearth, while the men who set the limits of their existence operated in the public sphere of business and politics. Women were idealised as mothers, icons of domesticity, models of moral stability, who operated in a realm of domestic furnishings and fussy interiors. Heavy curtains cocooned them from the grubby world of the foundry and factory outside. Few crossed the boundary.

One of those that did, though, was Lucy Townsend. Born in 1781, the daughter of a Church of England clergyman in West Bromwich, Lucy became interested in the anti-slavery movement as a young woman in the late 1790s after being inspired by the campaign of abolitionist Thomas Clarkson to boycott slave-produced sugar.

Over the following decades, her life followed a traditional course. In 1807, she married the Rev. Charles Townsend, and over the next few years gave birth to three daughters and three sons. But for one reason or another, she would soon be returning to the cause.

The moment came in the 1820s. Despite the Abolition of the Slave Trade Act in 1807, the harsh existence of slaves working on plantations in the British

Dominions of the Caribbean had continued unabated; and by now a new consensus was emerging among activists in London that the only way to end the suffering of slaves once and for all was to make slavery itself illegal. In 1823 the Society for the Mitigation and Gradual Abolition of Slavery Throughout the British Dominions (but more simply known as the Anti-Slavery Society) was formed, with Thomas Clarkson as one of its founders. Politics were the preserve of men like Clarkson. Notably absent from the leadership of the new society were women.

Whether the new movement revived Lucy Townsend's sense of youthful commitment or whether a sense of evangelical mission that she might have shared with her Anglican husband now drove her on, it is difficult to know, but soon the vicar's wife was writing to her one-time teenage hero Clarkson to propose the idea of a women's anti-slavery society. Writing back, Clarkson offered his full encouragement; on 8 April 1825, Townsend held a meeting at her home with Mary Lloyd, the wife of Quaker anti-slavery campaigner Samuel Lloyd, and other women from the Birmingham nonconformist community such as Sarah Wedgwood and Sophia Sturge.

It was the first meeting of the Birmingham Ladies Society for the Relief of Negro Slaves, later known more simply as the Female Society for Birmingham; and its mission, as set down in its first report, was that of 'awakening attention, circulating information, and introducing to the notice of the affluent and influential classes of the community a knowledge of the real state of suffering and humiliation under which British Slaves yet groan ...'[10]

What 'circulating information' meant in practice seems to have been something quite innovative for the time. A small army of female activists was now tasked with the job of visiting thousands of homes and shops, distributing pamphlets and publications, and talking to people, coaxing them to join public meetings of the anti-slavery movement or sign petitions. Under the leadership of Lucy Townsend and her fellow company secretary Mary Lloyd, the Society spread the word through distinctive forms of propaganda such as 'work-bags and albums'[11] containing poems, illustrations and the latest news clippings on the West Indies situation.

At the heart of this canvassing drive, there were two particular themes that the Society wanted to highlight.

The first was an emphasis on the particular sufferings of women under slavery, a determination to raise awareness of not only 'the bodily sufferings of female slaves' but also their 'moral degradation'[12] – a reference no doubt to the sexual exploitation that occurred on a regular basis on the plantations.[13]

The second was promoting a boycott of slave-produced sugar. The first report of the Society condemned the 'thoughtless consumption' of slavery produce that gave licence to 'the wretchedness in which 830,000 immortal beings were held on British ground'.[14]

Great effort was put into arguing the case for an embargo of slave sugar and recommending the consumption of free labour produce instead. By 1827 'more than half the town of Birmingham' had been visited 'house by house' to do just that, with the female canvassers 'determined to proceed unweariedly in the work'.[15]

This illustration of a slave market was part of the publicity material that activists from the Birmingham Female Society distributed from door to door to promote the anti-slavery cause. (Niday Picture Library/Alamy Stock Photo)

By the following year, 'only about one sixth of the town of Birmingham' yet remained to be visited.[16]

That is not to say that it wasn't a struggle. 'Were the funds of this institution equal to the sphere of exertion opening before it, we might indeed rejoice in the prospect of its success,' the Society complained early on, 'but at present your Committee feel deeply humbled that so few professing Christians can be brought to ask themselves, "What have I done for much injured Africa? How have I shown my wish to alleviate the sorrows of our captives, in their house of Bondage, or to assist in delivering them from their oppressors? What aid have I given to those who are devoting their time and talents, and health, to this work of Christian charity?"'[17]

Still, as the donations, sales of work-bags and membership subscriptions began to build, the Society was able to offer financial support to partnership organisations, in particular to the Female Refuge Society in Antigua, whose object was the protection of young Black females. Money was also set aside for the establishment of schools for slave workers and their children.

In addition, the Birmingham Female Society made donations to the national Anti-Slavery Society based down in London. In so much as the London organisation backed by leading lights Thomas Clarkson and William Wilberforce had the ear of Parliament in Westminster, it could perhaps be seen at first glimpse as the driving force behind the abolition movement. But delve beneath the surface, and the observer might discern that things were possibly the other way round. After all, the Birmingham Female Society not only had important international connections in Antigua and so forth, but also lay, in its own right, at the centre of a developing national network of female anti-slavery societies for which it acted as the hub. After Lucy Townsend and her fellow campaigners pioneered the first group in Birmingham, others followed all across the country – from London to Leicester and up to Sheffield, Darlington and Glasgow.

It was this national network of women campaigners, moreover, which would in the 1830s grasp the initiative in the lengthy fight against slavery from the male leadership in London, which was so often disdainful of the female contribution to the cause. By this time, the Birmingham Female Society and its satellite groups were losing patience with the cautious nature of the 'gentleman's club' down in London, so much so that in 1830 it submitted a resolution to the National Conference of the Anti-Slavery Society for the organisation to drop its proclivity towards 'gradual abolition'. Instead, it should push for an immediate end to slavery in the British colonies.

In this argument, the female activists were joined by the secretary of the Birmingham branch of the Anti-Slavery Society, Joseph Sturge, the brother of founding Female Society committee member Sophia.[18]

Furthermore, the resolution was backed up with a threat devised by Birmingham Female Society treasurer Elizabeth Heyrick, who had previously written a pamphlet called 'Immediate, not Gradual Abolition' that had sold thousands of copies. Drop the word 'gradual' in their title or lose their annual £50 donation from the Female Anti-Slavery Society, she told the leadership in London.

In all likelihood, she had said it in the conviction that the female movement had some clout. She was right. At the national conference the following month, the Anti-Slavery Society agreed to abandon the word 'gradual' in their title. From now on, it would campaign for immediate abolition.

The time was ripe. Not only was Parliament already being deluged with petitions calling for the abolition of slavery, but now radical newspapers, workers' groups and chapels across the land were also clamouring for an extension to suffrage. In the autumn of 1831 and May 1832, there were huge demonstrations of more than 100,000 people in Birmingham and London calling for electoral reform – the perfect stomping ground for anti-slavery campaigners to win over opinion.

With the passing of the 1832 Great Reform Act, they pressed home their advantage to a Parliament now sympathetic to abolition. In August 1833, MPs finally passed the Act abolishing slavery throughout the British Empire.

There was a caveat, however. There was going to be a transition period in which every slave over 6 on 1 August 1834, when the law came into effect, would have to serve an apprenticeship of four years in the case of domestics, and six years in the case of field hands.

〰

If the great campaigners of Birmingham – both within the Female Society and the Anti-Slavery Society – had been made of lesser stuff, that might have been that. After all, surely the 1833 Slavery Abolition Act was a great victory for them?

As time went on, however, the victory took on a decidedly hollow ring. While the West Indian planters had been compensated handsomely by the British government to give up their slaves, it was soon found that the apprenticeship scheme did not appear much different to slavery. It gave planters the right to have their former slaves work for them for a further six years, working long hours. Absenteeism would result in imprisonment and attempts to leave the plantation penalised. This was slavery in all but name. Activists in Birmingham began to see it, soon realising that they could not let their struggle wither on the vine.

In Birmingham, it was Joseph Sturge who now took the lead. Born in 1793 into a Gloucestershire family with Quaker traditions, Sturge had moved to Birmingham in 1822, where he was a successful grain dealer before diversifying his business into railways and canals. By the early 1830s, however, he had left the day-to-day running of the business to his brother Charles while he now turned his attentions to the anti-slavery movement and philanthropic pursuits.

After agitating so effectively for the Slavery Abolition Act, the reformer now sailed for the West Indies to see for himself the results of his efforts and those of others. He travelled extensively, speaking with planters and African-Caribbeans – now 'apprentices', rather than being officially slaves – and found what he had probably suspected.

On his return to England, he published his *Narrative of Events Since the First of August 1834*, which used the testimony of an African-Caribbean witness, referred to as 'James Williams' to protect his identity, to show what the radical Birmingham businessman had seen at first hand – that far from being abolished, working conditions for Black workers on the Caribbean islands were as harsh as ever.

Nothing had improved when Sturge made another visit to the West Indies in 1836. Determined to do something about it, he became involved in working with Baptist chapels to establish the first 'free villages' in Jamaica – settlements that would provide homes for former slaves beyond the control of the plantation owners. In particular, he worked with the Rev. John Clarke, the minister at the Baptist Church in Brown's Town, in the St Ann parish on the north coast. Very soon, the two had identified land in the lush folds of the nearby Dry Harbour Mountains, and began to establish their new settlements.

One of them became Sturge Town. Established in 1839, it was located on 120 acres of a former sugar estate. Each house that was built for an African-Caribbean family came with a separate acre of land where sugar cane or pimento trees could be grown. Other tree crops such as mangoes and breadfruit could be sold in markets all across the island of Jamaica. By the following year, the village also had its own church and a school.[19]

By this time, the slaves of the Caribbean had finally been fully emancipated. In a final showdown with the British government, Sturge had returned to England in 1837 and published *The West Indies in 1837*, which outlined the cruelties and injustices of the apprenticeship system. With support

Joseph Sturge travelled extensively in the Caribbean to gather information about the cruelties of the apprenticeship system. His efforts were rewarded in 1838 when the system was abolished. (Classic Image/Alamy Stock Photo)

from Quaker abolitionists and other nonconformists, he now lobbied for immediate and total emancipation.

The government sat up and listened. In the summer of 1838, the apprenticeship scheme was dropped, and at midnight on 31 July 1838, the Black community of the Caribbean finally gained its total freedom.

On 1 August, Birmingham came out in force to celebrate. Joseph Sturge led a march from the neo-classical colonnades of the city's new town hall to Heanage Street in the Aston area, to open a place of learning called the 'Emancipation School'. Afterwards, in the evening, there was a great meeting at the Town Hall, an account of which can be found in the Birmingham Anti-Slavery Society minutes. 'The body of the immense building, as well as the galleries, were crowded to excess,' it reported. 'There was a large number of ladies among the auditory.'[20]

Several speeches were made by local dignitaries. Then, Sturge stepped forward and was 'greeted with loud and general cheering'. Thanks to 'the mighty moral influence of the people of England,' he stated, according to the minutes, 'the sun had risen for the first time upon the freedom of a large majority of their … brethren in the British Islands of the West.'[21]

Among 'the large number of ladies' in the auditorium looking on were, in all likelihood, members of the Birmingham Female Society, the efforts of which had greatly contributed to the victory being celebrated in the Midlands city that day. Not only had they been involved in delegations and petitions to Parliament all that year, but also in many ways they had laid the initial groundwork in the previous decade, canvassing from door to door to throw light on the suffering of enslaved men and women.

Arguably, this was their victory as much as Sturge's. But if anyone thought they were now going to retire to their cosy drawing rooms, they would have been mistaken. The ladies of Birmingham and their satellite organisations now turned their attention to slaves living outside the British Empire, to those shackled and suffering in Brazil and Cuba, or in East Africa or the United States. Their objective was now worldwide emancipation, the mission they shared with the British and Foreign Anti-Slavery Society, about to be founded by their Midlands compatriot Joseph Sturge. When this new society organised the world's first International Anti-Slavery Conference in London in 1840, they were there in numbers.

In the increasingly male-dominated world of Victorian Britain, however, their presence was not fully recorded by a famous painting of the event by Benjamin Robert Hayden. While some female campaigners such as Anne Knight and Elizabeth Pease and Amelia Opie were included in the picture, the early pioneer of the female anti-slavery movement, Lucy Townsend, was not, even though she was most definitely present.[22]

It is true, though, that by this time Townsend was loosening the reins. She had given up her post as honorary secretary of the Birmingham Female Society, but continued to be a committee member. In 1836, she had moved to the village of Thorpe in Nottinghamshire, where her husband became the clergyman at St Lawrence's Church.

And on 20 April 1847, at the age of 65, she passed away.

The Birmingham Female Society ran an eight-page obituary in their twenty-second report, noting that it was in large part due to her 'zeal and devotedness' that the Society had been founded and that she had been responsible for a 'great degree of the energy which animated its proceedings' thereafter.[23]

Joseph Sturge, meanwhile, continued his work. He was active in the Peace Society, a British pacifist organisation; and back in the West Indies he became involved in a project to promote free labour as the best way forward on the Caribbean plantations.

The Elberton Sugar Estate on the island of Montserrat would prove to be the last project of his life. It was a scheme born of estates that his brothers John and Edmund owned on Montserrat, that had been converted to the growing of limes so that they could use the juice in the manufacture of citric acid at their chemical works on Wheeleys Lane in Edgbaston. Joseph bought into the idea, and purchased the neighbouring Elberton Sugar Estate in 1857, wishing to convert the abandoned plantation to lime production and, more importantly for the Birmingham philanthropist, to prove that a free labour system he would employ on the plantation could be made profitable.

Unfortunately, he did not live to see it realise its full potential. He died in Edgbaston a couple of years later, leaving the family business to manage the estate. The Montserrat Lime Company, run by generations of the Sturge family, successfully ran plantations with the onus on a fairly paid workforce for many years afterwards.

Joseph Sturge himself was honoured with a huge memorial statue. Unveiled in 1862 and made of Portland stone, it still stands proudly on the Five Ways roundabout on the edge of Edgbaston. Clad in a lapel-less Quaker coat, the abolitionist and activist is posed as if he is teaching, with his right hand resting on the Bible, and his left hand outstretched. Below him on the lower plinth are two kneeling female figures: one holding an olive branch representing Peace; the other comforting an African-Caribbean child representing Charity.

A bronze plaque on the upper plinth, meanwhile, is inscribed with the words: 'He laboured to bring freedom to the negro slave, the vote to British workmen and the promise of peace to a war-torn world.'

To commemorate the bicentenary of the abolition of the slave trade in 2007, a blue plaque was also erected at the site of his former home in Wheeleys Road in Edgbaston.

There are no public monuments dedicated to Lucy Townsend.

NOTES

1   The Galton Papers in the Wolfson Centre for Archival Research, Library of Birmingham [MS3101/B/6/1]. Cited in Ian Grosvenor, Rita McLean & Sian Roberts (eds), *Making Connections: Birmingham Black International History* (Birmingham Futures Group, 2002), p.59.

2   Simon Schama, *A History of Britain* (London: BBC Worldwide Ltd, 2003), p.34.

3   Ibid.

4   Jenny Uglow, *The Lunar Men: The Friends who Made the Future* (London: Faber & Faber, 2002), pp.411–12.

5   Ibid., p.412.

6   Drawings and correspondence in papers of Boulton & Watt of Soho, Handsworth [MS3147/5/822-1029] in the Wolfson Centre for Archival Research, Library of Birmingham.

7   Equiano was an African writer whose experiences as a slave led him to become involved in the British abolitionist movement. In 1789, he published his autobiography, *The Interesting Narrative of the Life of Olaudah Equiano or Gustavas Vassa, the African*, and travelled widely to promote it. His visit to Birmingham during his promotional tour is covered in *Making Connections: Birmingham Black International History* (Birmingham Futures Group, 2002).

8. Ian Grosvenor, Rita McLean & Sian Roberts (eds), *Making Connections: Birmingham Black International History* (Birmingham Futures Group, 2002), p.59.

9   MS3782/3 in the Wolfson Centre for Archival Research, Library of Birmingham. Cited in Ian Grosvenor, Rita McLean & Sian Roberts (eds), *Making Connections: Birmingham Black International History* (Birmingham Futures Group, 2002).

10 The First Report of the Female Society for Birmingham, West Bromwich, Wednesbury, Walsall and their respective neighbourhoods for the relief of British Negro Slaves (1825–26) in the Wolfson Centre for Archival Research, Library of Birmingham [IIR62].

11 Ibid.

12 Ibid.

13 Niall Ferguson, *Empire: How Britain Made the Modern World* (London: Penguin Books, 2004), p.80.

14   The First Report of the Female Society for Birmingham (1825–26) in the Wolfson Centre for Archival Research, Library of Birmingham [IIR62].

15   The Second Report of the Female Society for Birmingham (1827) in the Wolfson Centre for Archival Research, Library of Birmingham [IIR62].

16   The Third Report of the Female Society for Birmingham (1828) in the Wolfson Centre for Archival Research, Library of Birmingham [IIR62].

17   The Second Report of the Female Society for Birmingham (1827) in the Wolfson Centre for Archival Research, Library of Birmingham [IIR62].

18   Sturge's involvement with the Anti-Slavery Society is summarised in *Making Connections: Birmingham Black International History*, pp.84–85.

19   Jamaica National Heritage Trust. *Free Villages, Sturge Town*. Available from www.jnht.com [Online]. Also, The Abolition Project, *Joseph Sturge: The Radical Businessman*, available on www.abolition.e2bn.org. Also *The Gleaner* newspaper, 'Sturge Town – A Truly Free Village', available at www.jamaica-gleaner.com .

20   Minutes of the Birmingham Anti-Slavery Society in the Wolfson Centre for Archival Research, Library of Birmingham [158748/IIR62].

21   Ibid.

22   Britain and Slavery, Lucy Townsend, www.spartacus-educational.com/ Lucy_Townsend.htm.

23   The Twenty-Second Report of the Female Society for Birmingham (1828) in the Wolfson Centre for Archival Research, Library of Birmingham [IIR62].

II. BOURNVILLE

About forty years after Joseph Sturge bought the Elberton estate on Montserrat, a son from his second marriage – also called Joseph Sturge, confusingly – boarded the fortnightly mail ship at Southampton docks and sailed for the West Indies.

Whether he had been before, whether or not he had been involved in the family business on Montserrat, or whether he had never ever set foot in the Caribbean, an eclectic collection of manuscripts, diaries and reports held at the Wolfson Centre for Archival Research at Birmingham Library cannot tell us. All we know is that is what he did.

And we only know that because he turns up in the account written by another character in history.

That character belonged to another great Birmingham dynasty, the Cadburys. William Adlington Cadbury was the son of Richard, one of two brothers – the other was George – who had taken over their father's struggling cocoa firm and transformed it into a confectionary behemoth, exporting chocolate bars and cocoa all around the world from its 'garden factory' at Bournville in Birmingham's hinterlands.

It is a story that is well known to many chocolate lovers and visitors to Cadbury World, the Bournville visitor attraction where the factory still stands today – the zeal of two brothers from a Quaker family to move their factory workers away from the squalid slums of inner-city Birmingham, and provide them not only with better working conditions but also, in George's case, to build for them a model village of cottage-style houses, each with their own garden, and all within walking distance of a village green and other civic amenities.

This was all in the 1880s and '90s when the firm was at take-off point. At this point in time, the brothers George and Richard are very much the central characters in the Cadbury saga woven together by the history books, while William, who will later take on a central role in the family firm, is still only a bit-part player. Far from being inactive, however, Richard's son, now in his 30s, did have a job to do, according to the papers available in the Birmingham Archives. This was to visit the cocoa plantations in the Caribbean that did so much to supply Cadbury's chocolate business.

This certainly seems to be what he is doing from his notes on a voyage to the British West Indies[1] from 16 December 1896 to 2 February 1897, together with a collection of letters from his trip, that now fill up a couple of boxes in Birmingham Library. Most of these papers are dedicated to his visit to the Cadbury cocoa estates on the islands of Trinidad and Tobago at the very southern tip of the Caribbean archipelago.

Despite this focus, William seems to have made good use of his outward journey through the Caribbean archipelago if the two magnificent photograph albums he assembled as a result of the trip are anything to go by. Twelve days out from England, Cadbury and Sturge arrived in Barbados, and images abound from their two days' sail onwards from Barbados to Trinidad. There are some striking photographs of the volcanic atoll that then made up the British Windward Islands: from the hillside capital of Grenada draped around an azure blue bay to local people milling around in a market on the island of St Vincent. The observer can almost feel the heat of the tropics seeping out from the sepia gloss of the old film paper: a heat tempered only by the trade winds buffeting the shorelines, the same winds from which these islands had taken their name.

Not that William was going to go all sentimental about the scenery. He had been brought up a Quaker, after all, and therefore a sense of social conscience was never far below the surface of his writings about his trip. We 'must never forget the terrible degradation through which the [African-Caribbean] race has passed,' he wrote, referring no doubt to the long era of slavery, 'bred, bought and sold like horses and cattle, and separated from wife or children at the whim of their overseer or owner'.[2]

☙❧

Still, there was business to attend to, and on 30 December 1896, aided by the 'path of light across the sea' cast by the 'intensely bright' stars and planets of the Caribbean night sky,[3] he and his travelling companion arrived at their destination: Trinidad.

'We are safely landed, have comfortable rooms at the excellent Queens Park Hotel, overlooking the Savannah – this is the large town playing fields, so to speak, a mile across,' William wrote in a letter back home from the hotel in

A Sunday in Brunswick Square, Port of Spain, as captured by William Adlington Cadbury in his photograph album, *Views in Trinidad*. (Reproduced with the permission of the Library of Birmingham. MS466/42)

Trinidad's capital, Port of Spain. On the other side of the savannah were the Botanical Gardens and Governor's House, and behind that 'hills 2,000 feet high dotted with woods to the top'.[4]

In those hills lay the Maracas Valley, which was where Cadbury would be spending the next couple of weeks. A number of his photographs give the reason why: pictures of a bulbous fruit hanging from the branches and trunks of a particular tree. Growing in abundance in mountain plantations in and around the valley, this was the cacao tree, and hiding inside the fruit were cocoa beans, made in large part of cocoa butter, the amber nectar of all confectionery firms the world over. It was the tree that Cadbury had come to see.

He seems to have had a good time of it, accepting a number of invitations from plantation owners to ride up into the hills on horseback and inspect their groves of cocoa. One night he spent in the 'Oruna Basin', 'cocoa and coffee on all sides'; and on another, he rode up amongst hundreds of 'cocoa huts' and stayed up late in a 'solitary empty house, talking cocoa' and 'quoting Burns'.[5]

It was at the cocoa huts, he noted, that most of the processing took place. Here, the cocoa beans were shovelled onto a drying tray where workers – mostly female – would tread and stamp on them: 'dancing the cocoa' as it was called. Many of the workers on the plantations, as illustrated by Cadbury's photographs, were indentured labourers from the Indian subcontinent. This was a system of imported cheap labour that the British employed throughout their empire in the nineteenth century following the abolition of slavery, which accounts for the large Indian diaspora populations now living in former British colonies such as Singapore, Mauritius and Trinidad. People of Indian heritage now make up more than a third of the population of independent Trinidad & Tobago.

Also apparent in all his photographs was, as the young Cadbury observed, the 'universally glorious and abounding vegetation' of the island. In short, Trinidad was one huge tropical garden. The cultivated estates of cocoa in which he roamed were established in clearings on hills carpeted with tropical rainforest. Here, huge trees, climbers, shrubs and ferns jostled for space in a riot of deep green undergrowth, broken up only at the end of the rainy season each year by the flaming orange of the immortelle flower. This grows in the canopies of trees, regarded as the 'mother of the cocoa' because it is under the shade of these trees that the cocoa fruit thrives. Cadbury was in Trinidad at exactly the right time to witness this annual liturgy.

Later on, as he descended from the northern hill slopes to the island's central plains on his way to the sugar factories of San Fernando, he would have been in the sugar cane area – row after row of grass stalk growing as high as 7m, their long, sword-shaped leaves rustling in the damp warmth of the tropical lowlands. An ethereal scene perhaps for the traveller from Europe, but, in reality, the result of the hard labour of the plantation workers, furrowing, tilling and weeding until each field was ready to harvest.

Afterwards, he headed on to the town of San Fernando and the flat, watery margins of the western coastline fringed with swaying palm trees, before returning to Port of Spain, home to a wide expanse of mangrove swamp where the estuary of the River Caroni meets the Gulf of Paria. There are views of the Gulf, and numerous groves of wild coconut palms, in William's collection of photos.

Given the beauty of these pictures, one wonders whether the Midlands company man entertained the thought of just remaining in this beautiful tropical garden for ever. Perhaps just for a moment, he did.

Never to return to the grimy chains and cables of a Birmingham canal wharf.

Yet, even as he thought that thought, supposing he ever did, he would have known that another garden of sorts awaited him on his return. Not quite as magical as the verdant palms of a Caribbean island, but green and nourishing all the same. This was the 'garden' that his Uncle George was creating around the model factory he had established in a countryside setting on the edge of the Worcester & Birmingham Canal in 1879. There was indeed a canal wharf feeding the factory at Mary Vale Road, but spanning out from it, from 1893 onwards, was the gradual emergence of George Cadbury's 'garden village'.

The village was to feature hundreds of Arts & Crafts style[6] cottages influenced by the vernacular architecture of rural Worcestershire and Warwickshire, orbiting around 'ample open spaces, including a village green, children's playgrounds, girls' and youths' gardens, a public park, well-wooded recreation grounds and allotments' and soon to have 'well-appointed schools, an institute and places for worship'.[7]

It was a settlement deeply rooted in George's Quaker beliefs that the natural world was Eden-like and God-given, and there were 'spiritual benefits' to be gained from reconnecting with that world.[8] It was no coincidence too that George himself was a keen gardener, never quite forgetting a happy childhood spent in Edgbaston helping out in the family vegetable patch, gathering fruit and vegetables.[9]

All this infused his vision of the garden city that was being realised at Bournville as his nephew visited the Caribbean in 1896, and also when, tragically, his brother, Richard – William's father – died unexpectedly on a visit to the Holy Land in 1899.

The business continued to thrive, however, and as the new century opened George was still tending to his vision, sowing innovative product lines at the factory, nurturing social schemes for the well-being of his workers, and digging up new ways to carry out his philanthropic work.

The new lines at the factory, introduced during the Edwardian years, included Cadbury's Dairy Milk and Bournville Cocoa, which became instant and enduring success stories. The company looked increasingly overseas during this period, becoming the dominant chocolate producer for the British Empire markets of Australia, New Zealand, South Africa and India.[10] Success abroad was replicated by better rates of pay, as well as welfare benefits and pensions for his workers at home.

But, for George, there was always a much wider plot to hoe and plant. His Quaker faith had imbued in him the importance of working actively for a better world in the conviction that a new 'Jerusalem' could be achieved in the here and now. This led him not only to invest in schools, sports clubs, musical societies and so forth on the Bournville estate, but also to become involved in improving the lot of people in Birmingham and beyond. He established colleges for the training of Quakers and other Christians in theology, teaching

By Edwardian times, Cadbury exported chocolate all over the British Empire; but for George Cadbury and his wife Elizabeth, social reform was also of prime importance. (World History Archive/Alamy Stock Photo)

and missionary work; and after implementing a pension scheme for his own Cadbury workers, he funded a successful national campaign to win old age pensions for everyone.

Much of the struggle for pensions was led by the London newspaper he owned, the *Daily News*, which also fought to improve working conditions for the poorest workers and to give local authorities the power to buy land to create small holdings and allotments for ordinary people who wished to grow their own fruit and vegetables. Along with pension reform, both campaigns realised success in the progressive welfare reforms of the 1906–14 Liberal government.

By and large, progressive politics in Edwardian Britain proved to be fertile soil for George Cadbury's altruistic tendencies. Matters on the international stage, however, would offer up much stonier ground for the liberal business-man with good intentions.

To be a Quaker is to have a lifelong commitment to pacifism. So when that other giant of Midlands politics, Joseph Chamberlain, became Colonial Secretary in the government of Lord Salisbury in 1895, and subse-quently became embroiled in a classic piece of British military adventurism in South Africa, the Boer War, Cadbury was horrified. He hated the jingo-istic, imperialistic tone that accompanied the politics of the war, and the barbaric turn the hostilities increasingly took. When it was revealed that the British military had been using something akin to concentration camps to incarcerate Dutch-Afrikaner families, his newspaper, the *Daily News*, led the charge of outraged liberal opinion against it. His chocolate firm made a stand of sorts, too. Prior to the war of 1899–1902, Cadbury Bros had been typical of many companies in that it relied on depictions of colonial travellers and explorers to advertise its products. After the war, George dis-carded all this colonial paraphernalia in favour of a softer advertising front, centred round the home and housewife.[11] Nothing was enough to stop the tragedy of the Boer War, though – a conflict we will hear more about in a subsequent chapter.

His political differences with Chamberlain notwithstanding, Cadbury's main focus would always be the dynasty he was building at Bournville. His sons Edward and George Junior – also devout Quakers – were soon to step into his shoes as heirs to the business, and its philanthropy. George Junior was responsible for the launch of one of Cadbury's most famous products, Milk Tray. Edward developed Cadbury's export markets in Australia and South

America, and became a leading light in the garden city movement, for which Bournville Village still to this day remains an inspiration.

Meanwhile, William Adlington Cadbury – George Senior's nephew and the central character of our Trinidadian tale – pioneered the commercial production of cocoa on the Gold Coast in West Africa.[12] He went on to become the Lord Mayor of Birmingham between 1919 and 1921, after which he established a charitable trust, still very much in operation today, which has been responsible for supporting various worthy causes including the building of Birmingham's Queen Elizabeth Hospital.

So much for the men of the Cadbury dynasty. But what about the women? It is worth asking the question because one in particular stands out as making a significant contribution to the story of Bournville and of Birmingham. We have met her before. Her name was Elizabeth Cadbury, and while the males in the Cadbury line were busy tying in the growth and good works that Richard and George had already established, she was planting philanthropic roots of her own.

We met her in the previous chapter on Birmingham's links with India, so we already know that she was George's second wife, and that, already well-versed in Quaker good works, she helped her husband in the setting up of Bournville Village.

But she was also a social campaigner very much in her own right. She supported the suffragists fighting for the woman's vote, and later 'blazed a trail for women in politics',[13] becoming an Independent councillor for the local King's Norton borough in 1919 and standing as a Liberal candidate in the 1923 general election; while for many years acting as the Treasurer of the Union of Women Workers.

The preoccupation with women's rights naturally took her on to the international stage too, and over many years she attended and addressed the congresses of the International Council of Women. In 1936 she led the British delegation to, and spoke at, the World Congress of the International Council of Women held in India.

This is where we met her in the last chapter, and where we will leave her. By this time, she was well into her 70s, and George was long gone.

But the 'garden' that the Cadburys had built at Bournville endured. The business that George and Richard and their successors built, and the cottages in the village with their high chimneys, gabled roofs and small private gardens, prospered. Year after year the dahlias and the chrysanthemums grew, the autumn leaves blew away to feed the growth of the following spring, and the milky glow of porch lights lent warmth and cordiality to a winter's night.

൭ඪ

However, for a while in the 1940s, everything in the garden did come to an abrupt halt. Elizabeth invited the Friends Ambulance Unit to set up a training centre in the grounds of her home at The Manor, belongings were put away into storage, and Cadbury workers went away to the battlefields. The Second World War had arrived.

As is very well documented, the storm clouds had been gathering over Europe since the middle of the 1930s. The rise of the Nazis and Britain's initial appeasement of it has been so well recorded, in fact, as to render what was going on in Britain's global empire almost invisible.

But history had not stopped in Britain's colonies any more than history seemed to be accelerating in Europe. Over on the other side of the truculent expanses of the Atlantic Ocean, the British West Indies was witnessing a particular storm of its own. This was born of the hardships of plantation work during the 1930s Depression, which had led to protests and riots in the colonies of Guyana, Trinidad, St Kitts, Jamaica, St Vincent and Barbados.

Yet when the moment came, the people of the West Indies rallied behind the 'mother country'. This can be ascribed to several factors. For some it was the motivation to defeat the racist evil of fascism, for others loyalty in the here and now was seen as a route to reform and possible independence after the war. For others still, it was just the chance to leave home and have an adventure. Perhaps, though, the biggest factor was the colonial upbringing. On islands such as Jamaica or Barbados – the latter known as 'Little England' – people were brought up with pictures of the Royal Family, and were used to reciting Shakespeare at school. So, when war was declared, there was nothing more natural than doing their bit for King and Country.[14]

In the end, thousands of British Caribbeans saw military service during the war, most joining the RAF, but some serving in the merchant navy running the gauntlet of the German U-boat attacks in the Atlantic. A number of Caribbean women were recruited into the Women's Auxiliary Air Force (WAAF) and its army equivalent. Hundreds more West Indians – as they were termed in those days – worked in Britain's munitions factories.

൭ඪ

Not all West Indians or those of West Indian descent living in, and fighting for, Britain during the Second World War were newly arrived, though. On the contrary, some had been in Britain for quite some time. Take Warwickshire's Turpin Brothers, one of Britain's most famous boxing families, for instance. Randolph, Dick and John 'Jackie' were the sons of a First World War veteran from British Guiana who, after the war, settled in Leamington Spa – the Warwickshire town that will host the lawn bowls competition in the 2022 Commonwealth Games. Lionel Turpin had been badly wounded in the trenches on the Western Front and had ended up in a hospital in Coventry. Afterwards he had settled in Warwick, where he met local girl Beatrice Whitehouse. The couple married in 1921 and had five children before Lionel sadly passed away from his war injuries in 1929.

The youngest brother, Randolph, was by far the most famous of the three sons for the simple reason that he beat American boxing legend Sugar Ray Robinson to become the world middleweight champion in 1951. There is a statue of him in Warwick's market square. His two siblings did not perform totally in his shadow, however. After serving on the Royal Navy destroyer HMS *Myngs* during the war, the middle brother and featherweight fighter, John

Boxing brothers Jackie, Dick and Randolph Turpin (from l-r) chat with World Heavyweight champion Joe Louis in 1948. The brothers were sons of a First World War veteran from British Guiana who settled in Leamington Spa. (PA Images/Alamy Stock Photo)

'Jackie', went on to become the first British boxer to win in America after the war. Meanwhile, the eldest of the three, Dick, who had fought his first professional fight in 1939, managed to tuck the Commonwealth middleweight title under his belt in May 1948.

Just a month or so later, on 28 June, 40,000 spectators filled out Villa Park football stadium in Birmingham to watch him take on British title holder Vince Hawkins. Dick won on points over fifteen rounds, and thus became Britain's first Black boxing champion.[15]

NOTES

1   William Adlington Cadbury, Diary, letters and photographs from visit to the West Indies [MS466/42-43; MS466A/538] in the Wolfson Centre for Archival Research, Library of Birmingham .

2   William Adlington Cadbury, Notes on a Voyage to the West Indies, 16 December 1896–2 February 1897 [MS466/42-43; MS466A/538] in the Wolfson Centre for Archival Research, Library of Birmingham .

3   Ibid.

4   William Adlington Cadbury, Letter to Barrow Cadbury, Trinidad, 30 December [MS466/42-43; MS466A/538] in the Wolfson Centre for Archival Research, Library of Birmingham.

5   William Adlington Cadbury, Letters to Barrow Cadbury, Trinidad, 30 December and 9 January [MS466/42-43; MS466A/538] in the Wolfson Centre for Archival Research, Library of Birmingham.

6   A reaction to the worst excesses of Victorian industrialisation, the Arts & Crafts movement put the emphasis back on traditional craftsmanship in everything from jewellery to interior decoration and architecture. Arts & Crafts houses tended to reference local and historical traditions, and often featured asymmetrical roofs, often with gables. A good introduction to the movement can be found on the Victoria & Albert Museum website, www.vam.ac.uk/articles/arts-and-crafts-an-introduction. Early exponents were textile designer William Morris, and Pre-Raphaelite artist and King Edward's old boy Edward Burne-Jones.

7   Andrew Reekes, *Two Titans, One City: Joseph Chamberlain and George Cadbury* (Alcester, Warwickshire: West Midlands History Ltd, 2017), p.33.

8   Ibid., p.98.

9   Ibid., pp.112-3.

10 Ibid., p.11.

11 Ibid., p.79.

12 Ibid., p.86. William Cadbury's involvement here was not without controversy, as Chapter 7 of *Two Titans, One City* shows.

13 Ibid., p.116.

14 As the wartime memories of Black servicemen such as Cy Grant and Billy Strachan testify to in Stephen Bourne's *The Motherland Calls: Britain's Black Servicemen and Women 1939–45* (Stroud: The History Press, 2012).

ᴄᴐ

15 The Turpin Brothers' story is covered by Stephen Bourne's *Black Poppies: Britain's Black Community and the Great War* (Cheltenham: The History Press, 2019), as well as in David Olusoga's *Black and British: A Forgotten History* (London: Pan Books, 2017).

III. WINDRUSH

A few days before Dick Turpin's victory in Birmingham, an old British troop-ship had shuffled up the River Thames and docked at Tilbury Docks. In the aftermath of the war, there would have been nothing unusual about that. Even though the London docklands had been heavily bombed in the Blitz, they still sat at the centre of a vast, if ailing, empire.

But there was something unusual about this ship. Of the thousand passengers on board, well over half had come from the Caribbean, mainly from Jamaica, Trinidad and British Guiana; and as the ship docked a Pathé News film crew was on hand to record the event, asking a Trinidadian calypso singer wittily called Lord Kitchener to perform a song he had recently composed.

'London is the Place for Me' was the song that then rippled out along the quayside like the sunlight flickering on London's great old river on that bright summer's day; and, on the Pathé newsreeel everyone looked enchanted.

But if the gathering was lost for a moment in the light-hearted, tropical trills of Trinidadian calypso, no one was totally immune to the importance of its message. For the London welcoming party on the pier, the Caribbean passengers of HMS *Windrush* had come to help Britain, the mother country, recover from the devastation of war: to help man the factories so that they could belch out their rancid smoke into Albion's leaden industrial skies once again. By the same token, for the West Indian migrants – around half of whom had already served in Britain during the war – a job in Britain was the chance to escape economic hardships back in the Caribbean and find a better life for themselves. Within a month all but twelve of them had found work.[1]

Due to the huge labour shortages that British industry faced in the late 1940s, the work was everywhere: in the construction and manufacturing sectors as cities such as Birmingham sought to rebuild after the Luftwaffe air raids; in the service sector as cities including London got their transport systems up and running again; and in healthcare as just about everywhere sounded the clarion call for nurses to staff the newly created NHS.

Initially, there was hardly a rush to migrate to Britain after HMS *Windrush* had made its pioneering trip. Although the British Nationality Act of 1948 changed the status of people living in Britain's colonies from British Subject to Commonwealth Citizen, therefore giving them the right to settle in the UK, only about 5,000 West Indians had entered the country by 1950. This all changed in the early 1950s, however, after the US took the decision to curb Caribbean immigration, and after a devastating storm – Hurricane Charlie – hit Jamaica, resulting in thousands losing their homes and livelihoods. Now those with ambition or those with little alternative looked to the 'mother country' more than ever. About 10,000 West Indians entered Britain in 1954. The following year it was 45,000.[2]

Many made their way to Birmingham. If the unemployment rate was only about 2 per cent in the UK as a whole in the 1950s, it averaged less than 1 per cent throughout the decade in the Midlands as the city rode the wave of the post-war transport revolution. African-Caribbeans now found work at the British Motor Corporation in Longbridge and all the nuts and bolts firms, metal rolling mills, car component outfits and machine tool companies swimming in its orbit.

One of them was a Jamaican called Henry Gunter. Born in Portland Parish on the north-east coast of the island in 1920, Gunter studied accountancy in the capital Kingston before being recruited for wartime service for the USA, first working on the Panama Canal, then at a tractor plant in Milwaukee. In America, he experienced appalling racial discrimination, which led him to start a newsletter standing up for the rights of Jamaican workers there.

Back home after the war, the young man decided to emigrate after a British colonial representative visited Jamaica on a recruitment drive for rebuilding the 'mother country'. He arrived in Birmingham in 1949, where he already had friends, and was soon at work at a brass rolling mill in Deritend. Afterwards, he moved on to Moss Gear in Tyburn, which made gearboxes for top-end car manufacturers such as Jensen, Jaguar and Morgan, before moving on to become a tool cutter and grinder at Larches Tool Factory.[3]

By now, Lord Kitchener and his calypso band were being fêted by London's clubland, splashing out 'London is the Place for Me' into the capital's Saturday nights. Above the mellow tones of the clarinet, and the carnival-style rhythms, the willowy voice of Lord Kitchener, aka Aldwyn Roberts, would move on into the second stanza. 'To live in London you are really comfortable. Because the English people are very much sociable,' he would warble. 'They take you here and they take you there. And they make you feel like a millionaire.'

Unfortunately, though, for Henry Gunter, this was not his experience up in Birmingham. Far from English people making him 'feel like a millionaire', he was soon encountering the racism that would blight the experience of the growing Black Caribbean community in the UK for years to come. In fact, he had moved on from the factory in Deritend after challenging the union shop steward over racist verbal abuse of a colleague.

In contrast, he found a more supportive atmosphere at his subsequent places of employment. At Moss Gears, the union shop steward encouraged him to become more active in the labour movement, and at Larches, he joined the Amalgamated Engineering Union (AEU). Having become a member, he was soon elected as a delegate to the Birmingham Trades Council, the body that brings together trade unions from across the city. He was the first ever Black delegate, and given this opportunity, he became active in raising awareness of the issues facing Black workers in the city.

Among these was the difficulty Black people faced in obtaining decent accommodation. In a lead article for the newspaper *Caribbean News*, in February 1953, he hit out at the failure of local government to provide decent housing. West Indian newcomers were being forced to live in terrible conditions in inner-city slum areas such as Aston, Bordesley and Small Heath, he reported. In some instances, three or four male workers were sharing a small room with no bedding or proper facilities.

He elaborated on this theme in a more extensive piece he wrote the following year entitled 'A Man's a Man – a study of colour bar in Birmingham, and an answer', which was published as a booklet by the local branch of the Communist Party of Great Britain, based at Dale End. In this long essay, he identified racial prejudice as a major contributor to the inability of his compatriots to find good places to live. Not only did they end up in substandard housing in the inner-city wards earmarked for slum clearance, but also local landlords, landladies and boarding house keepers were turning them away because of the colour of their skin. The most recurrent excuse, Gunter noted witheringly, was: 'I don't mind myself, but there is no telling what the other white lodgers or the neighbours might say.'[4]

Moreover, the racism did not stop there, the trained accountant wrote, in his devastating social audit of the city. 'Colonials' were often refused service in pubs and hotels, and also 'several of the City's main ballrooms will not admit a coloured man unless he comes by special invitation', he wrote.[5]

There had also been the issue about work on the city's public transport system. Unlike other cities in the UK such as London, Birmingham's transport department had initially refused to employ Black drivers or conductors on its buses. Only a determined campaign by Henry Gunter, with the help of the Birmingham Trades Council and white liberal opinion, managed to get the decision overturned – a small success alluded to in the booklet.

There were also other small steps being made in the right direction, Gunter noted, as people of the Black community began to find their feet in the Midlands. Some of them had joined trade unions or the Labour Party, others had tried to form clubs of their own; and in Balsall Heath, where Gunter lived, the Clifton Institute had been established, offering social and educational activities for Black people.

The institute was a good initiative, Gunter commented, but still needed Black people serving on its committee to be truly representative, as did other social bodies seeking to improve the lot of Caribbean migrants to the city. A proposal to this effect had been suggested by one of Birmingham's city councillors, D.G. Allen, who, Gunter noted, was keen to ensure the well-being of Black people in Birmingham: a well-being that, he said, quoting Allen, 'they were entitled to as members of the Commonwealth'.[6]

Towards the end of his very critical report on Birmingham's 'colour bar' Gunter took a more upbeat stance. West Indian men were very keen sportsmen, he remarked, and it was 'good to know that the Midlands cricket clubs have given coloured players opportunities who have proved their worth by their high places in batting and bowling averages'.

Despite 'the many day to day hardships and rebuffs' Black people have also made 'some very good friends' in England, and there is 'an excellent chance that good relationships will develop', he continued.

'At the same time,' he concluded, 'it is necessary for a determined fight to be made by all men and women of good-will against the colour-bar and practices.'[7]

⁊⁊

Thankfully, the 'colour bar' was soon eradicated by pieces of legislation at the national level. But discrimination in its many forms was much harder to stamp out. Gunter continued to raise awareness of the conditions faced by Black Caribbean people, and to call for legislation to remove discriminatory practices. He became chairman of the Afro-Caribbean Association in Birmingham, and also became the Birmingham correspondent of the *West Indian Gazette*, which had been founded in Brixton by the activist Claudia Jones in 1958.

In 1966, though, he left the Midlands to take up a job in Kent, and did not return to live in the city again until after his retirement in 1985.

Returning to Birmingham in the 1980s, he would have found a city far more proactive in tackling racial injustice. To a certain extent this was due to the Handsworth riots of 1981 and 1985, which had served to turn the spotlight on the problems of 'ghettoisation' that the local Caribbean community had endured for years.[8] Now, armed with the Race Relations Act of 1976 that had bestowed upon local authorities the duty to eliminate racial discrimination, and promote equality of opportunity and good relations between different ethnic communities; Birmingham City Council was taking action. It created a Race Relations Unit overseen by a Race Relations and Equal Opportunities Committee; and within a few years the unit had formulated a number of race equality policies relating to housing, education and social services. It also organised a ten-day multicultural festival to promote the heritage of the city's BME (Black and Minority Ethnic) communities.

Alongside this initiative, the council 'began making links with community groups on a systematic basis',[9] formalising the relationships it had long cultivated with the Black-led churches and African-Caribbean organisations as well as with other ethnic and faith-based groups from the Yemeni, Bangladeshi, Hindu, Pakistani and Sikh communities, and the Chinese and Vietnamese communities.

This was backed up in the 1990s by a council commitment to have '20 per cent of its workforce from a BME background and helping specific percentages of BME pupils obtain good educational outcomes'.[10]

The local authority's emphasis on education paid off. By the turn of the century, more than 40 per cent of the city's school intake was from a BME background, and, by 2013, 85 per cent of Caribbean boys were attaining five or more GCSEs, with 92 per cent of their female counterparts achieving the same. This was in line with the average attainment levels across all the city's different communities – from white inhabitants and those from the Indian subcontinent to more recent arrivals from Africa – which had been raised across the board.[11]

This was a city now fully embracing its multi-ethnic make-up. The conurbation that once barred Black people from driving buses was now '"mainstreaming" equality into core business', according to a report drawn up by Birmingham-based equalities charity Brap.[12] In a city of 187 nationalities, where more than one in three people were now from a Black, Asian or other ethnic minority, it was the natural thing to do.[13]

Arguably, this 'mainstreaming' of 'equality' has been a long time coming, but in the meantime, despite all the racism they have encountered in the past, many Brummies of Caribbean descent have got on with the business of achievement. In fact, they have been doing so for quite some time. Like their Asian counterparts, they have made their mark in various fields, not only producing sporting heroes such as Denise Lewis from West Bromwich, who won heptathlon gold at the Sydney Olympics in 2000 and gold at two Commonwealth Games, but also leaving a strong cultural stamp on the city. In this, the Caribbean community has transformed a once rather grey industrial heartland into a place also for musicians, artists and performers.

෧෨

One of Birmingham's most famous sons, for instance, is Lenny Henry. Born at Burton Road Hospital in Dudley in 1958 to Winifred Henry, who had recently emigrated to the UK from a village in Jamaica, this much-loved comedian and entertainer grew up in a large family (he was the fifth child of seven) in the Buffery Park area of the Black Country,[14] experiencing the racist abuse that was commonly meted out to Black boys in Birmingham at that time. He soon found out, however, that making his secondary school tormentors laugh with jokes and impersonations got him out of scrapes. The realisation led him into pursuing a dual existence after he left school: serving an apprenticeship at British Federal Welders and attending West Bromwich Technical College during the day, while performing comedy gigs at pubs, working men's clubs and discotheques at night. Revellers at old Birmingham pubs such as The Ship & Rainbow and the Saracen's Head, and clubs including Club Lafayette, all witnessed his unique mix of impersonations and comedy stand-up.

Then, just before Christmas in 1974, he received the phone call. He had won a slot on the TV talent show *New Faces* in the new year. Appearing in January 1975, he won the contest with impressions of Muhammad Ali and Frank Spencer, and was thenceforth thrust into a TV world of light entertainment. He soon became a stalwart on the iconic Birmingham-based children's entertainment show *Tiswas*; and later, in the 1980s, landed his own BBC programme, *The Lenny Henry Show*, which blended stand-up comedy with sketches.

His TV comedy career carried on flourishing in the 1990s, although by then he was already showing a serious side, teaming up with screenwriter Richard

෧෨

Curtis in 1985 to launch Comic Relief, the TV charitable effort that has been running ever since. In 2009, he played Othello at the West Yorkshire Playhouse to widespread acclaim. Always a strong advocate for Birmingham and the West Midlands, and for greater Black, Asian and ethnic minority representation in the broadcasting industry, Henry was appointed chancellor of Birmingham City University in 2016. As home to the Birmingham School of Acting, the Birmingham Conservatoire and the Birmingham School of Media, the university is reportedly the biggest generator of creative professionals outside the South-east.[15]

Growing up at the same time as Lenny Henry, but up the road in Handsworth, was another African-Caribbean boy who was to make his mark on the British arts scene. Benjamin Zephaniah was born on 15 April 1958, and, although he was not a success at school, was writing poetry from an early age. His first real public performance of his poetry was in a church at the age of 10, and by the age of 15 he had developed a strong following in Handsworth.

The local appreciation of his hard-hitting poetry was not enough to keep Zephaniah in the Midlands, however; and in 1979 he moved down to London to seek a wider audience for his work. His first book of poetry – *Pen Rhythm* – was published the following year. This was followed up in 1985 by a second collection, *The Dread Affair*, which contained a number of poems attacking the British legal system. The political themes continued into his subsequent anthologies.

Despite moving down to London at an early age, however, this poet, novelist and playwright still sees his roots as being in Handsworth, calling it 'the Jamaican capital of Europe' on his website.[16]

It is the Jamaican make-up of Handsworth that has made it the cradle for cultural endeavour. This was the area of north Birmingham where many Caribbean people settled in the 1950s. But even if they were kept busy building new lives in the booming Midlands factories, they never quite forgot the old life they had left behind. If Jamaica was the place of street parties and street music, of calypso and ska, then some of that could not fail to end up in the elegant avenues of this once well-to-do Birmingham district. The street gatherings of rural tropical Jamaica morphed into the noisy parties held in the basements and front rooms of the neighbourhood's old Edwardian terraces.

Towards the end of the 1960s, the music coming out of Jamaica was the Rastafari reggae of Bob Marley, and this began to wield its influence over the sons and daughters of the first generation of Caribbean immigrants in Birmingham. Reggae became the signature soundtrack of record shops all over Handsworth, from the Soho Road to Grove Lane; and soon Birmingham had its first home-grown reggae band. Steel Pulse was formed in 1975 by a group of friends at Handsworth Wood Boys School who were never going to pull their punches. In 1978, they played in Victoria Park in Hackney at the first music festival organised by the Rock Against Racism movement.[17] The same year, they released their first album, *Handsworth Revolution*, which included their broadside against racism, 'Klu Klux Klan'.

Other Birmingham reggae acts such as Musical Youth and UB40 followed in Steel Pulse's wake, and following the other Handsworth/Jamaican tradition of fusing different musical styles were two mixed-race bands that combined ska, reggae and punk – The Beat from Birmingham and The Specials from Coventry.[18] These two groups burst onto the British music scene in the late 1970s with hits such as 'Tears of a Clown' and 'Ghost Town'. Musical genres in Birmingham have been mixed still further in recent years with a Punjabi bhangra scene.

Back in Handsworth itself, the blend of musical cultures around the Soho Road has also spawned singer-songwriter Joan Armatrading, soul singer Ruby Turner and Punjabi reggae DJ Apache Indian, who combines Caribbean and Asian vernaculars in his music.

Born in Handsworth in 1967, Apache Indian started off his career working with sound systems, which was the other musical phenomenon pumping out of the north Birmingham neighbourhood. This all started in the 1960s and '70s with impromptu 'blues parties' held in private houses – often derelict ones wired up to the street lighting outside – in which visitors paid at the door to groove to the sounds of a group of DJs, MCs and engineers gathered around a turntable and a stack of speakers. The speakers would be belting out an eclectic mix of ska, reggae and electronic dub manipulations, while the DJs and MCs would improvise mantras, 'toasts' and incantations over the top. As early as the 1960s, a sound system grouping called Quaker City had formed in Handsworth. Another one called Wassifa Sound System soon followed.

David Hinds of Steel Pulse performing in Bristol in 2004. Steel Pulse was formed by a group of friends at Handsworth Wood Boys School in 1975. (Lebrecht Music & Arts/ Alamy Stock Photo)

There is a black-and-white photograph of a group of Rasta-capped MCs and DJs gathered around a turnstile sitting in the Birmingham Archives. They are members of Wassifa Sound System pictured in Handsworth Park in 1983 by a photographer who is another product of Handsworth's great creative outpouring in the past half century.

Often described as the 'Godfather of Black British Photography', Vanley Burke was born in the shadow of the Blue Mountains in Jamaica in the early 1950s when the island was still a British colony. For his 10th birthday his mother, who had already gone to live in England, leaving Vanley in the care of his aunt, bought him a Kodak 'Box Brownie' camera, and in one stroke set the tone for the rest of her son's life. At the age of 14, in 1965, Vanley joined his parents living in Handsworth, Birmingham; and soon he was roaming the streets of the neighbourhood with a very definite mission in mind – to document the lives of the Caribbean diaspora to the city before it was lost to history.[19]

Some of them appeared in his first major exhibition, *Handsworth from the Inside*, shown at the Ikon Gallery in Birmingham and then the Commonwealth Institute in London in 1983.

But like his artistic counterparts in Steel Pulse who played the first Rock Against Racism festival, his interests were never limited to the Midlands. Inspired by the imminent release of Nelson Mandela in 1990, Burke undertook a six-week visit to South Africa, travelling the length and breadth of the country to chronicle Black lives under apartheid. Returning with thousands of images, he produced a critically acclaimed exhibition called *No Time for Flowers*, the success of which led to a second visit to the African nation, this time working with the African National Congress (ANC) to produce a tribute to the veterans of the liberation struggle.

On his return, he recurated his photographs for an exhibition at Soho House Museum in Handsworth called *Nkunzi: Photographs of Birmingham and South Africa*, which made connections between the country recently liberated from apartheid and his hometown.

It was to prove to be the catalyst for a programme of partnership projects between the cities of Birmingham and Johannesburg, which have been twinned as 'sister cities' ever since.[20]

Among other things, the Exchange Project involved the swap of Burke's pictures of South Africa with South African photographer George Hallet's pictures of Handsworth taken on a visit to the UK in 1971. Hallet's photos were exhibited at Soho House, while the Birmingham cameraman's work was shown at Bensusan Museum in Johannesburg.

A project worthy of note on its own terms. But there was an extra twist in the tale. In one of those strange soft-shoe shuffles of irony, Hallet had taken a picture of two boys outside their mother's grocery shop during his visit to Birmingham in 1971. On closer inspection by all concerned, they turned out to be Vanley Burke's brothers.

NOTES

1   David Olusoga, *Black and British: A Forgotten History* (London: Pan Books, 2017), p.494.

2   Ibid., p.498.

3   An accompanying letter to the *Financial Times*, 10 August 2001. Papers of Henry Gunter in the Wolfson Centre for Archival Research, Library of Birmingham [MS2165].

4   Henry Gunter, *A Man's a Man – a study of colour bar in Birmingham, and an answer* (Dale End, Birmingham: Communist Party of Great Britain, 1954), p.9, in Papers of Henry Gunter in the Wolfson Centre for Archival Research, Library of Birmingham [MS2165].

5   Ibid., p.11.

6   Ibid., p.13.

7   Ibid., p.14.

8   Chris Upton, *A History of Birmingham* (Stroud: Phillimore & Co./The History Press, 2011), pp.207–209.

9   Brap (A Birmingham equalities charity) report. *From Benign Neglect to Citizen Khan: 30 years of equalities practice in Birmingham*, 2015, p.16.

10   Ibid., p.16.

11   Ibid., pp.36–38.

12   Ibid., p.22.

13   *Birmingham Mail*, 'The figures proving Birmingham is more diverse than ever', 3 September 2018 [Online].

14   Lenny Henry tells his own story in *Who am I, Again?* (London: Faber & Faber, 2019).

15   Information can be found on Birmingham City University's website, www.bcu.ac.uk.

16   benjaminzephaniah.com.

17   The Rock Against Racism movement emerged in the mid-1970s in response to the growing number of racist attacks in the UK. Primarily a musical movement, it organised a number of festivals and gigs, including the Victoria Park concert, which attracted an audience of 100,000 people who had marched from Trafalgar Square to attend.

18   The Coventry Stadium and Arena will host three sports at the Commonwealth Games 2022 – rugby sevens, judo and wrestling.

19   A collection of Vanley Burke photographs [MS2192] is held at the Wolfson Centre for Archival Research, Library of Birmingham.

20   The twinning is part of Birmingham City Council's European and international Strategy. More information can be found at distinctlybirmingham.com/partner-cities/johannesburg.

CHAPTER FIVE

SOUTH AFRICA

If the tale of Vanley Burke and his photo swap as Black Africans born of apartheid finally found their freedom was a heart-warming moment in Birmingham's relations with South Africa, then a monument sitting in Cannon Hill Park, an elegant public space sandwiched in between the southern suburbs of Edgbaston and Moseley, tells quite a different story.

Unveiled on 23 June 1906, the Boer War Soldiers Memorial features a granite base surmounted by a sculpture of a female figure symbolising peace looking down on a gun carriage flanked by two soldiers. Meanwhile, brass bas-reliefs on the pedestal itself carry the names of the Brummie soldiers who fell in the killing fields of South Africa. Gunner Wilks, Sapper Potter and 510 others listed here were among the 22,000 British servicemen who perished in a vicious campaign conducted by Birmingham's most famous son, its Lord Mayor from 1873 to 1876, Joseph Chamberlain.

So, how did the town councillor who had driven a welfare revolution in Birmingham before becoming a government minister become embroiled in Britain's bloodiest war since the Crimean conflict of the 1850s? Well, the answer lies, as many historians argue, in the complex character of a man who is widely regarded as the 'most dynamic politician of late Victorian and early Edwardian Britain'.[1]

'Arrogant', 'pushy' and 'ruthless' have been some of the adjectives pinned on the Birmingham industrialist turned politician, although on the flip side he was lauded in Parliament for his 'remarkable business ability', and for being one of the 'best speakers'[2] in the House of Commons. Chamberlain was a man who got things done but also a man who made enemies easily, and his formidably articulate debating style at Westminster made him an implacable opponent.

Even more galling for his detractors was the fact that he was probably the most effective populist of his age. Well-armed with the dark arts of oratory, this distinctive politician with the monocle over his right eye and the orchid in his buttonhole could, and often did, rally the people behind his way of thinking, his latest

With the trademark monocle over his right eye and the orchid in his buttonhole, Joseph Chamberlain was a nonconformist by nature as well as by religion. (Reproduced with the permission of Cadbury Research Library: Special Collections, University of Birmingham)

political cause. The problem, say his critics, was that his political causes were often destructive: his opposition to Irish Home Rule in the 1880s and his advocacy of tariff reform in the early twentieth century managed in large part to break up the very governments to which he belonged.

Destructive, contrary, competitive – whether or not Chamberlain's nonconformist upbringing contributed to his taciturn nature it is difficult to tell, but one thing is certain: at times he had Britain's cosy political and social establishment on the run.

As a Unitarian, and thus naturally inclined to oppose any form of privilege, he probably would not have had it any other way. As we have seen before in this book, nonconformity is what made Birmingham tick. Unitarians were at the heart of the Lunar Society, while Quakers formed the core of Birmingham's anti-slavery movement; and it was the business acumen of both nonconformist sects that dominated the Midlands economy, despite together making up less than 5 per cent of the town's church and chapel attenders.[3] Excluded from public office or universities by England's Anglican elite until well into the nineteenth century, it was as if those who did not conform to the practices of the Church of England threw themselves into philanthropy or business instead. Chamberlain himself came from a London Unitarian family, which had connections in Birmingham. In the autumn of 1854, at the age of 18, he caught a train up to the Midlands to make contact with them, joining the firm owned by his uncle, John Sutton Nettlefold.

As we have seen, rather than being a town of large mills like Manchester, Birmingham at the time was a city teeming with small workshops making everything from pins and nails to jewellery. This was not going to change, but what we were beginning to see was the emergence of some very large outfits as well. With the young Joseph Chamberlain's restless entrepreneurial energy and his flair for marketing and accountancy, Nettlefolds was about to join this premier league. Within little over a decade, Nettlefold and Chamberlain – as it soon became known – had become the main manufacturer of screws and fastenings in the Midlands, employing more than 2,000 workers.

At the same time, Chamberlain was establishing himself in local civic life. He was appointed as treasurer and taught Sunday school and evening classes at the Unitarian's Church of the Messiah in Broad Street, and became President at the well-connected Edgbaston Debating Society. Honing his speaking skills at the Society, it was not long before the entrepreneur would be turning away from industry in order to turn his hand at politics. He became involved in an educational crusade in the late 1860s to establish locally managed, non-sectarian schools across the country in direct challenge to the Church of England's monopoly of primary education, becoming a member of the new Birmingham school board and a town councillor into the bargain. In 1873, he became the mayor of Birmingham.

The Liberal councillor's three-year tenure at the helm of the Birmingham local authority would prove truly transformative. Recognising that only radical reform could transform the health and environment of Birmingham's working class, he swept aside any opposition to drive through the purchase of the town's two gas companies in a two-pronged strategy that would see his newly municipalised gas supply yield enough profit for reinvestment in a public-owned water company as well. With thousands of new gas lamps appearing on Birmingham streets, no councillor dared to vote against Chamberlain's subsequent takeover of the water supply, especially after the headstrong Unitarian had argued forcefully for the eradication of the tainted water wells that were the source of so much disease in the city's slums. This second piece of reform was truly significant. 'No single policy in nineteenth-century Birmingham did more for the health of its inhabitants,' according to historian Andrew Reekes.[4]

The success of gas and water reform paved the way for the third pillar of Chamberlain's legacy for Birmingham – a revitalised city centre. Using new powers under the Artisans' Dwelling Act of 1875, the mayor tore down 40 acres of slums in the city centre and replaced them with fine shops, offices and public buildings, many of which lined a handsome new thoroughfare called Corporation Street. With only a few dozen working-class houses constructed, it was an audacious move that never quite lived up to the spirit of the Act, but instead gave Birmingham a commercial and civic centre to rival any provincial urbanity across the world.

In just three years, the man with the monocle had reinvented his adopted town as a model of municipal progress, and in doing so, incidentally wired the capacity for reinvention firmly into the city's political DNA.[5]

For Chamberlain himself, wielding power in Birmingham had whetted his appetite for something more, and despite being struck by personal tragedy during his tenure as mayor, he went on to fight a successful by-election to win a seat in Parliament in 1876. The loss of his second wife, Florence, in childbirth would weigh heavily on him long after his arrival at Westminster, but soon his undoubted talents as an organiser and political operator were to be recognised. Forming his second ministry in 1880, Liberal Prime Minister William Gladstone appointed Chamberlain as his trade minister.

The Birmingham MP now had the power he craved on a national basis. Just as important, however, for the legacy that he would leave behind was the intellectual journey that he would go through with that power. As President of the Board of Trade in Gladstone's Cabinet, he was in charge of furthering British business interests overseas, which had expanded rapidly in the past decade with the opening of the Suez Canal. With 80 per cent of the commercial traffic travelling along this vital shipping lane in British hands, it lay with Chamberlain to defend it, while also making strategic inroads into the Arabic and North African lands surrounding it. This experience seemed to provoke a sea-change in the Birmingham politician's thinking, according to historian Travis L. Crosby, especially after the timely reading of a just-published justification for British imperialism.[6]

Full of pomp and circumstance, *The Expansion of England* by Cambridge historian J.R. Seely argued that Britain's colonies were not merely far-flung possessions, but instead were a family of nations closely tied to the mother country through bonds of blood and institution – an extension and expression of England rather than something remote.

It was an idea that the nonconformist was taking on board as Gladstone's ministry faced increasing Irish agitation for a parliament devolved from Westminster. When Gladstone committed the Liberal Party to Home Rule and held a vote on it in the House of Commons in 1886, Chamberlain joined with other Liberal dissidents to defeat it. The split in the Liberal Party would prove damaging. The party lost the general election that year, and would be consigned to the political wilderness for the best part of two decades.

Having contributed to his own government's fall, Chamberlain was now out of office too; and although he was still an MP, he now had more time to develop his estate at Highbury Hall, the house that had been built for him in 1880 in the Birmingham suburb of King's Heath.

With its red-ochre brickwork and tiered series of stone-lined bay windows, Highbury had been built in the neo-Venetian Gothic style, fashionable at the time. The style extended to the exuberant use of coloured tiles, parquet floors and marbled pillars inside the house, and to Chamberlain's study in one corner of it, which was lined with oaken bookshelves.

Lavish as the building was, though, Chamberlain's real domestic passion lay at the end of the stone paths that led out of the house and into his landscaped gardens and greenhouses sitting in acres of ground. The man with a signature orchid always planted firmly in his jacket buttonhole spent many hours in his greenhouses – there were two dozen of them – cross-fertilising and developing new varieties of this delicate flower. In the same way as he absorbed himself thoroughly in political causes, he became an expert in botany, winning awards from the Royal Horticultural Society for the orchids he had nurtured.

But 'there was more to Highbury than orchids', writes historian Andrew Reekes. The eclectic mix of 'bamboo, tropical ferns and magnolias from the East' in the gardens and hothouses also 'reflected the owner's own imperial vision'.[7]

It was this vision – very unlike the wholesome, back-to-nature outlook of fellow Birmingham nonconformist and keen gardener George Cadbury – which now animated Chamberlain, especially after a tour of British-occupied Egypt in late 1889 and early 1890. During this visit, he had been impressed by the British development of public works in the country, particularly the irrigation scheme that was increasing agricultural output in the Nile Valley. This chimed nicely with the public work programmes he had initiated in Birmingham, and he returned to the UK to become the 'most prominent and articulate spokesman of Britain's imperial mission'.[8]

Britain now had to invest more heavily in its overseas possessions, he was now urging. In the same way as he had endowed Birmingham with its own 'improvement scheme',[9] what the colonies needed were more things like irrigation pipes, and trains running on railway tracks. (It also just so happened Birmingham manufacturers made this sort of thing, as in the case of rolling stock manufacturer Metro-Cammell, which employed thousands of workers locally.)

'Great Britain, the little centre of a vaster Empire than the world has ever seen, owns great possessions in every part of the globe, and many of those possessions are still almost unexplored, entirely undeveloped,' he said in a speech during the election campaign of 1895.[10]

As landlord of such a large estate, the orchid grower argued, it was Britain's duty to develop it.

Like the orchids in the greenhouses at his Highbury home, Joseph Chamberlain believed the British Empire needed nurturing. (Reproduced with the permission of Cadbury Research Library: Special Collections, University of Birmingham)

It was an aspiration that received ready support from both his working-class constituency in Birmingham and nationwide. After all, the 1890s were a time when British jingoism was running high. Books such as *King Solomon's Mines* that told tales about British derring-do in exotic locations were all the rage.

In the election that followed, the political faction he now led – the Liberal Unionists – were swept into power as part of a Conservative–Unionist alliance, and Chamberlain was installed as Secretary of State for the Colonies.

He was now free to develop his new political cause. The repercussions would soon be felt thousands of miles away on the South African veldt.

෧෨

In 1892, when Joseph Chamberlain was nursing his political ambitions and tending to his orchids at the Highbury estate, a boy was born in a city known as the 'fountain of flowers'. The boy's parents were Midlanders who had moved to the city to make a new life for themselves. Arthur had tried to make a career at Lloyds Bank in Birmingham, but with prospects of promotion slow, he had looked to South Africa where banks were booming on the back of recently discovered gold and diamond reserves. In the late 1880s he had landed a job with the Bank of Africa, and at the beginning of 1891, his betrothed, Mabel, had sailed out to join him. After their marriage at Cape Town Cathedral on 16 April 1891, the couple had made the long railway journey up and onto the dry, dusty plateaus of southern Africa to the place where they would be based.

This was the capital of Orange Free State, Bloemfontein, so-called because of the profusion of rose bushes lining its streets and filling its parks with vivid colour. In addition to the rose bushes, it was a place of sturdy European buildings such as the neo-classical Parliament House and the neat, Victorian railway station, which was the terminus of the newly opened Cape Town to Bloemfontein railway line.

But while Cape Town was firmly in British hands, as part of Britain's strengthening grip over southern Africa, the Europeans in charge in Orange Free State were the Boers or Afrikaners, farmers of mainly Dutch descent who had migrated onto the veldt when the British had replaced them on the Cape during the Napoleonic Wars. This made Arthur an outsider, an *uitlander*, of which there were many – adventurers, mostly British, who had been lured to the Boer lands north-east of the Cape by the exciting prospects offered up by gold and diamonds, but as *uitlanders* denied full citizenship rights by the Boer governments.

Whatever the disadvantages of being a second-class citizen, the opportunities must have outweighed them, because by all accounts Arthur had thrown himself into his work as a bank manager in an area sandwiched between the Kimberley diamond mines to the west and the gold mines of Witwatersrand to the north. Soon, too, he was a proud father. Mabel had given birth to boy on 3 January 1892, and on 31 January 1892, the couple had him christened at Bloemfontein Cathedral.

The name recorded in the register was John Ronald Reuel Tolkien.

Later on in life, J.R.R. Tolkien, or Ronald, as he was more simply called by his parents and relatives, would have few memories of his very early years spent in the dusty heat of South Africa. There was one memory, however, of a hot day and 'running in fear through long, dead grass'.[11] Just beginning to walk in the garden, he had stumbled on a tarantula, which had bitten him. Fortunately, the family nurse had been on hand to snatch him up and suck out the poison.

Perhaps the giant spiders that would later weave their grisly influence in *The Hobbit* and *The Lord of the Rings* sprung somehow from a subconscious inkling of that far-off day in Bloemfontein. Whatever the truth of the matter, most of the remainder of his early life in Africa followed fairly regular routines. In the early afternoon and later afternoon the child would be taken out into the garden, where he could watch his father tending to a small grove of trees and saplings. In between times he was kept indoors out of the blaze of the subtropical sun. By early 1894, when he was joined by a baby brother, he was growing up fast, sporting a mop of fair hair and blue eyes, and 'talking volubly'.[12]

His mother, however, had long yearned for some home leave away from the intensity of the African climate and the 'endless social calls' and 'tedious dinner-parties'[13] of Bloemfontein life. In 1895 she got her wish. Arrangements were made, and at the beginning of April that year, she and her two boys boarded a ship bound for Southampton.

Three weeks later, she was holed up in the house of her parents at 9 Ashfield Road, King's Heath – a stone's throw from Joseph Chamberlain's Highbury Hall – enjoying the change of scene no doubt and waiting for Arthur Tolkien to join them.

He never did. First, it was work commitments that detained him, and quite possibly a love of the African climate that always saw him making excuses for not returning to England, even for a short time. Then, in November, news arrived that he had gone down with rheumatic fever, and a visit to England in the depths of winter would do little to aid his recovery. Mabel sat tight until after Christmas, when she started to make arrangements to return to Bloemfontein so that she could care for him.

She never returned to South Africa, nor did her son J.R.R. Tolkien. On 14 February 1896 she received a telegram, telling her that her husband had suffered a severe haemorrhage. The next day he was dead.

⟨ᴏ⟩

How much Arthur Tolkien knew, if anything, about the goings-on in Johannesburg, the gold mining settlement to the north-east of Bloemfontein, in the final few weeks of his life, will always remain one of history's hidden and irrelevant footnotes. Perhaps a headline in a newspaper glimpsed from a hospital bed? Who knows? Who will ever know?

⟨ᴏ⟩

How much the newly appointed Colonial Secretary in the British government, Joseph Chamberlain, knew about them will also be forever lost in conjecture. However, in his case, unlike that of Tolkien senior, what he knew or did not know remains an important piece of historical inquiry.

One thing is certain: right from the outset of his tenure at the Colonial Office, Chamberlain was embroiled in South Africa. In one sense, this was all part of a more proactive engagement with empire pursued by the new Colonial Secretary, which saw him setting up loans for new infrastructure projects in British West Africa and the West Indies, founding Schools of Tropical Medicine in Liverpool and London, and beefing up the South African department in the Colonial Office to keep an eye on Britain's growing interests, predominantly in gold and diamond mining, in the region. In another sense, though, it was going to be in South Africa where events would gather so much momentum that he would be sucked into their wake.

The key driver behind those events was Cecil Rhodes, the founder of the mining company De Beers, which controlled the Kimberley diamond mines and also had substantial interests in the gold mines up in the Transvaal. The problem for the freebooting Rhodes, who was also Prime Minister of the Cape Colony, one of two British possessions on the coast of southern Africa, was that the Boers held sway in the Transvaal as they did in the Orange Free State; and even though the mines there were overwhelmingly staffed by British and German engineers, these foreign immigrants were treated poorly by the Boer government.

As *uitlander* resentment grew against their lack of civil and voting rights in Boer territory, though, Rhodes saw his chance: foster an uprising among the *uitlanders* in the Transvaal, send in troops to protect the 'rights of British subjects', and then grab total control of the gold mines. That was the plan, anyway, when on 29 December 1895 collaborator Leander Starr Jameson led a force of 470 men on horseback over the border of British Bechuanaland (now part of Botswana) into the Transvaal and headed for Johannesburg. Contrary to expectations, however, there had been no *uitlander* uprising in Johannesburg at all and the raid was quickly supressed by the Boer military. Jameson was thrown into jail, and with him Rhodes' idea of bringing the Transvaal to heel, and extending British influence.

As Cecil Rhodes' ultimate boss, Joseph Chamberlain would face speculation for many years to come as to how much he had known beforehand of the Jameson Raid. Despite much parliamentary scrutiny, though, the allegations did not stick, and Chamberlain survived the inquiry intact, ready to fight another day.

That other day came soon enough, with the appointment in 1897 of a new High Commissioner for South Africa, Alfred Milner. Like Chamberlain, Milner was an enthusiastic imperialist, convinced that the British Empire was a benevolent force in the world, bringing order and prosperity – in their minds at least – to areas where chaos once reigned.

Suffice to say, the Boers of Southern Africa didn't quite see it that way, and before too long, the two sides were engaged in a heated war of words over the long-standing issue of *uitlander* rights. Whether or not, below the surface, the real motives for their provocations were imperial expansion and control of the goldfields, the clarion call from Chamberlain and his diplomat were indisputably about political rights for the *uitlanders*, most of them British. How could subjects of the world's pre-eminent power suffer the oppression and injustices of Boer government? Britain had a right to defend its citizens. All Britain wanted was franchise reform, common justice and so forth. Paul Kruger, the president of the South African Republic (the Transvaal), did not buy it; and in October 1899 war broke out.

Unfortunately, Joseph Chamberlain's verbal brinkmanship had not extended to providing enough British troops on the ground, and the beginning of the Boer War did not go well for the Colonial Secretary. Within days of hostilities erupting, Boer fighters had surrounded the British garrison at Mafeking in Bechuanaland, and were soon besieging Ladysmith in the British colony of Natal, as well as the diamond mining centre of Kimberley. In December 1899, over the course of just one week, they inflicted three major defeats on increasingly bewildered British troops.

After 'Black Week', as it was known in Britain, it was time for changes in the military top brass and reinforcements. Generals Roberts and Kitchener arrived in the new year with 40,000 reinforcements, and began to turn the tide. By the end of February, Kimberley and Ladysmith had been rescued. In March, Roberts occupied Bloemfontein, and in May British troops marched into Johannesburg. The same month, after a siege of 217 days, the British garrison at Mafeking was saved. In June, the British army entered Pretoria, the capital of the Transvaal.

In a post-election address in 1900, after the Conservative and Unionist government had been returned to office, an exuberant Chamberlain, still Colonial Secretary, proclaimed the British Empire, with its 400 million subjects comprising 'almost every race under the sun', as 'one family' bound together by mutual sentiment, common ideals and noble aspirations. It was an altruistic empire, he continued, having brought 'freedom and justice and civilisation and peace' to all its 'dependent races'.[14]

For the Birmingham entrepreneur, it seemed, the Empire had now taken on almost mystical proportions.

It was all a little premature, however. Even as the Birmingham MP spoke, the Boers were regrouping, this time as guerrilla fighters, cutting supply lines, derailing trains, attacking British posts. It took the mighty resources of the British military machine, and two very dubious practices – a scorched earth policy of burning Boer homesteads and crops, and resettling women and children from those homes into 'concentration' camps – to finally bring the defeated Afrikaner republics to the negotiating table in May 1902.

The war memorial in Birmingham's Cannon Hill Park offers testament to the heavy cost that the British army paid in trying to win that war, but British casualties were easily matched by victims on the other side, including thousands of South African civilians who perished in the ineptly run concentration camps where crowded and insanitary conditions lit the touchpaper of disease. Chamberlain maintained that the camps were a humane policy intended to protect innocent people caught up in a war zone,[15] but all the justifications in the world were not going to bring back all those people in the camps who had died of dysentery, measles and pneumonia. On the outskirts of Bloemfontein, where the Tolkiens had once lived, there stands an imposing monument to the Boer women and children who died in those camps.

Still, never lacking in political courage, in November 1902 Joseph Chamberlain set sail for South Africa to investigate the situation for himself and to try to reconcile the Boer republics as to the benefits of now being included in the British Empire.

Having received a hearty send-off by cheering crowds in Birmingham city centre the week before, the Birmingham politician, together with his third wife Mary Endicott and three aides, boarded HMS *Good Hope* at Portsmouth, and after a rough passage in the Bay of Biscay, arrived soon afterwards at Port Said in Egypt. After a detour to Cairo – the city that Chamberlain had last visited in 1890 – his ship carried on through the Red Sea and into the Indian Ocean towards Mombasa, the main port of British East Africa, a vast swathe of British occupation extending from the African Great Lakes region to the coast. A railway completed just the year before by British engineers and workers from India then took Chamberlain and his entourage inland as far as Nairobi, though the railroad itself continued on to the shores of Lake Victoria.

Whether or not he noticed the preponderance of Asian faces on the sides of the railroad, the Indian workers who had decided to stay on and settle in East Africa and form the communities that would later have to flee to Britain in the 1960s and '70s amid political persecution, one cannot say. But now the Birmingham MP continued his own journey southwards: a trip that took him back to sea, past Pemba Island where Birmingham Quaker Maria Albright would spend some time visiting the Society of Friends mission station eight years later,[16] and past the spice island of Zanzibar, before finally docking at Durban on Christmas Day 1902.

Once in South Africa, the politician threw himself into a punishing schedule that took him not only to the most important centres of power in Johannesburg and Pretoria, but also to former battle sites such as Mafeking and small country towns high up on the veldt. Sometimes he had to travel in covered wagons drawn by mules and sleep under canvas, and sometimes he risked assassination at the hands of vengeful Boers; but everywhere his message was the same:

The programme for a banquet given to the British Colonial Secretary at the end of his two-month tour of South Africa. (Reproduced with the permission of Cadbury Research Library: Special Collections, University of Birmingham)

accept the peace treaty, work in partnership with benign British rule, and all will be well.

One might assume that many Afrikaners did not quite revel in the light, but Chamberlain himself sailed out of Cape Town on 25 February 1903 thoroughly convinced by the power of his own argument. The unification of South Africa under the British flag was just another step towards ever-increasing imperial unity. The time was now ripe for him, Joseph Chamberlain, to initiate the next step.

What he did next would split his own government right down the middle and bring his own tempestuous career to its final denouement.

◌◌

It all started in typical Chamberlain fashion. A pugnacious speech at Birmingham Town Hall on 15 May 1903, a couple of months after returning from overseas, set out his stall. A new nation was being forged in South Africa, one that could take its place in a British Empire standing together, 'one free nation, if necessary, against all the world'.[17] Britain and its empire were at a critical junction in their shared history, he continued. There was already an 'empire of sentiment', but this needed to be strengthened now by ties of trade and commerce. In order to build imperial unity, there needed to be 'a community of interest'.[18]

What Chamberlain was tracing out here was a programme of tariff reform, or 'Imperial Preference', as the MP came to call it. The idea was to transform the Empire into one giant Customs Union, with Britain waiving duties on imports from its colonies while reimposing them on goods coming in from countries outside the Empire. Canadian wheat coming into Britain, for example, would be exempted from duty, while American or European wheat would be saddled with a tariff. Under such schemes the colonies would win a greater share of UK markets, but, of course, in return they would have to reduce their tariffs on British goods.

All of his experience as a local politician and as a minister in two governments suggested to Chamberlain that this new programme made complete sense. As President of the Board of Trade he had seen how protectionist policies in Europe, the United States and elsewhere were blocking British trade, while Britain's own free trade stance allowed for a continuous flow of cheap foreign imports. For years he had heard the complaints of Birmingham industrialists being undercut by their European and American rivals. An imperial free trade bloc could reverse the tide.

Moreover, there had been a growing movement towards freer trade arrangements within the Empire. A succession of colonial conferences had mooted them; and for some years Canada had been unilaterally reducing its tariffs on British products, calling for Britain to do the same in return. Now, in Chamberlain's mind, it was time to act.

What was a matter of conviction for Chamberlain, however, turned out to be political dynamite. Ever since the Repeal of the Corn Laws in 1846, which had dumped protectionism for British farmers, Britain had stood for free trade, an almost sacred idea that free commerce between all nations would promote peace and harmony. The questioning of this orthodoxy was almost heresy. Not to mention the fact that taxing food would drive those living on the margins of society to anarchy. Chamberlain's Town Hall speech caused a sensation, sparking a storm of opposition from MPs on all sides of the House and driving a rift between tariff reformers and free traders in the government itself.

Rather than deterring the Birmingham politician, who had started his parliamentary career as a free trader himself, the uproar only drove him on. After all, he had already split a government over Irish Home Rule. He was by nature a heretic and he was going to persist in his crusade regardless. He quickly established a war room of advisers and loyalists, resigned his Cabinet post to focus all his efforts on his new obsession, and hit the campaign trail.

From Glasgow to Liverpool, from Cardiff to Birmingham, he was met with large and excited crowds who warmed to his central theme of industrial decline if cheap tariff-protected imports were not stopped in their tracks. In Liverpool, he warned of the foreign business threat to the shipping business. In South Wales, it was coal mining, tin plating and steel making being hung out to dry, and back at Bingley Hall in Birmingham in November 2003 it was brass, pearl buttons and bicycles sinking under the weight of unfair competition from abroad.

The answer was commercial union with the colonies that would see British-manufactured goods finding a ready market, while slapping duties on foreign imports from outside the imperial yoke could also free up funds for a domestic social reform agenda.

But there was always a heady whiff of mysticism in Chamberlain's message, too. The British people needed to accept the overtures from colonies such as Canada to increase commercial links if there was any hope of transmitting to their descendants 'untarnished in lustre, undiminished in power, the sceptre of our Imperial dominion', he intoned in a decidedly religious incantation.[19]

It was the Empire, he argued, that 'ennobled our national life' and discouraged 'petty parochialism'.[20]

For a while, this heady concoction of economic self-interest and imperial pride contained in the Birmingham politician's message, together with the zeal with which he delivered it, struck a chord with the electorate.

೧೦

Had the embattled Unionist government gone to the country in 1904, more momentum might have been behind Joseph Chamberlain and his tariff reform disciples. But Arthur Balfour, who had taken over from Lord Salisbury as Prime Minister in 1902, prevaricated over the divisions in Parliament and in his own Cabinet that the Birmingham thorn in his side had created. Unable to declare for one side or the other – for free traders or tariff reformers – he stumbled on to December 1905 when, after all the procrastination, he abruptly resigned.

In the intervening period, the tariff reform campaign had lost its head of steam, and when a general election was set for January 1906, the opposition Liberal Party with its rising political stars such as David Lloyd George were able to raise the rallying cry that free trade meant cheap bread. They were swept into power in one of the biggest landslides in British electoral history.

That is not to say that Joe Chamberlain did not go down fighting. Ignoring Balfour and the other party moderates, he had campaigned furiously against the Liberal Party through most of January, giving speeches almost every day. When the polls finally closed, all seven Birmingham Unionists had been returned. Nationwide, however, there had been a decisive rejection of tariff reform. The Birmingham maverick's dream of an imperial customs union had been thwarted. And perhaps much more besides – it is no secret that Chamberlain even contemplated a federated imperial union one day, presided over by an imperial parliament.

But at least the people of Birmingham still loved him. For several days that July, factories and shops all across the city were shut down in order to allow people to join in with his 70th birthday celebrations. Thousands of them lined the streets cheering his open motorcar cavalcade as he went on a tour of the city. The following evening, the elder statesman gave a heartfelt speech at Bingley Hall about his commitment to the people of Birmingham, and was

೧೦

then escorted back to his home in Highbury by 5,000 torchbearers. The celebrations ended with a huge fireworks portrait of the city's favourite son being blasted into the night sky.[21]

Two days later, after returning to his London house in Prince's Gate, Kensington, he suffered a stroke.

For the final eight years of his life, he remained an MP and, showing his trademark stamina and determination, continued to issue political advice and directives to his followers. He was, however, consigned to a bath chair, and his health never really recovered. He died on 2 July 1914, and was buried, according to his wishes, at Key Hill Cemetery in Birmingham's Jewellery Quarter.

Ever the maverick, he had spurned a plot at Westminster Abbey.

∽

Ronald Tolkien was a student at Oxford University when Joseph Chamberlain was finally laid to rest among the Victorian obelisks and catacombs of Key Hill.

Growing up in Birmingham after his mother's return to the Midlands, Ronald had proved himself to be a gifted school pupil, ending up at the school for Birmingham's brightest – King Edward's. Having already produced one languages expert and philologist in Frederick William Thomas, the neo-Gothic cloisters of this famous educational institution were about to produce another. Tolkien had considerable linguistic gifts, mastering not only the Latin and Greek languages but also becoming well-versed in the Germanic languages and Anglo-Saxon. Academia aside, he also had a close circle of friends, a group of boys who met together after school in the tea room of Barrow's Stores in Corporation Street. They called themselves the Tea Club and, later on, the Barrovian Society.

On the face of it, then, Ronald was a clever, sociable boy who was destined for academic success. Conversely, though, he was also 'capable of bouts of profound despair',[22] owing to a difficult childhood. Shortly after the death of Arthur Tolkien in South Africa, Mabel and her two sons had settled in a rented cottage in Sarehole, now most definitely a suburb of Birmingham sandwiched between Hall Green and Moseley, but then a rural hamlet. Ronald spent many a happy summer's day there with his brother Hilary, exploring the area that is said to be the inspiration for 'The Shire', the home of the Hobbits in the great fantasy novels he would later write. But the peace of the countryside would not last. Soon the Tolkien family had moved into more cramped surroundings in industrial Birmingham, first in Moseley and King's Heath, then in Edgbaston;

and shortly afterwards tragedy struck again. Mabel, who had long suffered from diabetes, collapsed. On 14 November 1904, she died.

Now orphans, Ronald and his brother were sent to stay first with an aunt in Edgbaston, and then later to a local boarding house run by a Mrs Faulkner.

Yet, even as bereavement and harsh living conditions in dark, squalid Birmingham threatened to overwhelm the young Ronald Tolkien, new horizons opened up for him, mainly due to his academic strengths. In December 1910, he sat for Oxford and passed. In the autumn of 1911, he arrived at Exeter College to study Classics.

He was there for four years, swapping course halfway through to English Language and Literature, and notwithstanding the hostilities that had broken out in Europe in 1914, achieved a first-class degree the following year.

War beckoned, however, and soon Tolkien had enlisted as a second lieutenant in the Lancashire Fusiliers and was heading out to the Western Front. Before he left, he had the foresight to marry his childhood sweetheart, Edith Bratt, who he had first met at Mrs Faulkner's boarding house back in Birmingham. Shortly afterwards he was at the Somme.

One can only imagine the horrors that met him there: the mud, the cacophony of the guns, the suffering of the injured. Luckily – if that ever could be the right word – it was the insanitary conditions that got to the young Oxford graduate before a sniper's bullet. After four months in and out of the trenches, he developed the typhus-like infection known as 'trench fever', and was sent back to Birmingham to spend six weeks in the temporary

The clock face of the 'Old Joe' tower at Birmingham University is said to have provided J.R.R. Tolkien with the inspiration for the eye of Sauron in *The Lord of the Rings*. (Photograph by Tupungato, Shutterstock.com)

military hospital that had been set up at Birmingham University. There, from the hospital ward, he had a view of 'Old Joe', the soaring clock tower that had been erected at the insistence of the university's main fundraiser, Joseph Chamberlain. The tower's brightly illuminated clock face at night is said to have provided Tolkien with the inspiration for the terrifying Eye of Sauron in *The Lord of the Rings*.[23]

With his illness recurring throughout 1917 and 1918, Tolkien never returned to the terrors of France. Old friends from the King Edward's Tea Club were not so lucky. By the time the guns fell silent at the eleventh hour of the eleventh month, all but one of them had been killed in action. For Tolkien, the fellowship of the Tea Club must have died with them.

Things had to move on, however, and after the war, the old Edwardian began to build up the academic career for which, given his intense interest in philology, the science of words, he seemed destined. In 1920 he took up the post of Reader in English Language at the University of Leeds. In 1925 he returned to Oxford as Professor of Anglo-Saxon.

In many ways, his life at Oxford was a typical don's life. Cycling to college meetings, giving lectures in large halls filled with excitable undergraduates, socialising with colleagues in common rooms filled with pipe smoke. Afterwards, returning home through the foggy Oxford streets in the evening to his children and wife Edith tucked up in their quiet house on Northmoor Road in Summertown.

What was untypical about Tolkien was the corpus of writing that he was beginning to put together around a whole mythology he was creating. Inspired by Norse legends and old Anglo-Saxon lore and language, this was Middle Earth, a time when elves and dwarves and malevolent orcs had walked the planet. It was a fantasy that would make its way into his first published novel, *The Hobbit*.

This great children's classic was published in 1937, introducing to the world Bilbo Baggins, Gandalf and Gollum. There was also Smaug the dragon slumbering in his mountain chamber of jewels and gems, and the great spider that tried to tie Bilbo up in a sticky web of silken thread.

Whatever the demons that inspired the spider scene – the deaths of his parents when he was a child, the trenches of the Somme, or the spider that bit him in the garden all those years before in South Africa – the spider in the sequel to *The Hobbit* was even more frightening.

It took him more than sixteen years of pipe-smoking and beer-drinking at the Eagle & Child pub with fellow Inklings – a literary club he formed with the likes of *Narnia* creator C.S. Lewis – to produce his masterpiece *The Lord of the Rings*, but when the Fellowship of the Ring, the Black Riders and Sauron were finally unleashed they took the reading public by storm.

One of the standout scenes in the book was the hobbit Frodo's encounter with the monstrous spider called Shelob. This hideous beast with her huge swollen belly, great horns and deadly venom traps Frodo in her cliff-side lair. It takes all the courage of his faithful sidekick Sam, armed with a sword and the Phial of Galadriel, to defeat the monster and save him.

⁖

By the time *The Lord of the Rings* was published in the mid-1950s, South Africa – the country of Tolkien's birth – had created a monster of its own: a political system called apartheid.

Although voting rights in Britain's original Cape Colony with its distinctive 'Cape Coloured community'[24] had been based on property ownership rather than skin colour, when the four provinces of the region came together in the Union of South Africa in 1910, an exclusively white parliament was announced.

This was very much to do with a 'cosying up' between Great Britain and the Afrikaner leaders of the Orange Free State and the Transvaal. Despite winning the war, Britain realised that there had to be some accommodation of the Boers, while on their side the new Afrikaner leaders were willing to be subsumed under the British Empire's sphere of influence so long as they called the shots on their own turf. This spelt trouble for the native Black Africans and Asian immigrants of the region. Tough and self-reliant, the Boer farmers were strict Christians who, generally speaking, saw themselves as a 'chosen people', racially superior to Black South Africans.

This sense of exceptionalism was only boosted as South Africa experienced in the ensuing years the same sort of spectacular economic growth as enjoyed by the other white settler colonies of Canada, New Zealand and Australia, which, like South Africa, all had dominion status within the British Empire. As economic fortunes soared and with them a growing sense of arrogance, Black people's rights to hold land and to exercise their vote were steadily eroded.

Worse was to come. Much worse. In 1948, the National Party came to power in South Africa on a platform of apartheid, enshrining racial segregation firmly into law. The Population Act of 1950 classified all South Africans as either Bantu (all Black Africans), Coloured (those of mixed race) or White. A fourth category of Asian was added later. Then a series of 'group areas' and 'land' acts cordoned off specific residential and business districts for each race and established 'Black homelands', while the existing 'pass laws' were extended to make sure that people of colour could not enter white areas unless they were carrying the right documents. Yet more laws separated public and education amenities and forbade most social contact between the races.

The scene was set for confrontation. In 1960, a demonstration against apartheid gathered in the Black township of Sharpeville. The police fired into the crowd, killing sixty-nine and wounding many more.

In response to the Sharpeville massacre, the African National Congress (ANC), which had been set up as early as 1912 to fight for Black constitutional rights, abandoned its long-standing commitment to non-violent protest and adopted a policy of armed struggle. In 1963, Nelson Mandela, Walter Sisulu and other ANC leaders were sentenced to life imprisonment on charges of treason, sabotage and violent conspiracy after an arms cache had been discovered in Rivonia, a fashionable suburb of Johannesburg.

A decade or so later, a group of Black schoolchildren on the other, significantly poorer, side of town, in Soweto, were shot by police for protesting against classes in the Afrikaans language – an incident that sparked a violent uprising in which some 600 people, mainly young, were killed.

༄

Perhaps, though, there is no reach of the world so dark that it cannot be illuminated by light. The British Anti-Apartheid Movement originated in 1959 as a small group of South African exiles and other African students living in London who got together to promote a boycott of South African goods. After the Sharpeville massacre of 1960, its ranks were swelled by British people horrified by the actions of the Pretoria regime, while support came in from politicians including Labour MP Barbara Castle, who organised a vigil outside London's Lancaster House during the Commonwealth prime ministers' meeting in 1961, calling for South Africa's expulsion from the organisation. With newly independent African states joining in the outcry, South Africa was forced to withdraw its membership of the organisation.

Meanwhile, beyond the bubble of London politics, the Anti-Apartheid Movement begin to build a network of groups and alliances around the country, and it was not long before Birmingham entered the fray. Boxes and boxes of archive material belonging to the Anti-Apartheid Movement now sit at the Wolfson Centre for Archival Research at Birmingham Library,[25] bearing witness to the efforts of Midlanders over a period of three decades to bring down the brutal system of apartheid. One of the most significant moments was the 'Stop the Seventy Tour' when thousands of agitators marched from the Council House in Birmingham to Edgbaston Cricket Ground to protest against the South Africa cricket team's summer tour of England. In unison with other demonstrations around the country, the action had the desired effect, and the visit was cancelled by Harold Wilson's Labour government.

That was 1970, and as the decade progressed the Anti-Apartheid Movement increasingly turned its attention to a disinvestment campaign, showing how British firms had profited from the apartheid regime. For their part, Anti-Apartheid campaigners in Birmingham pointed to Midlands firms with interests in South Africa. These included such industrial giants as ICI, GKN, British Leyland and Metal Box. Given the extent of British interests in South Africa, though, it was always an uphill struggle. The campaign to encourage the UK to pull its investments out of the country was also not helped by the arrival at Downing Street in 1979 of Prime Minister Margaret Thatcher, who blew distinctly cold over doing anything concrete about apartheid.

Despite her recalcitrance, though, by the mid-1980s the tide had begun to turn on apartheid. In Birmingham and elsewhere in Britain people continued to march and petition, while on the international stage, Commonwealth leaders in 1986 agreed a programme of economic sanctions against the Pretoria regime. In their communiqué from a mini-summit in London, the Commonwealth Heads of Government called for the 'dismantling of apartheid and the establishment of a non-racial and representative government in South Africa as a matter of compelling urgency'.[26]

Bowing to increasing pressure, meanwhile, Barclays Bank pulled out of the country in 1986, with more than fifty British companies following suit. Still more reduced their investments.

Even more perplexing for the government in Pretoria was now the beat of another drum, isolated and muffled at first, but each year getting louder: the call to release Nelson Mandela. Incomprehensible as it may seem now, Mandela's name did not carry much meaning outside South Africa at the beginning of the 1980s. The freedom fighter's name was also unknown to Coventry musician Jerry Dammers, who heard it for the first time at a concert at Alexandra Palace in London in 1983 that had been convened to celebrate the imprisoned activist's 65th birthday.

Returning home, the founder of the group The Specials, which had split up messily a couple of years before, realised he had a new song on his hands, a song for his new band, the Special AKA. What resulted was an irresistibly catchy tune that became the unofficial anthem of the international anti-apartheid movement. Called simply 'Free Nelson Mandela', the final song on the Special AKA's debut album caught everyone's imagination; and soon, from the young audience at a 70th birthday concert in honour of Mandela at Wembley Arena in 1988 to Black people in the townships of South Africa, everyone was singing and dancing along to it.

Another concert was held at Wembley two years later. After artists such as Jerry Dammers, Simple Minds and Tracy Chapman had left the stage and

as darkness fell, a figure of a man appeared on stage. After years of incarceration with often only the complete works of a Midlands-born playwright called William Shakespeare to keep him company, he had been released from prison. It was Nelson Mandela.

The great man was to pay visits to the UK on a number of occasions afterwards, at one point visiting Birmingham just months before he became president of a multi-racial and democratic South Africa in 1994, a country that would now re-join the Commonwealth after years in the wilderness.

He was welcomed by crowds at Handsworth Leisure Centre, and greeted in nine languages

Nelson Mandela visited Birmingham just months before he became president of South Africa, and was greeted by children at the Nelson Mandela School in Sparkbrook. (Commonwealth Secretariat photo by Tony Edenden/Sportsphoto)

by children at the Nelson Mandela School in Sparkbrook, named a few years before in his honour.[27]

⟨⟩

If Coventry, preparing to host three sports at the 2022 Commonwealth Games, played a walk-on, but not insignificant, role through Jerry Dammers in the final dismantling of apartheid, Birmingham itself was ready to do its bit for a post-apartheid South Africa.

Birmingham has a long tradition of twinning with cities around the world. Lyon in France, Chicago in the US and Guangzhou in China, to name a few, all have close links with the Midlands conurbation. In 1997, another was added to the list when the City Council signed a 'sister city agreement' with Johannesburg.

First and foremost, the agreement has seen the two cities exchanging expertise over the past twenty-five years on a series of local government issues. This started with talking about mutual youth work strategies in the wake of not only the apartheid years in South Africa but also the race riots in Handsworth in the 1980s and '90s. Later on, this widened out into joint school improvement programmes. One of these was a project that involved Birmingham teachers providing IT training to teachers in Soweto.

Johannesburg and Birmingham are also both members of the Commonwealth Inclusive Cities Network (ICN). Co-ordinated by Birmingham City Council, the ICN brings together sixteen Commonwealth cities from Vancouver to Brisbane to share ideas on how to deliver services to their most disadvantaged citizens.[28]

⟨⟩

This sort of collaboration between equals – between different parts of the Commonwealth, and between Birmingham and Johannesburg – seems a far cry from the warmongering in South Africa of city father Joseph Chamberlain, the focus of most of this chapter.

It is probably true to say that the British Empire does not have a good look these days, and when people in the twentieth-first century look on 'Old Joe', as J.R.R. Tolkien once did when he spotted the soaring clock tower from his hospital bed at Birmingham University, they too might see the terrifying Eye of

⟨⟩

Sauron. As Lord Sauron wielded power over the hellish landscape of Mordor, a place of mines, forges and foundries filling the night sky with fire, so too did Chamberlain preside over a devastating war. After all, he did hail from a city of pits, ironworks and blast furnaces himself.

Yet it might be argued that there was something of 'the Shire' in the Liberal politician too. Whatever the twists and turns of his distinctly topsy-turvy career, his political language always remained peppered with Liberal ideals. Even if we might doubt his sincerity, he did often speak about a liberal sort of empire bringing 'freedom and justice' to all its different peoples.

And while we can deplore his callous imperialism, it might be debated that in the Commonwealth collaborations Birmingham now seeks there is the hidden hand of the maverick MP. His central message was always one of building international ties rather than falling back into a 'petty parochialism'. It was in this spirit that the people of Birmingham marched on Edgbaston cricket ground in 1970, that their city twinned with Johannesburg and their council now works with other Commonwealth cities to tackle urban depravation.

Chamberlain may well have approved. His commitment to improving people's lives and well-being was evident from his tenure as mayor of Birmingham. However, when historians are asked to look back at his subsequent political career, they often only see failure. He played a large part in splitting two governments, oversaw a controversial war, and went down to political defeat in 1906 over his great cause celebre – tariff reform.

But, as we shall see later in this book, his ideas around preferential tariffs on the global stage would never quite drop out of the British political psyche.

Nor did the orchid grower's ideas about overseas investment.

Tropical territories were poor, in his view, because they lacked investment. They could not attract investment because they were not seen as commercially viable. If only he could open up the funding sluice gates as he had done in the rejuvenation of Birmingham in the 1870s, then the situation could be remedied.[29]

It was a principle of investment in underdeveloped and developing economies that would later be taken up by the Colonial Development Act of 1929, and then, in the founding of the Commonwealth Development Corporation after the Second World War.

But Chamberlain would get there first, as we shall see as we turn to the next chapter.

NOTES

1   Travis L. Crosby, *Joseph Chamberlain: A Most Radical Imperialist* (London, New York: I.B. Taurus & Co., 2018), p.1.

2   *Sketch of the Public Career of the Hon. Joseph Chamberlain MP* (1887), pp.2–3, in the Chamberlain Collection at the Cadbury Research Library, University of Birmingham.

3   Roger Ward, *The Chamberlains: Joseph, Austen and Neville 1836–1940* (Stroud: Fonthill Media, 2015), p.13.

4   Andrew Reekes, *Two Titans, One City: Joseph Chamberlain and George Cadbury* (Alcester, Warwickshire: West Midlands History Ltd, 2017), p.37.

5   The line of continuity between Joseph Chamberlain's reforms and the innovations of modern Birmingham administrations is drawn in the preamble to this book, pp.6–11.

6   Crosby, p.43.

7   Reekes, p.112.

8   Crosby, p.114.

9   Roger Ward, p.47.

10 Crosby, p.115.

11 Humphrey Carpenter, *J.R.R. Tolkien: A Biography* (London: HarperCollins, 2016), p.21.

12 Ibid., p.22.

13 Ibid., p.22.

14 *The Times*, 25 October 1900. Cited in Crosby, p.151, and Reekes, p.77.

15 Crosby, p.153.

16 Her letters home from the Chake-Chake mission station on Pemba Island can be found in the Wolfson Centre for Archival Research, Library of Birmingham [MS1509/4/65 & 66]

17 *The Times*, 16 May 1903. Cited in Crosby, p.162.

18 Ibid.

19 'Trade and the Empire: Preference, the true Imperial policy' (A speech made by Joseph Chamberlain MP in Gainsborough, 1 February 1905), p.20, in the Chamberlain Collection at the Cadbury Research Library, University of Birmingham.

20 *The Times*, 7 October 1903, cited in Crosby, p.171.

21 Crosby, p.182.

22 Carpenter, p.41.

23 See the Birmingham Tolkien Trail at www.birminghammuseums.org.uk.

24 See P.J. Marshall (ed.), *The Cambridge Illustrated History of the British Empire* (Cambridge: Cambridge University Press, 1996), p.228, and www.britannica.com/place/Cape-Province .

25 Records of the Birmingham Anti-Apartheid Organisation [MS2209] at the Wolfson Centre for Archival Research, Library of Birmingham.

26 From the Commonwealth archives: thecommonwealth.org/media/news/archive-sanctions-agreed-against-apartheid-era-south-africa.

27 Birmingham remembered him twenty years on www.birminghammail.co.uk/news/local-news/birmingham-remembers-nelson-mandelas-visit-6381061.

28 More information can be found here: distinctlybirmingham.com.

29 More information on Chamberlain's colonial economic programme can be found in Chapter 10 of Crosby, *Joseph Chamberlain*.

CHAPTER SIX

WEST AFRICA

Imagine a train rattling and rolling through the African bush. High-pitched, mournful whistles blow out from the steam locomotive at the front of a string of dilapidated carriages as they weave their way through a dusty landscape of scorched grassland and ramshackle villages. A man is sitting with a female companion in an airless compartment in one of the carriages, his hands drenched in sweat due to the muggy equatorial heat seeping in through the open window. His face is soaked in shadow.

This is a scene from one of Graham Greene's many melancholic works set in the tropics, *Journey Without Maps*. In 1935, the celebrated English writer set out to explore the remote African republic of Liberia, and in order to do so he had to travel through the British colony of Sierra Leone, disembarking his ship at the capital Freetown – a typical English town in the tropics, full of smart bungalows, tin roofs and little churches – and then catching the train to the Liberian border from a railway terminus called Water Street Station. In the resulting travelogue, the author compared the countryside of Sierra Leone to 'a piece of drab cloth along a draper's counter, grey and dull green and burnt up by the dry season …'[1]

It is a characteristically downbeat picture, one might argue, written by a master of words writing during a time when the British Empire was on the decline amid the 1930s Depression.

But it is a picture that bears little resemblance to the upbeat imperial pomp and circumstance with which the railway was created, or to the effervescent self-confidence of the man who fashioned it.

Rarely prone to doubt, it seems, Joseph Chamberlain set in motion his grand plan of colonial economic development within months of taking up office as Colonial Secretary in 1895, with West Africa lying at the very heart of it.

From being the worst perpetrator of the horrific slave trade between the western coast of Africa and the Americas in the eighteenth century, Britain had now for nearly a century acted as the world's policeman in trying to block it, making Freetown in Sierra Leone the naval base for its anti-slave-trade squadron, and as a result substantially growing its influence in the region. Where the military went, commerce and religion had followed; and very soon the Boulton & Watt forges in Birmingham were supplying coinage for the new crown colony of Sierra Leone, British merchants in general were trading in West African palm oil and timber, and Birmingham Female Society member Hannah Kilham was sailing for Sierra Leone and the Gambia to set up schools for children rescued from slave ships. Freetown, in particular, became a boomtown where liberated Black Africans (Sierra Leone had been set up by freed slaves arriving from England, Jamaica and elsewhere) became merchants and businessmen alongside drifters and chancers from Europe arriving in port in pursuit of a quick buck.

In the late nineteenth century, however, things had slowed down as European firms began to encounter difficulties opening up the African hinterland to their commercial ambitions, and industrial pressure groups across the UK, including the Birmingham Chamber of Commerce, had started lobbying government to help further their interests. This is where the imperially minded Chamberlain was only too happy to step in.[2]

He had just the answer for the three colonies of British West Africa: railways. By bringing in the railroad, he argued, heavy crushing machinery could be taken to the gold mines of the Gold Coast (now Ghana). Likewise, the bulk commodities of Lagos and Sierra Leone – rubber, timber and palm oil – could be transported from plantation to coast quickly and efficiently. Such improvements in distribution would also spur the production of other plantation crops such as tobacco, cotton and groundnuts.

As with all of Chamberlain's schemes, the proposal is likely to have been put forward in the most grandiose terms, so much so that it received a distinctly lukewarm response from the Treasury, which did not share the Colonial Secretary's enthusiasm for splashing cash on risky capital ventures in Africa. Nor did the rest of the Cabinet like Chamberlain's counter-proposal to launch a colonial development fund based upon the British government's revenues from the Suez Canal.

Faced with this intransigence, Birmingham's maverick MP did what we would half expect him to do, and carried on regardless. Casting aside the immediate need for Treasury backing or parliamentary scrutiny, he gave the go-ahead under his own authority as Colonial Secretary for railway construction to begin in Lagos and Sierra Leone, while route surveys would start in the Gold

Coast. Empowering the relevant colonial governors to start construction and to issue colonial stock for railway loans on the London market, he also let the crown agents under his employ off their leash, allowing this group of colonial administrators to negotiate engineering contracts and raise additional finance.

Stumbling behind, as seems so often the case, in a trail that Chamberlain had blazed, the British government now took his colonial investment principle on board and passed a Colonial Loans Act in 1899 that authorised payments to thirteen different colonies, including infrastructure projects under way. Under this new initiative, it is true to say that the West African lines carried less shine for investors than projects such as the Canadian railroad. Nevertheless, by the time Chamberlain left office as Colonial Secretary in 1903, a line had been built inland from Sekondi on the Gold Coast, another had been built from Lagos up-country into the lands of the Yoruba people, and the Sierra Leone railway had chugged into Bo, a town about 100 miles away from the capital city of Freetown.

Some three decades later, Graham Greene, in his 'tiny, lamp-lit train',[3] would have passed through Bo, the second largest city in Sierra Leone, on his way to the Liberian border.

Much later still, in 1981 to be exact, Bo formed a friendship with the district of Warwick in the Midlands, which includes within its borders Leamington Spa where the bowling tournaments of the 2022 Commonwealth Games will be held. The One World Link (OWL), as the initiative is called, has seen connections being forged between hospitals and schools in both communities, and is still going strong. In its 2019 Awards, OWL was 'highly commended' by the Commonwealth Association of Planners[4] for the training and support it had offered Sierra Leonean colleagues in the field of urban planning.[5]

৩৬

While One World Link, in the parlance of our twenty-first century, talks of equal 'partnerships' between the people of the UK and the people of West Africa, it is safe to assume that Joseph Chamberlain did not quite see it that way. The past, after all, is a 'foreign country'. They do things differently there.[6]

So, just to prove his point to the twenty-first-century historian, the Colonial Secretary was soon forming a battalion to deter French military advances in the region. Formed in 1897, the West Africa Frontier Force was made up of troops from the local Hausa and Yoruba ethnic groups, and was commanded by a British military man with a wealth of experience in Africa: Frederick Lugard.

The French were suitably deterred, and stood aside as Lugard and his army mopped up in the Niger Valley. The British were now not only overlords of the settlement of Lagos, but also of its hinterland, which soon became the British protectorate of Nigeria with Lugard himself as its first governor-general.

By now, the era of Chamberlain was well and truly over; so it was what Lugard did next that now set the tone for British rule in West Africa. Building on the time-honoured tradition of British governance, Lugard established a central government comprising an appointed governor, an executive and a legislative council. But in a crucial departure from tradition, he left local governance to traditional rulers and institutions. This put a well-established class of Western-educated Africans, educated in institutions such as the Fourah Bay College in Freetown – founded in 1827 by the Church Missionary Society – out in the cold. Against the grain, indirect rule became the rule of thumb for all of British West Africa.[7]

It was a balancing act that the British Empire managed to perform for a while until the forces of modernity finally overwhelmed it. The main reason for this was perhaps the relative success of its four fiefdoms in the region.

Easily the most buoyant was the Gold Coast. The railway built inland from Sekondi had been designed to support the gold mining industry inland, to which from 1919 onwards was added another valuable commodity – diamonds. However, the real mainstay of the economy was something that did not glitter at all, but instead just hung around on trees. In the last few decades of the nineteenth century, local farmers working in forest plots had started to harvest the cocoa bean; and by 1913 cocoa was outranking gold as an export, soon constituting somewhere between a third and a half of the world's supply.

The revenues generated by this staple crop allowed the colony's governor in the 1920s, Sir Frederick Gordon Guggisberg, to finance a programme of social and economic development, and before long the cocoa-producing forest lands boasted an extensive road and rail network, new schools and hospitals were opening their doors, and Sekondi's twin city Takoradi saw the country's first deep-water seaport.

Nigeria, meanwhile, saw an explosion of its railway network, and by the 1930s it had 1,900 miles of track, boosting the production and distribution of its staple commodities – palm oil, cocoa and peanuts. The narrow strip of land in a river valley that constituted The Gambia, and Sierra Leone, had a harder time of it; but even they did moderately well. The Gambia generated good revenues from peanut production, and fortunes took a favourable turn for Sierra Leone with the discovery of diamonds in the 1930s.

Yet, indirect rule remained the elephant in the room. The Western-oriented Africans of the coastal cities such as Freetown and Lagos grew increasingly frustrated by their lack of involvement in the political system. The traders, professionals and officials sitting on the original legislative councils of these cities in the nineteenth century had been almost as likely to be black as white, and therefore had been a vehicle, however constrained, for the expression of African interests and feelings about British policy. While the British cultivation of traditional African rulers might have gone down well in the interior, such as with the Ashanti farming communities, it was not proving to be a hit with the urban elites.

A couple of generations of these city types had also been sending their children to British universities. A hundred or so in the 1920s grew to more than a thousand after the Second World War. These were clever young people who did not appreciate the discrimination they often faced as Black people in the mother country, and as a result began to form organisations agitating not only for their student rights, but for reform in their homelands. At first, this reform was the limited hope for more representation in legislative councils, but gradually the call grew for independence.

It was not as if West Africans had not done their bit for the Empire. During the Great War, the Gold Coast Regiment had been sent to fight the Germans in East Africa, alongside regiments from the West Africa Frontier Force and soldiers from Nigeria. West Africans had also been deployed in various conflict zones in the Second World War, including the Far East.

Reform did arrive; but too little, too late. After the Allied victory in 1945, legislative councils were reconfigured so that African representatives outnumbered European officials, but all too often these were nominees of the traditional order.

Particularly on the Gold Coast, tensions rose. In 1948, European trading houses were boycotted and some rioting broke out in the larger towns.

The following year, a young British academic arrived at the University College of the Gold Coast. His name was John Donnelly Fage, and he would later play an important role not only in West Africa, but also in the Birmingham story.

☙❧

Although it wasn't on the Gold Coast itself, Fage had spent a bit of time in Africa during the war, flying seaplanes for the RAF. Flying Tiger Moth biplanes in Southern Rhodesia (now Zimbabwe) before graduating to the Catalina flying boats in East Africa and the Indian Ocean, some of the missions he was involved in were quite obviously filled with danger. If it was not flying anti-submarine sorties, it was battling with capricious weather. One December day, he was part of a Catalina crew caught in a tropical front over the Mozambique Channel. Unable to climb high enough to pass over the line of turbulent black cloud, there was no alternative but to fly under it, through the narrow gap between the cloud and a stormy spume-streaked sea. Pulled in all directions by violent gusts of wind, the plane managed to get through, but as Fage remembered later, it was the most frightening experience of his flying career.[8]

The experience, however, did nothing to dent a new-found interest in Africa, and when the young RAF man returned home to his former life as a History student at Magdalene College, Cambridge, he looked outside the traditional academic emphasis on European history at the time for an African subject for his doctorate. The result was a thesis tackling the question of why, a couple of decades before, Britain had granted self-government to its colony of Southern Rhodesia.

It was not immediately apparent that this would lead to a first university appointment in the British Gold Coast, but this is where Fage, now armed with his PhD, ended up. Casting around UK universities for his first posting in 1949, the young academic found a handful that had an interest in extra-European history, namely Glasgow, Birmingham and the School of Oriental and African Studies in London, but by now he had more or less decided. If he were to specialise in the history of Africa, it would be better if he actually lived there. A lectureship in history came up at the University College of the Gold Coast, which had been established just the year before. He applied.

And so it was that John Fage and his wife Jean arrived at Accra airport shortly after midnight on 5 October the same year. The expression of discontent in the colony was still in full swing, with a committee on constitutional reform that very month proposing wider African involvement on the Executive Council, and a new Legislative Assembly, to try to accommodate the rising aspirations of the colony's Black citizens. For a group of young, radical politicians led by activist Kwame Nkrumah this was still not good enough, and a campaign of protests and strikes calling for 'self-government now' quickly followed. It was an exciting time to be in the Gold Coast as the country embarked on its journey towards independence, as Ghana, in 1957.

⁊⁌

But John Fage's main concern would have been his new job at the university. In this respect, he was soon heavily involved in trying to move the fledgling History Department's Euro-centric syllabus towards something that could be considered to be 'a mature and balanced Honours Degree syllabus for an African university institution'.[9] This meant the introduction of at least two courses in African history, and the education of a generation of

The General Post Office in Accra was built during the height of British power on the Gold Coast, but by the time John Fage arrived to take up his university post in 1949, the colony was calling for independence. (Photo by R.W. Wilcox)

African graduates who would take over the teaching of African history from him. Throughout the decade Fage was at the University College of the Gold Coast, he was the only member of a History department mainly comprising European, American and Australian academics who was teaching African studies. After his departure in 1959, the university was able to recruit from its own graduates. When two of his students in particular, Adu Boohen and Isaac Tufuoh, who had moved on to postgraduate work in the UK, took over the mantle of African studies from him, Fage felt he had 'really achieved' what he had 'left Britain to do'.[10]

Besides teaching, Fage also needed to look to his own academic research. Here, again, he charted a new course. If his PhD thesis had been about British colonial administration in Africa, this was not the route he was going to follow now. Living in West Africa was making him increasingly 'inquisitive about the nature and development of its society before it had come to be influenced and ultimately dominated by Europeans'.[11] So, now he turned to accounts of Arab and European travellers to the region from the fifteenth century onwards in order to gain new insights into West African society and history at the time. By the same token, he began to study the oral traditions of pre-literate Gold Coast societies. This was no mean feat because there were about seventy separate ethnic groups in the country, each with its own distinct social-political structure and language. As a result, Fage took a broad brush approach, building up a picture of the interrelationships between various historical traditions, rather than delving into a particular polity in depth. With the help of an anthropologist called David Tait, this led him to the official traditions of the old royal courts of the region to see how they intertwined with those of subordinate chieftaincies.

In 1953, he and Tait travelled around the upper reaches of the Volta River to investigate the Mole-Dagbane family of kingdoms. How they did this was in typical anthropological fashion: using local trusted informants to 'translate' drum recitals often performed at royal occasions – 'drum histories' as they were called – so that the two academics could examine and interpret the 'history' being communicated.

A picture of a broader sweep of West African history was now emerging for John Fage, and this no doubt found its way into his first book, *An Introduction to the History of West Africa*, which was published in 1955.

Save for his explorations in the northern territories of Ghana with Tait, who died tragically in a motor accident in 1956, Fage did not travel widely in Africa during his time at the university college near Accra. Busy with departmental work or his writing, except for getting away to the nearby beach at the weekend or the town of Takoradi down the coast, where he and his family would some-times stay for a short break, the lecturer who would later set up the Centre for West African Studies at Birmingham University rarely left his campus-based academic life.

However, there was one major exception when he joined other historians at a major academic conference at Bukavu, sitting on the shores of Lake Kivu in the Belgian Congo. He used it as a bit of an opportunity to see more of Africa, travelling westwards to the sprawling city of Leopoldville, now Kinshasa; north-wards to Goma at the northern tip of the lake; and then onwards to Uganda.

But perhaps the land that struck him most was the territory of Rwanda sitting just on the opposite shore of Lake Kivu. He was taken on a trip to see the 'rural tranquility' of this land 'in which the masses of Hutu cultivators lived alongside the tall and willowy cattle-owning aristocracy of the Tutsi'. As Fage recalled in *To Africa and Back*, 'it was impossible to think that less than forty years later Rwanda would have all but destroyed itself in Hutu-Tutsi strife and that the lovely rural and urban countryside from Goma to Bukavu would have been devastated by the influx of refugees from Rwanda'.[12]

The historian is not alive to see it, but fast-forward a few decades on from the Rwanda genocide of 1994, and, generally speaking, Rwanda is now hailed as a success story, both of national reconciliation between ethnic peoples once in conflict with each other, and of economic transformation. As part of Rwanda's economic rebuilding, the country joined the largely English-speaking East

African Community in 2007, and the following year changed its medium of education from French, the language of its former colonisers, to English, in order to become more competitive in the global marketplace.

The tilt towards the English-speaking tendencies of its neighbours in the African Great Lakes region saw its apotheosis in Rwanda's admittance into the Commonwealth in 2009, despite having no links with the former British Empire.

From the Great Lakes region of Africa to the Great Lakes of North America. A few years after his trip to Bukavu and its surroundings, John Fage spent a semester as a visiting Professor of History at the University of Wisconsin not far from Lake Michigan. There, he gave a series of lectures on how a colonial polity in Ghana had emerged from 'the interaction between African traditions of commerce and statehood and European and increasingly British expansion, and then how and why this polity had become an independent state'.[13]

∽

While Fage had been away in North America, the colonial polity he had talked about in his lectures at Wisconsin had finally secured its independence as Ghana, and joined the worldwide community of nations as a member of the British Commonwealth and the United Nations. When Fage returned to his lectureship up on the hill above Accra in September 1957, it was now at the University College of Ghana, not the Gold Coast. Meanwhile, down in the town below, Kwame Nkrumah was Ghana's first Prime Minister.

A wind of change had swept through the place that had been home for the Fage family for almost a decade, and before too long change was in the air for the Fages too. In January 1959, John accepted the offer of a lectureship back in London at the School of Oriental and African Studies where, reunited with fellow African specialist Roland Oliver, a collaboration began that would transform the study of African history. In 1960 the two academics became the founding editors of the *Journal of African History*, and in 1962 their writing partnership produced the *Penguin Short History of Africa*. This was just the beginning of a long-standing partnership that culminated in the joint editor-ship of the eight-volume *Cambridge History of Africa* between 1975 and 1986, which sought to establish Africa's past as an integrated whole rather than as a series of colonial incursions from outside.

In the meantime, Fage had moved to the University of Birmingham. Driven by a desire to offer its students at least a sampling of society and

∽

culture outside the usual Judaeo–Graeco–Roman tradition, and aware of the fact that Birmingham itself had significant commercial connections with West Africa, most notably in cocoa production that supplied the chocolate manufacture of Cadbury Bros, the university was keen in the early 1960s to set up a West Africa centre, and they had a particular person in mind to head it up.

Attracted to the idea of finally running his own show, Fage took up the posts of Director of the Centre for West African Studies (CWAS) and Professor of African History at Birmingham University in April 1963. Although he was very much a southerner, having being brought up in London before going up to Cambridge, one gets a sense from his autobiography that he was very happy to be teaching at an institution built to 'the red-brick Byzantine plans'[14] of architect Aston Webb (who also built the main building of the Victoria & Albert Museum in London), and also just a stone's throw from the Edgbaston Cricket Ground – cricket being a lifelong interest!

The same could not quite be said for his wife Jean, who was 'never wholly at home with the strange flat tones which issued from Brummie mouths'![15] Nevertheless, the couple found a pleasant home in Harborne, the neighbourhood next door to Edgbaston, and settled down to two decades in the city.

This was of enormous benefit to the African expertise that Fage was establishing at the city's university. As well as courses for undergraduates, the professor described in a *Guardian* obituary in 2002 as 'classically English, tall, rangy, preposterously boyish well into middle age'[16] established postgraduate Degrees at the CWAS, and by the mid-1970s was welcoming a good number of PhD and Masters students not only from the UK, but also from Africa and the rest of the world.

It was in this 1970s heyday that the CWAS received two significant donations that continue to benefit Birmingham University today. In 1970 John Cadbury, the grandson of Cadbury founding father Richard Cadbury, paid John Fage a visit. The result was the establishment of the Cadbury Fellowship Scheme, which funds a short tenure of a visiting scholar from an African institution at the university each year.

Cadbury money also helped to secure the Danford Collection of African Arts and Crafts for the university. Assembled in the 1940s and '50s by John Danford, an artist working for the British Council in Nigeria, the collection features more than a thousand objects, ranging from wooden sculptures and musical instruments to pottery and textiles, and is considered one of the finest of its kind in Europe. It now sits in the Department of African Studies and Anthropology, the successor to John Fage's creation at the CWAS.[17]

This is all part of John Fage's compelling legacy at Birmingham University. Wind back to the 1970s, however, and unfortunately for the university's pioneering Professor of African History, fortunes for British universities were soon to take a turn for the worse. The decade that opened with the leftovers of 1960s optimism would end with Thatcherite cost-cutting that left institutions like his seriously strapped for cash.

By the mid-1970s, though, John Fage was in the middle of a work that would provide the climax to his career – a sweeping overview of the African past from its Neolithic beginnings to the present. *A History of Africa* was published in 1978. Six years later he retired and went with his wife to live in Wales. He could never get Africa quite out of his hair, however, and from a study somewhere in a wet Welsh valley, he returned to some of his original research as a young lecturer in Accra looking at early accounts of West Africa written by European travellers. The result was a comprehensive catalogue of original sources for pre-colonial West Africa.

જી

Whether or not John Fage ever bumped into Ronald William Wilcox, the father of this book's author – either at an official Birmingham function or just in a local pub in Edgbaston – will never be known. But it is likely their paths never crossed, Fage being an academic and my father being a business journalist. I do not recall the name from my childhood, and my father is no longer around to ask. He passed away a long time ago – in the late 1980s.

It is all a bit of a pity because, had they met and got chatting, they would have soon found out they had something in common – the Gold Coast.

Like the West African historian, my father had been enlisted into the RAF in the Second World War, but unlike Fage he was not going to become a flying ace. Instead, he was trained up in the dark arts of Morse code in order to perform a humbler, but by no means a less significant role, as a wireless operator.

This might have been because he had been employed at the age of 15 as an apprentice reporter on a rural newspaper just before war broke out, and knew something about secret codes, having been compelled to learn shorthand as part of his training on the *Banbury Advertiser*, avidly squiggling in his novice notepad as a local lady of the manor told him how pleased she was to be opening the village fete or when a local constable tipped him off about a house fire that appeared to be a little on the suspicious side.

It was this compulsion to record – learned on the coal face of journalism – that my father would take through to his call-up to the war effort. A rather earnest young man, he kept a diary of all the goings-on and his impressions of everything he heard and saw as he was shipped out in July 1943 to serve eighteen months in West Africa.

His adventures could not have started more dramatically. A few days out of Glasgow, his troop ship was bombed by German planes, and he found himself on a rope scrambling down the side of a sinking vessel into a flimsy life raft below. Plucked out of a burning sea by another ship in the convoy a few hours afterwards, he and his fellow raft survivors finally made it to Casablanca a week later.

From Casablanca, a Greek vessel called the *Nea Hellas* took servicemen onwards to Freetown in Sierra Leone, and in the diary notes he typed up many years later my father recalled how from the ship's deck at night he could see the lights on shore – 'a fascinating sight after the blackouts of the past four years'.[18]

The next day, he went ashore in a motor launch with other RAF recruits, gazing at the brick and plaster houses lining Freetown's waterfront looming larger as the gap between boat and quay narrowed. Once they had made landfall, the squadron climbed a hill to the railway station to board the narrow-gauge train service that novelist Graham Greene had boarded nearly a decade before. As they rattled and rolled through the Freetown suburbs, Ronald Wilcox was struck by how the railway 'passed directly through the streets, and there was no fencing or division of any kind'.[19]

'At one point,' he added, 'the railway track crossed a deep gorge, and we were given the feeling of being suspended in space as the train crawled across a suspension bridge.'

By nightfall, they had arrived at Hastings – a camp in the forest with an RAF seaplane base next door. The forest was very dark and it was pouring with rain, the water dripping off the trees, and there was some difficulty in finding anywhere to sleep that night. Finally, however, a hut was found for some valuable rest before lorries arrived early the next morning to ferry the servicemen back to the *Nea Hellas* for the final voyage on to the British Gold Coast. Three days later, on a Sunday evening, my father and his compatriots arrived in the harbour of Takoradi.

It was at an RAF station just up the coast near the capital, Accra, that Ron Wilcox would spend the next eighteen months in a jungle wireless hut, urgently tapping out Morse code messages between the base and military air traffic. There were also dealings with the Takoradi Air Base, which was a key staging post for RAF planes flying reinforcements on to the North Africa campaign.

It was a routine life dominated by shift work, but what always shines through from my father's memoirs is his youthful ambition. Beyond the Morse code operating system that he had to learn, he wanted to learn the local African dialects of Fante and Ga, and he also wanted to have a frank exchange with his African assistants to learn more about their lives. Paradoxically, what he probably learnt but what a British man of his time could not quite acknowledge was that these young Ghanaian men were very well-educated. They had gone to

People on the Gold Coast were involved in raising money to keep Britain's Spitfires flying. Many of these fighter planes were built at Castle Bromwich in Birmingham. (Photo by R.W. Wilcox)

very good local schools such as the Achimota College, they spoke several local languages as well as English, and they were better than my father – initially at least, at twiddling the right knobs on the telephone switchboard to establish the right frequency between West Africa and the 'mother country'.

Still, Ronald Wilcox always worked diligently to keep an enquiring journalistic mind. One day, he was on a local beach when an African man sitting on the sand remarked to him about the weather. The two got talking, and it turned out that the African was a prominent politician locally. His name was Dr Danquah, a barrister and leader of a political movement on the Gold Coast calling for self-government for the country; and although the two men diplomatically avoided talking about politics and the RAF, they did have a wide-ranging conversation about Accra and the Gold Coast, and the local cocoa farms.

Seemingly a trivial digression in my father's memoirs, this chance meeting took on more significance later on, as the author of this book learnt from his father when he was growing up. J.B. Danquah was actually one of the founding fathers of modern, independent Ghana, but when he fell out with its first prime minister, Kwame Nkrumah, over the increasingly dictatorial style of his government, he was imprisoned. Jailed twice for subversion in the early 1960s, he died of a heart attack in prison in 1965.

In my mind's eye, I can still see my father now telling me the story around the dinner table in our house in the Birmingham suburb of Sutton Coldfield in the 1970s. What I also remember vividly are the three albums of photographs he took while on the Gold Coast (which are still in my possession). Whenever he had a day off, 'R' – as many of his fellow servicemen called him, and as many of his newspaper colleagues would do later – would slip off into the local villages or the capital Accra armed with his Kodak Brownie.

The first album of my father's collection – embossed smartly as it is with a little logo featuring an elephant under a palm tree – contains pictures of his RAF friends in baggy service shorts and cigarettes hanging from their mouths, as well as their RAF camp in the bush where 'R' would always take a torch to the washrooms at night in case he met a scorpion or a black mamba. There are also images of buildings in the capital Accra, including the 'Bombay Bazaar' run by Indian and Syrian traders.

The third album captures seven days on leave in the little coastal town of Winnebah. There are pictures of palm trees on beaches, local fishing villages and waves swirling around rocks.

But perhaps it is the second album that is most striking. There appears to be more of an emphasis on local people here: a young tribeswoman paddling her canoe down river, a goat herder, hawkers displaying their wares on an Accra street corner.

But one photograph probably stands out. She is a woman from Accra, likely to be from the Ga tribe, with her three children. Although the picture is in black and white, you can see she is wearing the bright handwoven cloth of her ethnicity, wrapped around her chest and colourfully braided around the waist. There is some light etching on her

A woman from Accra, probably from the Ga tribe, with her family. (Photo by RW Wilcox)

arms, stripes that suggest the cultural expression of a local people, and a beaded necklace that falls below her neck.

She is staring at the camera, fixing its gaze with her powerful eyes.

NOTES

1   Graham Greene, *Journey Without Maps*, first published 1936 (London: Vintage Books, 2006), p.41.

2   Travis L. Crosby, *Joseph Chamberlain: A Most Radical Imperialist* (London, New York: I.B. Taurus & Co., 2018), pp.115–116, and Ian Grosvenor, Rita McLean & Sian Roberts (eds), *Making Connections: Birmingham Black International History* (Birmingham Futures Group, 2002).

3   Graham Greene, *Journey Without Maps*, xxvii. Preface to Second Edition by Greene (London, November 1946).

4   More information about the Commonwealth Association of Planners can be found at www. commonwealth-planners.org.

5   More information about One World Link can be found at oneworldlink.org.uk.

6   'The past is a foreign country; they do things differently there,' is a quote from the novel, *The Go-Between* by L.P. Hartley, first published in 1953.

7   The online Britannica Encyclopaedia gives us a very good account of British rule in western Africa, www.britannica.com/place/western-Africa.

8   J.D. Fage, *To Africa and Back: Memoirs* (Birmingham: Centre for African Studies, University of Birmingham, 2002), p.60.

9   Ibid., p.89.

10 Ibid., p.91.

11 Ibid., p.94.

12 Ibid., pp.101–2.

13 Ibid., p.107.

14 Ibid., p.135.

15 Ibid., p.136.

16 *The Guardian*, Obituary, John Fage, 2002. www.theguardian.com/news/2002/oct/07/guardianobituaries.highereducation.

17 More information can found on the University of Birmingham website, www.birmingham. ac.uk/schools/historycultures/departments/dasa/facilities/index.aspx.

18 R.W. Wilcox, *Diary of Wartime Experiences of Ronald Wilcox: West Africa – 1943/1944* (Unpublished), p.5.

19 Ibid., p.6.

CHAPTER SEVEN

TO AUSTRALIA
AND BACK

As Ronald Wilcox arrived on the Gold Coast, so too did he depart. Such had been the success of the Takoradi air base in combating the German threat in North Africa that by the end of 1944 the whole West Africa operation was being wound down, and one day in December a ship arrived in the harbour to take a consignment of troops home.

Hugging the coast of West Africa just as the *Nea Hellas* had done eighteen months before on the way out, the Dutch boat *The Johan de Witt* was at Freetown in a few days. There it anchored up for forty-eight hours to take on hundreds more soldiers before sailing on to Gibraltar, where my father went ashore and had 'a really nice tea in a modern café'.[1] After Gibraltar, the ship ran into some very stormy seas, but finally, on 28 December, it slipped into the River Clyde. In a matter of two weeks, the heat and humidity of Africa with its verdant forests and khaki brown rivers and tribeswomen with powerful eyes had given way to the cold chill of a Glasgow winter.

Before too long, though, as memories of his African adventure began to fade, the old life as a newspaper reporter sprang back into existence. Still only 21 years old, he had a whole career before him, and soon he had taken up the Bognor Regis beat at the *Portsmouth Evening News*, covering everything from local council elections to the cancellation of a local cricket match because of 'the condition of the wicket'.[2] This was followed by two years on the *Southend Standard* reporting on the colourful life of a seaside town slowly recovering from the war. This life included the court case of an estate agent who was allegedly receiving deposits for houses that were never built, the 14ft python from Singapore that escaped his owner and slid up the Royal Mews, and the hypnotist who turned up at the beachfront Palace Hotel one evening and managed to get Wilcox of the *Standard* to answer to the name of Hollywood film star Alan Ladd.

Then, one day in 1949, Ron Wilcox, obviously none the worse for his evening with the hypnotist, arrived at a grand entranceway on Birmingham's Corporation Street. He had a new job on the *Birmingham Gazette*.

The Midlands was now booming on the back of rising post-war demand for goods of all kinds, and as industrial correspondent it was my father's job to put on his trademark reporter's mackintosh and head out to the factories and the workshops, noting industry and innovation. It was his duty to open his notepad in the managing director's office and get the figures; and then return to the clattering typewriters and cigarette smoke of the newsroom to file his copy.

Five hundred words on the 58,000 job vacancies in the Midlands because of booming export orders, 300 words on the first-ever gas-turbine engine for a merchant ship designed by Midlands engineers, 200 words on the 'secret' location somewhere in a Warwickshire wood where Rover was test driving an experimental turbo jet car – there was no shortage of things to write about in the 'city of a thousand trades'.

And even though the glittering era of Birmingham industry always had its mirror image in the increasing frequency of workers' strikes fuelled by tensions with management, in the 1950s this was still part of the Birmingham success story as workers lobbied for a greater share of the fruits of their labour. Besides, it also provided more copy for a journalist on the up. 'Day shift workers at the Austin motor works, Birmingham, yesterday played cards and cricket and stood talking in groups while nearly 600 cars were lost to the export market,' Ronald Wilcox wrote one day in June 1951,[3] his acerbic words on one particular strike lobbed out of the pages of the *Gazette* like sharp metal objects produced in a Black Country foundry.

Regardless of its worsening industrial relations, the Austin Motor Company, and its chrysalis as the British Motor Corporation after its merger with Morris Motors in 1951, was probably the biggest success story in town, even eclipsing that of the BSA Motorcycle company at Small Heath, which for a while was the largest motorbike producer in the world. Over the course of a decade, my father followed its progress. A new version of the company's classic vehicle, the Austin Seven, would soon be launched, my father announced in December 1950 after having a few words with managing director Leonard Lord on the sidelines of the company's AGM. A new final assembly building would soon be in action at Austin's Longbridge plant in south-west Birmingham, he also learnt, which would no doubt help things along. Not that things were going at all badly. Export sales to the US had more than doubled in the last financial year, had soared by 275 per cent to Canada, and almost doubled just about everywhere else.

The following summer, the *Gazette*'s man was at Longbridge to witness 'the opening of the most modern car assembly plant in the world'.[4] The new factory was bringing something entirely new to British engineering, and was going to be the focal point of the whole works at Longbridge. From now on, all car parts – engines, bodies, axles and suspension units – would travel on 24 miles of chain conveyors to the assembly lines where they would be 'raised on elevators and dropped exactly into place on the chassis'.[5] Moreover, when fully operational the plant would be capable of producing 4,000 cars a week.

There could be no doubting the sheer innovation of this new operation at the time. No less startling though, was that the firm started in 1905 by engineer Herbert Austin when he took over a small, derelict printing works at Longbridge at the foot of the Lickey Hills, was also expanding fast in Australia. It had acquired its first assembly plant in this Commonwealth country in 1948, and by the time the state-of-the-plant assembly line was opening in Birmingham, more than 30,000 cars a year were being churned out for the market Down Under.

The Commonwealth connection was key. When Austin merged with Morris Motors of Oxford to form the British Motor Corporation (BMC), the strategy was to extend its reach across the 'British Commonwealth', and within five years the conglomerate had sales operations in Australia, Canada, South Africa and East Africa. In 1954, BMC sold 42,000 vehicles in Australia, 25,000 in Africa, 27,000 in the Americas and 13,000 in Asia – all together easily eclipsing the 50,000 vehicles sold to Britain's European neighbours.

⌒⌒

That the Commonwealth was the key to the BMC's fortunes was, at first glance, unsurprising, and yet on second glance, a little paradoxical. If the British Empire had been teetering on the brink of collapse on the eve of the Second World War, with colonies in Africa, Asia and the Caribbean seething with unrest against imperial rule, it would be the war itself that delivered the final *coup de grace*. Despite the fact that the empire had managed to head off full-blown revolt in India, had managed to walk back into Malaya as liberators after the ignominious fall of Singapore in 1941, and had been ultimately victorious against Nazi Germany and Japan, the post-war Labour administration led by Clement Atlee saw its mission as one of slowly dismantling it. It had little choice. Britain was virtually bankrupt, its cities were in ruins and the likes of Burma, Ceylon and India were now clamouring for independence. Those three countries achieved it very quickly; others would have to wait a bit longer to gain their freedom as Britain initiated a process of democratisation in her colonies in preparation for self-governance.[6]

In other words, the writing was on the wall for the largest, most populous, most global imperium the world had ever seen.

Yet, at the same time, something was stirring. An idea had been circulating for quite a while – since at least the Imperial Conference of 1926 – that Britain's colonies should in the end all become 'self-governing members of a multi-racial commonwealth'.[7] The white settler dominions of Australia, Canada, New Zealand and South Africa, who all attended the 1926 summit, were already semi-independent of Britain and regarded as members of the 'British Commonwealth of Nations'; but now India, which was also represented in 1926, was also being promised that it could follow suit.

While people in every corner of the empire were fighting for their very survival during the Second World War, the idea was naturally put on hold, but as former colonies began to gain their freedom after the hostilities had ended, the notion was, rather oddly as it may seem, resurrected. The crucial moment arrived when Jawaharlal Nehru, the first prime minister of independent India, came on board. Although Nehru insisted that as an independent and nascent republic, India could not possibly pledge allegiance to a British king or queen as the likes of Australia had done, or be a member of a Commonwealth that had 'British' in the title, he was also a moderniser who was sympathetic to the notion of an international association based on British and western values of democracy, the rule of law and religious toleration.[8]

The die was cast. At a meeting in London in April 1949, Nehru and Atlee, together with political leaders from Australia, New Zealand, South Africa, Pakistan, Ceylon and Canada, declared that they were all 'free and equal members of the Commonwealth of Nations, freely co-operating in the pursuit of peace, liberty and progress'.[9] Other countries and republics were welcome to join; and with this, the 'London Declaration', the modern Commonwealth of Nations was born.

Still, the London Declaration would have been of little significance to places like Birmingham if there had not been another factor: the continuing economic importance of Britain's former empire. Pruning his orchids at

Highbury Hall, Joseph Chamberlain had dreamt of some sort of commercial union between Britain and its colonies, but it was actually his son Neville who implemented it. Faced with the Great Depression and the protectionist policies abroad in the 1930s, the Chancellor of the Exchequer in the new National Government had to think of the financial survival of Britain and its empire. The result was a system of Imperial Preference agreed at the Commonwealth conference in Ottawa in 1932, whereby preferential tariffs were agreed between Britain and the countries in its orbit based on a principle of 'home producers first, Empire producers second, foreign producers last'. The share of British exports going to its colonies and territories duly rose from 44 per cent to 48 per cent, while the Empire's share of imports into the UK grew from 30 to 39 per cent.

It was a system that would survive well into the post-war world despite the general liberalisation of global trade after 1945, the loosening of Commonwealth ties and the increasing importance of European trade to our tiny littoral island that culminated in membership of the European Economic Community (EEC) in the 1970s.

Meanwhile, there might have been something of 'the empire of sentiment'[10] of Joseph Chamberlain's deepest imaginings. On the British side, there was the Empire Marketing Board (EMB) formed in 1926 by Colonial Secretary Leo Amery, which, in a series of poster campaigns, 'Empire Shopping Weeks' and radio talks, sought to encourage Brits to 'buy Empire'. It was a campaign that spawned the hugely influential EMB film unit that created iconic documentaries such as *Song of Ceylon* about tea pickers,[11] and must have played a part in the fact that in the post-war world – before EEC membership changed everything – the British only had eyes for Canada, Australia and New Zealand when it came to buying their wheat, meat and dairy products.

In the other direction, more than 40 per cent of British exports still went to the Commonwealth in the 1950s, with British machines finding their way to every corner of the world.

Some of the main beneficiaries of this phenomenon were Midlands enterprises that went out into the world and came home with a succession of success stories under their belts. This was not only Austin, but also the likes of Norton Motorcycles, the Triumph car firm and many others. In the early 1950s, my father reported on how Gilbert Smith, the 49-year-old managing director of Norton, hoped for a great many orders from India, Malaya, Australia and New Zealand after 'travelling 35,000 miles round the world in nine weeks', and how the Standard-Triumph motor firm of Coventry had an assembly plant in New Zealand churning out hundreds of cars a day.[12]

And throughout the '50s, Birmingham's famous railway carriage maker, Metro Cammell, rattled along nicely on the export tracks that emerged from its Saltley works – twenty railcars for Jamaica, steam railcars for the Nigerian State Railways, and electric trains for Calcutta and Bombay just a few of the contracts it won during the decade. In the Indian trains, the floors and the lower side panels were painted burgundy red 'to conceal stains from betel nut juice'.[13]

Things were rattling along so nicely, in fact, that one day my father and twenty-eight other journalists received an invite in the post to what must be one of the greatest press trips of all time. A four-week, all expenses paid pilgrimage to see the British Motor Corporation's operations in Australia.

☙

In my mind's eye, I can see them now freezing on the tarmac on a cold night at Heathrow on 22 February 1956. Men from the nationals such as Norman Dixon of the *Manchester Guardian* and Harold Nockolds of *The Times*, and men from car magazines including Harold Hastings of *The Motor*.

Then there were the local men: my father's lifelong friend Clem Lewis, who was now industrial correspondent on the *Birmingham Gazette*; Jack Hay of the *Birmingham Post*; and last but not least, my father, who was now industrial and motoring correspondent on the *Birmingham Evening Despatch*. Soon they would all be boarding a Stratocruiser propeller plane belonging to the British Airways Overseas Corporation (BOAC) in order to bump across the Atlantic to a refuelling stop at Gander in Newfoundland in the middle of the night.

From there they would touch on the broad expanses of Canada – across the Gulf of St Lawrence and over Prince Edward Island – and into the airspace of the United States. Perhaps as they did so, my father thought of the article he had written a few years before about a small firm in West Bromwich that had opened a plant in Canada to take advantage of the 'rapidly-increasing demand for its type of goods'[14] over there. The facility just outside Toronto would be used to finish off the making of steel storage products the firm would ship over as partly processed components. How were they doing now, my father might have wondered. Who knows?

Alternatively, he might have just been wondering when, at last, he would be able to get off the plane and stretch his legs. He had already been in the air for about twelve hours by that time. It would be another two hours or so before they would touch down in New York.

They landed in New York in the early hours. Perhaps the press pack had seen the neon lights of the jagged skyline from the plane windows as they circled to land; but there would be no lingering in the city of Frank Sinatra. Four hours later, they were all on a plane again – this time a United Airlines DC-7 – heading for Denver, and then onwards to San Francisco. Thankfully, there was a night's respite here on America's west coast with the weary travellers coached off to the Sheraton Palace Hotel for the night.

They would need a good night's sleep because early the next morning another coach was waiting for them outside the hotel, ready to whisk them back to the airport, and the Antipodean embrace of a Qantas service bound for Sydney. Sydney and the Antipodes were still an awfully long way away, however. It was another nine hours to Honolulu alone, and another seven hours to an airstrip perched on a narrow atoll in the middle of the Pacific Ocean. Whether or not Ron Wilcox, likely to have been half-asleep, noticed the familiar red livery of a post office stationed amid the scattered palms fringing the atoll's lagoon in the early hours of the morning, I will never know now, but this was Kanton Island, then part of the British Gilbert Islands, but now part of Kiribati.

The British press trip had now crossed the international date line, halfway round the world, but it was still another twelve hours across the wide blue expanses of the Pacific Ocean until their Lockheed Super Constellation finally touched down in Sydney. There is a photograph in an album that my father

Happy to be on the ground again, UK journalists on arrival at Sydney Airport. (Pictorial Record of the British Press Visit to Australia, February–March 1956. The British Motor Corporation (Australia) Pty Ltd)

kept of his Australia trip of journalists, looking a bit bleary eyed and dazed, tumbling out of the plane and onto what must have been the welcome tarmac of an Australian summer's day. They had been travelling for more than four days, of which fifty-three hours had been spent in the air.

∾

Gruelling as this journey must have been, their trip only started in earnest at this point.

Well, perhaps 'in earnest' is overstating it. By today's standards – when journalists are probably lucky to get a night at an airport hotel after a frantic day of meetings and tours somewhere overseas – the BMC event in 1956 seems to have been one long drawn out piece of indulgence. The evidence stacks up with each page one turns of the leather-bound programme that my father brought back home with him. In Sydney a welcome lunch was followed by a tour of Palm Beach and then a welcome dinner; the day in Brisbane opened with a reception with the Lord Mayor at City Hall and closed with cocktails at the Lennon's Hotel; the whole day in Adelaide was devoted to a tour of the vineyards of the Barossa Valley with a barbecue at the Stonyfell Saltram Winery thrown in. Seldom did sobriety appear to get a look in.

Yet it did, occasionally. In between the drinking and the back-slapping in this very male 1950s world of industry and journalism, there were at least a few instances of serious endeavour. They spring out of the musty pages of my father's booklet years later, the shiny typeface of the letters twinkling like a Birmingham-made button. Just before a reception held by the Lord Mayor of Sydney, for example, the press pack squeezed in a tour of the BMC factory at Victoria Park; and in the morning before lunch at the Savoy Plaza Hotel in Melbourne the journalists visited both the Austin plant on Dudley Street and the commercial vehicle assembly plant at Fishermen's Bend, in the heart of the city's docklands.

These visits were, in all likelihood, to have been the set-piece events of the entire trip – the ones that BMC boss Sir Leonard Lord really wanted to plug – because quite simply they lay at the very heart of the British car operation in Australia. The 50-acre Victoria Park site, situated on a disused racecourse, had been bought by Lord Nuffield, aka William Richard Morris, in 1947; and in 1950 the first factory building sprung up for the assembly of a range of cars including the iconic Morris Minor saloons. Staff numbered more than 2,000 by

∾

the time the British press descended on them in 1956, and the production rate three times more than that originally planned. A new BMC engine-making facility based on the one back at Austin's Longbridge plant had also just been erected.

In contrast to the brownfield site in Sydney, the Austin body building factory at Dudley Street, Melbourne, had been purchased in 1948 as a going concern. It was a large factory, with 4 acres of floor space, and the latest in up-to-date equipment. In the seven years since its inception, it had produced more than 60,000 Austin-branded vehicles.

However, it was still not quite large enough or up-to-date enough to match the high ambitions of parent company BMC (Australia) and, as a result, another factory had been bought down the road at Fisherman's Wharf with additional land available for future development. Assembly operations had already commenced at this new plant for the building of commercial vehicles; but, as Leonard Lord was quick to point out to his assembled gathering of journalists, the company was not going to stop at that.

The move was a strategic one, he announced as the reporters flicked open their notepads. The site was not only 2 miles from Melbourne city centre, but also adjacent to a deep water frontage filled with wharfage facilities. From here, in the not-too-distant future, he could launch his export invasion of Southeast Asia.[15]

No doubt Herbert Austin, who himself had emigrated to Australia and worked as an engineer in Melbourne until he was called back to his native England to work at the Wolseley manufacturing firm in Birmingham, would have been proud.

After leaving Wolseley to set up his own company at Longbridge, Austin had gone on to build a motor empire that was the envy of many. By 1930 output at Longbridge had reached 1,000 vehicles a week, among them his seminal model – the Austin 7.

Launched to great scepticism in 1922, the Seven became an infant prodigy, a hallmark of Herbert Austin's genius. In many ways it was a large car in miniature. Less than 3m long, it could nonetheless provide seating for four people. In the 1930s it became one of the most popular small cars in the world, and, although Herbert Austin, by this point widely regarded as 'the father of the British motor industry', died in 1941, the company he founded continued to grow from strength to strength.

It was the 'New Austin Seven', or rather the Austin 30, together with the subsequent A40 and A50 models, which was on offer in Australia in 1956 as the British press pack followed up their factory tours in Sydney and Melbourne with visits to distributor showrooms. But it did not stop there. As the journalists tramped around car dealerships in Australia's two leading cities, and then in Brisbane, Adelaide, Perth and Hobart as well, they saw many more examples of the automotive design and engineering that they knew so well from home on sale there in Australia. There was the sportiness of the Austin Healey sharing the limelight with the burliness of the Wolseley Six Ninety. There was the lovable awkwardness of the Morris Minor standing bumper to bumper with everyone's last word in style: the MG sports car.

⌖

Having been the *Despatch*'s motoring correspondent for nearly three years, Ron Wilcox knew many of the vehicles well. He had test-driven the A40 and A50 models around the hills of the Lake District, declaring them in the male prejudice of the time as 'ideal cars for the women motorist' because the steering was 'light but positive'; and he had admired the work of Midlands suspension engineers as he bounced at the wheel of a two-door Austin Seven along a pot-holed street in West Bromwich.[16]

He also knew the classic family saloon that he would drive up to the Snowy Mountains near Canberra during the trip. It was less than two years since he had written about the 'completely restyled' Morris Oxford with its 'revolutionary new engineering features',[17] and now he was part of a convoy of BMC vehicles heading up into the mountain range to see one of Australia's landmark construction projects.

If the press visit of 1956 was an enormous sales window for the British car industry, it was also an opportunity for Australia to sell its story back to Britain via the column inches and cameras of a band of British journalists; and as PR moments go, a tour of a huge hydro-electric project up in the mountains presented a good chance to show off Australian engineering in its best light.

Certainly in its scale and ambition the scheme was impressive. With construction beginning in 1949, the idea was to build a series of dams to divert the waters of the Snowy River emerging on the slopes of Australia's highest peak, Mt Kosciusko, through large tunnels buried in the mountains and into the valleys below, thereby generating huge quantities of hydro-electric power and helping to irrigate all the vineyards and citrus groves sitting on the banks of the Murray River to the south.

⌖

At the Brisbane car distributor (above) and elsewhere, Ron Wilcox came across the cars he knew so well from home, like the Morris Oxford he drove up to the Snowy Mountains. (Pictorial Record of the British Press Visit to Australia, February–March 1956. The British Motor Corporation (Australia) Pty Ltd)

Another great engineering works in progress, but one much closer to frui-tion, was the Melbourne Olympic Stadium being built against the clock for Australia's second city to host the Games that summer. After Canberra and the Snowy Mountains, the British press pack flew to Melbourne and, after the all-important visits to factories and showrooms, they were treated to a tour of the Olympic sites. All steel girder and angular sloping roof, the stadium was the latest in modernist architecture. However, the thing that might have astonished the reporters still more is how much the building site's surroundings looked as if they had just been lifted out of an English city like Bristol on a Victorian afternoon. There was the fine white stucco of Government House and the neo-Gothic spires of St Paul's Cathedral and, very close, the huge grandstand of the Melbourne Cricket Ground, which would serve as the centrepiece venue at the Olympic Games later that year (as well as at the Commonwealth Games of 2006). Melbourne was one of those typical colonial port cities that had been built on an influx of British immigrants, and immigrants from elsewhere, cru-cially Asia, which had flourished in the nineteenth century. In Melbourne's case, the initial attraction had been the gold mines of nearby Ballarat.

Then, in contrast to the sturdy Victoriana of Melbourne, there were the golden creeks and coves of Sydney Harbour, which is where the British press tour ended up at the end of three weeks Down Under. Australia was a land of beauty and opportunity, and could still provide a good life for the British emigrant, my father commented in one of a series of articles he wrote for the *Birmingham Evening Despatch* based on his trip. 'Skilled men are particularly welcome in a country which has much to do to develop its immense resources,' he wrote. 'They receive good pay, are found temporary homes until they can make permanent arrangements – and in most cases they stay in Australia.'[18]

Of course, there were exceptions. One ten-pound Pom from Birmingham told my father that ever since he had arrived, 'the weather in Sydney had been "worse than Birmingham"'.[19] There was also the issue of the strict licens-ing laws that until very recently had seen many Australian pubs close up in the evenings.

But then there were the group of Birmingham workers who had taken up the challenge to work for the BMC factory at Victoria Park in Sydney on special contracts offered by the firm back in the UK. One of them, Jack Jones, an engine tester, had commented in an earlier report wired back to the Birmingham newsroom by my father: 'strange but very nice ... there is something about living in Australia which just strikes you'.[20] A group of these

Some of the Birmingham workers who accepted the challenge of emigrating to Australia to work for the BMC factory in Sydney, and my father's accompanying article: 'It can be a good life'. (*Birmingham Evening Despatch*, 26 March 1956)

workers all looked happy enough in a photograph that was printed with this particular piece.

In the end, Ron Wilcox concluded: 'Australia is a land of great opportunity for the migrant who is prepared to be without, for a short time, the small comforts he has enjoyed in Birmingham. The hard part of emigration is becoming established. Once that is accomplished, the possibilities are limitless.'[21]

∞

Whether or not there was a hint of envy in my father's typewriter key when he wrote this – he had been in Africa, after all, and was always to his dying day deeply interested in travel – I will never know. But what I do know is that his short adventure in Australia was now drawing to a close. There was barely time to hug a final koala and feed a final titbit to an expectant kangaroo – as two photos from his album of the press trip show my father doing – before all the journalists were gathered up again for the farewell dinner at the BMC factory in Sydney. There, they would hear – once again, probably – BMC chairman Leonard Lord's plans for world domination.

He had been most impressed by the progress British car production was making in Australia, the chairman probably said, if the press notes that accompanied the trip are anything to go by.[22] Spectacular as the growth had been, however, this was only the beginning. To date, the factories in Australia had been merely assembly plants, receiving vehicles from the UK in pack form ready for final processing; but from now on a large expenditure programme of £5 million would transform the Australian operation into a self-contained manufacturing business, more or less, using local iron and steel to make British branded cars from scratch.

At peak production, the BMC chairman predicted, the combined manufacturing facilities would produce a minimum of 50,000 vehicles a year and employ 10,000 men and women, making BMC (Australia) one of the country's major employers.

'Not so long ago … there was a tendency to "count out" Britain and the British Commonwealth,' Lord had told Australian journalists at a press conference at the Wentworth Hotel in Sydney just before the arrival of the British press visit. 'It was said that we had "had" it economically. We in the motor industry have done something, I think, toward disproving all that.'[23]

He probably said something similar at the farewell dinner of his British guests a month later.

∞

Despite all the fine words, however, some of the journalists sitting around the tables in their best suits perhaps had an inkling that this was putting things a bit too optimistically. Certainly, my father had written many articles on the rising competitive threat from the German and Japanese motor industries.

But after a substantial meal of oysters, asparagus in a vinaigrette sauce, roast chicken and pear belle helene, all washed down with sumptuous amounts of wine and champagne, I doubt if any of them cared too much. After all, tomorrow was another day.

෬෧

It certainly was. With heavy hearts and possibly even heavier heads, the journalists from the motor journals, British nationals and Birmingham press spent the next day packing up and taking in their last views of Sydney before the coach arrived to take them to the airport. At 10.30 in the evening of Sunday, 18 March 1956, their plane took off on the first leg of their long return journey to the UK.

This time they were to take the Asian route. By the early hours of the next morning they had landed in Darwin on Australia's northern fringes. From there it was a short hop to Jakarta, the capital of Indonesia, and then on to the British crown colony of Singapore.

This low-lying equatorial island perched at the end of the Malay peninsula was, however, going through the birth pangs of independence. Although the British authorities had introduced increasing levels of democratic assembly and self-government ever since they had returned to the city after the brief interlude of Japanese rule during the Second World War, there was no turning back the clock. The word 'Merdeka' – the Malay word for freedom – was out; and had been the rallying cry of a huge gathering held at the old Kallang airport on the east coast the night before Wilcox of the *Despatch* and his fellow journalists arrived in the colony. The members of the press were bussed to the famous Raffles Hotel for a night's rest from weary hours sitting in a plane seat; but ever the enquiring reporter, my father picked up a local newspaper as a memento of his visit.

'Merdeka Rally Runs Riot' was the splash story on the front of the *Singapore Standard*. Apparently, things had turned ugly after 'Communists' had 'sabotaged' an otherwise good-tempered gathering of supporters of Singapore's main political parties, which had even received a visit by a British Parliamentary

෬෧

delegation. After the delegation had left, however, 3,000 Communist 'stooges' had stoned the police 'in 60 minutes of rioting'.[24]

Having written some stories about 'Communist infiltrators' worming their way into the inner echelons of Birmingham trade unions, this front-page lead might have been of some interest to Ron Wilcox, probably more so than the report on the back pages that Birmingham City had reached the FA Cup Final after beating Sunderland 3 –0. During all my childhood, I never heard him express any particular interest in sport.

Two pictures of Singapore also turned up in the photo album that my father brought back from his trip. Working in Singapore myself nearly half a century later, they are scenes I recognise. One is of cargo barges anchored in the sultry Singapore River. Behind them is a row of grimy godowns (warehouses) on Boat Quay, the storage must-haves for every successful city merchant ever since founder of colonial Singapore Sir Stamford Raffles first set foot on the island in 1819.

And the other picture is of a side alley lined with Chinese shophouses running off Boat Quay. Chinese calligraphy runs down one of the pillars. It is the Ngai Wah Store. People are standing outside – some Malay, others Chinese. An Indian man is walking down the street. And there is a street stall nearby too. The Chinese man standing behind it is hawking durian fruit, perhaps the smelliest fruit in the world. It stinks of old socks, and I think I can catch the stench of it as I gaze at this photo typing these words.

Luckily, though, I can turn over and move on. I have now reached the final page of the album, and on it is a picture of my mother standing in a stylish two-piece with my father on his return, both posing rather woodenly with my uncle and aunt in a garden. And I know now that it will not be long.

Business as usual on a Singapore street in 1956, but times were changing – Singaporeans now wanted freedom from British rule. (Pictorial Record of the British Press Visit to Australia, February–March 1956)

Not long before my father boards a plane again, and flies on to Calcutta and Karachi, and then Beirut and Zurich, spending no more than a couple of hours in each airport before moving on again. He is almost home now.

Ron arrives in London at 3.50 p.m. on the afternoon of Wednesday, 21 March, and in my mind's eye I can see him battling over to London Euston Station clad in his raincoat, clutching his suitcase. He is back now in the wind and the rain of England, far away from the dusty heat of an Australian summer. He boards a carriage amid the bellowing steam of the locomotive, and sinks into a seat in a second-class compartment.

Not long now. A couple of hours later he catches a black cab from Birmingham New Street out to Perry Barr, the taxi splashing along Witton Lane in a sudden downpour, rain slugging at the passenger window as my father peers out into the city gloom. But he doesn't mind too much. He has missed her, and he knows the feeling will be mutual. The cab crosses the canal now, just beyond the Boar's Head.

In a few moments, it will be pulling up. She will be there. At the door of the pasty brick semi-detached on College Road. She will be there, the one who has missed him all these weeks. His wife, Joy.

NOTES

1   R.W. Wilcox, *Diary of Wartime Experiences of Ronald Wilcox: West Africa – 1943/1944*, (Unpublished), p.19.

2   Ronald Wilcox, 'Rain and Transport rule "no play"', *Portsmouth Evening News*, 30 May 1949.

3   Ronald Wilcox, 'Austins: 80 per cent out', *Birmingham Gazette*, 21 June 1951.

4   Ronald Wilcox, 'Pioneer sees a dream come true', *Birmingham Gazette*, 20 July 1951.

5   Ronald Wilcox. 'Revolutionary new assembly plant opened at Austins', *Birmingham Gazette*, 20 July 1951.

6   A number of historical works have looked at this process, including Martin Kitchen, *The British Empire and Commonwealth: A Short History* (Basingstoke and London: Macmillan Press, 1996), pp.86–89; and P.J. Marshall (ed.), *The Cambridge Illustrated History of the British Empire* (Cambridge: Cambridge University Press, 1996), Chapter 4.

7   Martin Kitchen. *The British Empire and Commonwealth: A Short History*, p.75.

8   Ibid., p.122.

9   The Commonwealth of Nations. London Declaration, April 1949, thecommonwealth.org/london-declaration.

10 Travis L. Crosby, *Joseph Chamberlain: A Most Radical Imperialist* (London, New York: I.B. Taurus & Co., 2018), p.162.

11 You can watch a copy of *Song of Ceylon* on YouTube.

12 Ronald Wilcox, '35,000 miles to sell motorcycles', *Birmingham Gazette*, 24 April 1950;

'More production records by Midland car firms', *Birmingham Gazette*, 7 April 1950.

13   Keith Beddoes, Colin & Stephen Wheeler, *Metro-Cammell: 150 Years of Craftsmanship* (Cheltenham: Runpast Publishing, 1999), p.67.

14   Ronald Wilcox, 'Small firm to open Canadian plant', *Birmingham Gazette*, 4 April 1950.

15   The British Motor Corporation [Australia] Pty Ltd, *Vital facts on a vital industry. Background information on the British Motor Corporation (Australia) for Australian journalists covering the British Press Visit of February 26–March 18, 1956*, p.38. (This booklet clearly formed the basis for speeches made during the press visit. It also laid out the itinerary of the trip and supplied potted biographies of all concerned, including those of the twenty-nine journalists from the UK. As mentioned earlier, there was also a booklet laying out the detailed itinerary for the visit. It was leather-bound and was called *BMC in Australia: Round the World with BMC. Programme of the Visit of the British Press to Australia February–March 1956.* There had been a couple of other overseas press trips to BMC operations in the years before the 1956 trip, including ones to Canada and South Africa.

16   Ronald Wilcox, 'The A40 and A50 are ideal for women', *Birmingham Evening Despatch*, 25 September 1954; 'The new Austin Seven has a "big car" performance', *Birmingham Evening Despatch*, 8 February 1954.

17   Ronald Wilcox, 'Morris put more into the new Oxford', *Birmingham Evening Despatch*, 19 May, 1954.

18   Ronald Wilcox, 'It can be a good life', *Birmingham Evening Despatch*, 26 March 1956.

19   Ibid., the Ten-Pound Poms were Britons who emigrated to Australia and New Zealand after the Second World War under a scheme introduced by both countries. They were attracted by the fare of only £10, and more than 1.5 million went.

20   Ronald Wilcox, 'Most like new life down under', *Birmingham Evening Despatch*, 5 March 1956.

21   Ronald Wilcox. 'It can be a good life', *Birmingham Evening Despatch*, 26 March 1956.

22   The British Motor Corporation [Australia] Pty Ltd, *Vital facts on a vital industry. Background information on the British Motor Corporation (Australia) for Australian journalists covering the British Press Visit of February 26–March 18, 1956*, p.37.

23   Ibid., p.36.

24   *Singapore Standard*, 'Merdeka Rally Runs Riot', 19 March 1956.

CHAPTER EIGHT

THE
COMMONWEALTH

Twelve months on from the Australia press trip, and it appeared that 1957 was already shaping up to be an eventful year. Anthony Eden had resigned early in January following his controversial handling of the Suez crisis; Ghana had become an independent country within the Commonwealth in early March; and at home on College Road in Perry Barr, Birmingham, Joy Wilcox had just given birth to a baby daughter. She was my parents' first child.

As the year wore on, there was the first meeting of John Lennon and Paul McCartney at a garden fête where Lennon's skiffle group The Quarrymen were playing, and there was another new member of the Commonwealth as Malaya gained its independence from Britain.

Back in Birmingham, after becoming a father for the first time, Ron Wilcox became an editor for the first time. Having written about Birmingham industry for so long, he was about to become its mouthpiece as the Birmingham Chamber of Commerce secured his expertise to become the editor of its journal. On the second day of September, he settled down behind a desk in his own office, uncluttered by the papers and cigarette ends of dozens of other journalists, and stayed there for the next twenty-five years, an influential voice amid the waxing and then waning of Birmingham's fortunes.

It was a sad story in a way. When he first sat down at his desk at the Chamber, Birmingham was an industrial powerhouse, still recognisably the 'the city of a thousand trades'; its nuts and screws, its metal fittings, its electrical appliances and its cars exported to every corner of the world. When he retired in 1982, the city he had made his home was on its knees, factory after factory shutting their doors for the final time, no longer able to compete in the global market and finally succumbing to the savage recession of early 1980s Britain. Metal grilles came down, workers were laid off, and factory after factory, like the Spon Lane

Works of the Chance Brothers glass factory this book discussed earlier, left to rust on the banks of rotting canals.

Running parallel to this decline in fortunes, too, was another story of fluctuating allegiances. At the beginning of the period it was Britain's former empire that commanded most of Birmingham's attention and took the lion's share of its exports. By the end, it was the European Economic Community. But throughout the period, it was very apparent that Birmingham, like the rest of Britain, was not sure which way to turn.

The confusion was there right at the outset. In the new-look relaunch of the Chamber's journal in January 1958, my father extolled the virtues of Birmingham as 'predominantly a city of small businesses'. The town, he claimed in his opening editorial, was 'resilient, hard working, and, yes, prosperous, a living example of private enterprise'.[1] But, as an article in the magazine by an expert from the Birmingham College of Technology illustrated, that private enterprise was already looking nervously over the English Channel. The European Common Market had come into being that very month after the signing of the Treaty of Rome the year before, at a stroke removing tariff restrictions between its six member countries, and on this side of the Channel making it more difficult for British firms to compete in Europe. However, as the article pointed out, the UK had 'declined an invitation to enter the Common Market but instead put forward proposals for the formation of a Free Trade Area in Europe'. The reason? Because the Rome Treaty members were 'subjected to a

Which way to turn – Europe or the Commonwealth? The confusion was already evident in the 1958 relaunch issue of the *Birmingham Chamber of Commerce Journal*.

common tariff policy' for trading with all countries outside the market. That could not possibly sit with the system of preferential rates that were already in place between Britain and other Commonwealth countries.[2]

Yet only three years later, the UK – one of the original signatories to the European Free Trade Association (EFTA) in 1960 – was seeking membership of the more integrated European Economic Community (the Common Market) in negotiations led by government minister Edward Heath MP. In so much as Britain had a long-term economic strategy, it was clearly prepared to throw in its lot with Europe's inner circle, even at the expense of favourable relations with its former empire.

Except it wasn't really. It was one thing to go where the economic growth was – and that in the 1960s was clearly the EEC. It was quite another to loosen the old ties. 'The future of Commonwealth trade is inextricably linked with the Common Market negotiations, and British entry could well mean some loss of our preferential position in Commonwealth markets,' Ronald Wilcox wrote for the September 1962 issue of the *Chambers of Commerce Journal*,[3] probably just glad to be typing away in his Edgbaston office rather than being at home with another screeching baby. His second child had come along in the spring that year. He and Joy had recently moved to a larger house – detached, with three bedrooms – in the suburb of Sutton Coldfield, and my arrival had come shortly afterwards.

All-consuming as a new baby was, prime ministers from around the world were turning up in London in September for the Twelfth Commonwealth Heads of Government Meeting, while a Birmingham and London Chambers of Commerce trade mission had recently returned from the British colony of Hong Kong; and, at least as far as work was concerned, this was concentrating my father's mind in the late summer of 1962. Would a full economic association with the EEC mean difficulties in maintaining exports to global markets such as Commonwealth member Hong Kong, he wondered. Should Midlands companies consider setting up manufacturing facilities in the Asian territory to take a stake in its future development, using it as a base for sales into nearby markets in the Far East?[4]

Like a Chinese junk tacking and turning in Hong Kong's famous harbour, buffeted by the changing winds, the 'Voice of Birmingham', as my father dubbed his journal in the relaunch issue of 1958, continued to rock to and fro for the next decade and more.

∽

One thing was certain: there was a pressing need to tack more towards the Commonwealth again. In May 1963, the journal was reporting on a speech made by Commonwealth expert Don Taylor at the Birmingham Chamber of Commerce on how the UK could maintain its share of Commonwealth trade in the face of growing competition from Japan and Germany. It was noted that British exports to the bloc had fallen from a high of 47 to 48 per cent in the 1950s to about 34 to 35 per cent. In a sidebar story about trade with Australia, it was seen that the UK's share of Australia's import pie had dropped from 40 per cent to 30 per cent in recent years.

The answer might be, as with the discussion over Hong Kong in 1962, more investment by Birmingham conglomerates and small and medium-sized enterprises (SMEs) alike in overseas operations, perhaps through joint ventures. There was no shortage of middlemen, go-betweens and finance houses that could help, if the journal's advertisement pages were anything to go by. Woodcocks of Melbourne could help you to acquire an interest in a local firm or find industrial premises for you at a reasonable rent;[5] National and Grindlays Bank, which had a network of 167 branches across India, Ceylon, Aden, East Africa and elsewhere, could assist with finance;[6] or the Bank of Montreal could provide you with a guide to establishing a business in Canada[7] if you requested a copy from their London office in Threadneedle Street.

Alternatively, the answer was Europe. By the beginning of the 1970s, the momentum was building. A survey of Birmingham Chamber members revealed overwhelming support for joining the EEC, by a margin of 4,164 companies to 11. It was a groundswell of opinion that Prime Minister Edward Heath applauded at a luncheon speech in Birmingham in September 1971, just weeks before the British Parliament at Westminster voted 'yes' to entry.[8]

Ron Wilcox reported on the speech enthusiastically in the Chamber's journal, now called *Midlands Industry and Commerce*. Yet, in the same issue, he gave column space for concerns about the uphill task British exporters now faced in New Zealand as the country's Commonwealth tariff preferences for British goods were gradually abolished under Treaty of Rome rules. He also reported on a Birmingham Chamber of Commerce mission to Zambia and Malawi that had returned with a sack full of orders from two Commonwealth countries that still held 'considerable goodwill towards UK quality and service born of the long standing trading associations'.[9]

Moreover, there was Singapore. The Commonwealth island nation had notched up astonishing rates of economic growth in the past few years,

and offered 'undoubted scope both for the exporter and for those consider-
ing setting up an operation overseas', according to an article provided by the
Chartered Bank on the next page. A company prepared to manufacture on the
island would receive a whole raft of tax breaks and other incentives, and benefit
from the fact that this jungle-covered island at the tip of the Malay peninsula
was a 'jumping-off point for the region as a whole'.[10]

৩৩

That very same year, Singapore also served as the jumping-off point for the
Commonwealth as a collection of nations 'freely co-operating in the pursuit of
peace, liberty and progress', as the London Declaration had stated. Since that
prime ministers' meeting in London in 1949 when the modern Commonwealth
of Nations was born, the organisation had grown steadily as more countries
had won their independence but also voluntarily decided to join up. However,
the whole exercise had not been without its difficulties.

On the one hand, there had been some very positive moves towards increased
collaboration. Proposed by Ghana, Nigeria, Trinidad and Uganda, the establishment of the Commonwealth Secretariat in 1965 took the administration of
the organisation away from British hands and placed it firmly under auspices of
an international agency capable of setting the agenda for a truly global club. It
was the role of the Secretariat to not only scope out the principles and priorities
for Commonwealth politicians to pursue on the international stage, but also
to co-ordinate an expanding network of civil society organisations teaming up
in collaborative projects across six continents and five oceans. As the Queen,
the head of the Commonwealth, put it in a speech in 1962, it is 'the thread of
personal concern and understanding between individual peoples that weaves a
strong fabric of the modern Commonwealth'.[11]

In other words, relations between 'students, engineers, doctors, and lawyers,
along with artists, writers and cricketers, would form the weft and warp of
the new Commonwealth of people rather than statesmen'.[12] Not to mention a
whole welter of sportsmen and women who were already turning up in some
corner of the world every four years to take part in the Commonwealth Games.

On the other hand, the Commonwealth Heads of Government Meeting
(CHOGM) held every two years was growing increasingly acrimonious. Many
member states saw 'Britain and the white Dominions as paternalistic and pat-
ronising', while 'the African states seemed to be obsessed with the question of

৩৩

While it was in London in 1949 (above) that the modern Commonwealth was born, it was at the 1971 summit hosted by Singapore PM Lee Kuan Yew (below left) when it truly came of age as a liberal institution. (Commonwealth Secretariat photos)

race' and 'the Indians and their followers were thought to be playing one side in the Cold War off against the other to their own advantage ...'[13] All these attitudes, reflecting as they did the shifting allegiances in the post-war world – Africans to Pan-Africanism, India to non-alignment and so forth – often found full expression at the biennial CHOGMs. There was also one standout issue that could always be relied on to provoke fury and division: the racist regime in South Africa. Pressured out of the Commonwealth after the Sharpeville massacre of 1961, apartheid South Africa always had the capacity to drive a rift into an organisation that at times looked distinctly shaky.

Things came to a head at the prime ministers' meeting in Singapore in 1971, when Britain's decision to send arms to South Africa as part of a global strategy to contain the Soviet Union (while making large amounts of money on the side) drew the ire of many member states. The war of words that followed was only finally ended by Canadian Prime Minister Pierre Trudeau, who put forward a proposal – widely accepted – that while members should respect the interests of other members, they also had the right to define their own vital interests.[14]

It was as the meeting pulled back from the brink, however, that a seminal moment in the evolution of the Commonwealth organisation was reached.

In a Declaration of Commonwealth Principles, the leaders declared: 'We believe in the liberty of the individual, in equal rights for all citizens regardless of race, colour, creed or political belief, and in their inalienable right to participate by means of free and democratic political processes in framing the society in which they live.'[15]

And with obvious reference to South Africa, the declaration continued with an unequivocal statement about racism: 'We recognise racial prejudice as a dangerous sickness threatening the healthy development of the human race and racial discrimination as an unmitigated evil of society.'

Emerging from the 'liberal empire' that British historians and politicians had promised in Victorian times, but in so many respects had failed to deliver, the modern Commonwealth had unequivocally set out its stall for 'the basic human rights and freedoms that are central to the liberal tradition'.[16]

୧୨

Back at home, however, Birmingham industrialists were not about to go all soft over a few fine words and some lofty ideals. The fact was that Commonwealth trade was now accounting for less and less of their overseas trade, while trade with other countries, particularly with European ones, was expanding rapidly. The European Common Market beckoned.

The UK joined in January 1973. The following month the Prime Minister, Edward Health, paid the Midlands another visit, this time to cut a tape to set in motion the building of the National Exhibition Centre located near Birmingham's airport. Internationally, world trade was on the move and 'we have achieved our major aim of membership of the European Community', he told his assembled audience, according to *Midlands Industry and Commerce*. 'British exporters have already begun to take advantage of these conditions. This is particularly true of our exports to Western Europe. Between the first and halves of 1972 our sales in Germany and the Netherlands rose by 8 per cent; in Italy by 11 per cent; in Belgium and Luxembourg by 13 per cent; and in France by as much as 17 per cent.'[17]

And that, as they say, seemed to be that. After all, you couldn't argue with the figures, could you? In any case, the Commonwealth was quarrelsome, often critical of Britain and always carried with it a whiff of neo-imperialism. Wouldn't it be better to consign it to history, taking with it the memory of all our imperial iniquities? Throw in our lot with modern, developed European democracies. Consign the Empire to history over a bottle of Chianti on the terrace of a Tuscan farmhouse.

Yes, Britain was making a new start.

◦◦

Or was it? Despite the fact that in 1975 the UK gave a referendum thumbs-up to European Community membership and went on to generally thrive in Europe,[18] it is undoubtedly true that it never quite forgot its former empire or the Commonwealth.

In one way or another, they were always there.

They were in the nostalgia for a lost age that swept through the nation in the early 1980s with the popular television dramas *Brideshead Revisited* and *The Jewel in the Crown*, and continued unabated with TV documentaries about the British Empire, books about white Mughals and Victorian pioneers, and films about just everything the British thought and did during their imperial heyday.[19]

They were also in the Commonwealth Games, often called the 'Friendly Games', which debuted in 1930 in Hamilton in Canada, and – except for a brief hiatus due to the Second World War – have provided us every four years with a spectacle of sport involving thousands of athletes.

Finally, in all the people we know and have known. One of my close friends at John Willmott School in Sutton Coldfield in the 1970s was a Greek Cypriot, from a community that had started to settle in Birmingham in the 1950s after poverty and conflict had forced them to leave the villages of their Mediterranean homeland in search of a better life. Cyprus was then, and still remains, a member of the Commonwealth. Among my close friends when I later lived in London, working in various editorial jobs, were colleagues whose parents had emigrated from the countries of the Indian subcontinent in the 1950s and '60s.

For all the success of the European project, there were still ties beyond it that bound.

And the proverbial junk still continued to rock to and fro in the harbour. Although the preferential trade with the Commonwealth was long gone, and sales to this unique group of nations had plummeted in the intervening years, in the 1990s it suddenly turned up again as an exciting business proposition. As if it had never really gone away.

It all happened with the Commonwealth Heads of Government Meeting in Edinburgh in 1997. When fifty-three heads of state wafted into the Scottish capital as the autumn leaves were beginning to carpet the ground, they had something new on the agenda, something that had not been discussed seriously in Commonwealth circles for many years: trade and investment. [20]

It was an idea that had come of age … again. The Cold War was over, globalisation was on the march, and after years of wrangling over apartheid, years that had sapped the energies of the organisation, South Africa was now a full democracy under the leadership of Nelson Mandela. The time was ripe for this diverse group of nations that had so much common – legal, political and educational systems often based on the UK model, not to mention a shared language – to look outside politics to see how it could increase mutual prosperity.

A new business forum bringing together politicians, company bosses and entrepreneurs had met in London just before Edinburgh to thrash out new ideas on how private sector enterprises across the Commonwealth could tap into each other's expertise. Investment was also on the agenda, with the Commonwealth Development Corporation (CDC) on hand to offer advice on how SMEs could tap into funding.

Born and bred in Birmingham, former International Development Secretary and Birmingham MP Clare Short (second from left) at the commemoration of the Commonwealth Development Corporation's fiftieth anniversary in 1998. (Commonwealth Secretariat photo)

Since its foundation in Britain in 1948 with a mandate to invest in businesses in the poorer countries of the Commonwealth, the CDC had notched up some important successes. Among these were helping Kenya to establish its tea industry, backing the Indian tech sector in its early birth pangs, and investing in shopping centres in Soweto. Now, it was at a major Commonwealth 'club' meeting, hoping to inject more pace into commercial discussions and free up the flow of cross-border investments further still. To that end it was poised to announce the formation of a regional equity fund of over $100 million for South Asia.

It is highly likely, I think, that the Birmingham maverick, Joseph Chamberlain, who had first established the development finance principle a century beforehand, would have approved.[21]

⁂

A few years later, a new job took me halfway across the world to Singapore to join the Money Desk on the city state's main newspaper. Not that I fully appreciated it when I first stepped out of the airport at Changi on a March day to be hit by a wave of humid equatorial heat – a lone Brummie in one of the great Asian cities – but I would be spending the next three years seeing things from quite another perspective. Although the links with the former colonial power were still strong – Singapore was a major investor in the UK, mainly in property development, transport and IT,[22] and there were around 700 British firms with a base in the city state – quite often it was what was happening on the US stock markets or in neighbouring countries in the Association of Southeast Asian Nations (ASEAN) that exercised the minds of Singaporeans.

What was most striking for me, though, was the sheer cultural diversity of the island. In this respect, it was very typical of an urbanity that had grown up as a British colonial port. They started flocking to the settlement as soon as East India Company man Stamford Raffles planted the British flag on the marshy, mosquito-infected island in 1819, drawn by the opportunities for trade and work. Mainly it was the Chinese – Hokkiens, Teochews, Cantonese and Hakkas – who had set sail from poverty-stricken southern China, looking for work in the docks. But it was also Malays from the peninsula, and Bugis sailors from Java and then Indian merchants and civil servants who appeared from other British trading posts on the other side of the Bay of Bengal. In time, the Indian professionals were supplemented by indentured labour from South India, mostly Tamils, employed on public works projects – a system that was widely criticised and finally banned in 1910.[23]

In the meantime, Parsis blew in from Bombay; and Armenians and Jews rolled up from the fringes of Europe. There were also the Peranakan or Straits Chinese, who had been born up the coast in Melaka or Penang, and who brought with them the distinctive cuisine of Nyonya.

Although the British authorities always liked to keep these communities living in separate areas – in a system of 'divide and rule' – it was cuisine that often brought these very distinctive peoples together, as they congregated to eat outdoors in the heat of the equatorial night at the hundreds of ramshackle hawker stalls that popped up all over the island.

They still do. Sitting on Boon Tat Street underneath the glitzy towers of the central business district, for instance, is a gable-roofed marketplace held up with wrought-iron pillars. Built in Victorian times, Lau Pa Sat houses dozens of sizzling food stalls fired up by the steady hiss of Calor gas cylinders. Crushed garlic and prawns will fizzle and spit in a wok on the *char kway teow* counter before they are joined by hurried handfuls of noodles, bean sprouts and chives. A sticky dough mixture will be flipped and stretched at the Muslim *roti prata* stall before being served up with a bowl of hot curry sauce. There will be the chop of the cleaver on a chopping board belonging to a hawker of Hainanese chicken rice.

And everywhere there will be the slops and gurgles of all kinds of broths as workers from the financial district spill out into the humid evening air for sustenance before they head home.

∽

Lau Pa Sat is a dynamic, energetic place that reflects the dynamism and energy of one of the world's most go-getting economies. For the past fifty years or so, independent Singapore has notched up an average GDP growth rate of more than 7 per cent per annum, taking it from third-world status to first. Under the tutelage of its first Prime Minister Lee Kuan Yew and then his successors, Singapore is now the world's fourth largest financial centre, has one of the world's busiest container ports, and has the highest number of millionaires per capita in Asia.[24]

It is this economic vigour of a Commonwealth country that seems to have figured highly in the calculations of Eurosceptic politicians and other Leave campaigners in the run-up to Britain's EU referendum in 2016. Always the mouthpiece of the Conservative right, the *Telegraph* newspaper ran a series of articles at the time pointing out that growth in Commonwealth countries had now outstripped that in the Eurozone, and would soon account for more of the global business scene than the European Union. Just look at India – it said – a rising tiger with an economy growing at 7 per cent or more, and yet Britain, hampered by its single market membership, was unable to negotiate a bilateral trade deal with it. With Europe now accounting for only 45 per cent of UK exports compared with 55 per cent a decade before, it added, it was time to leave the bureaucratic and protectionist mainland and play patsy with the emerging markets of the future.[25]

By this time, the Tory Eurosceptics had a new leader, Boris Johnson MP. 'It is absurd that Britain, historically a great free-trading nation,' he blustered in one of his campaign speeches, 'has been unable for 42 years to do a free trade deal with Australia, New Zealand, China, India and America.'[26]

All bar China, these nations had played an important part in Britain's history. Accompanied by drum rolls and bugle sounds, no doubt, Britain would re-establish trading arrangements after Brexit, not only with the old settler economies of Australia and so forth, but also with the new trade buccaneers of our age, Singapore and India.

The ghost of Joseph Chamberlain had come back to haunt Britain.

⌒⌒

As is well documented, Birmingham voted for Brexit by a whisker, shocking the forecasters, as the UK's controversial vote to leave did generally. While the country voted by 52 to 48 per cent to leave, 50.4 per cent of Brummies voted for it, by a margin of 3,800 votes. Whatever their reasons – whether it was concern over immigration, or resentment against Brussels bureaucracy, or a desire for Britain to become a free-trading nation again with a world outside

Europe – the city now had to look forward, and envisage what a post-Brexit Birmingham would look like.

Birmingham City University set up a Centre for Brexit Studies to explore what impact life outside Europe would have on society and the economy. Meanwhile, with the city's bid for the Games in mind, the Birmingham Chamber of Commerce, or rather the Greater Birmingham Chambers of Commerce (GBCC), as it is now known, launched a new arm to help its members develop trade links with the Commonwealth.

In a press statement on 5 December 2017, it stated its belief that 'Commonwealth countries represent a largely untapped market … which has been overshadowed by the UK's relationship with the European Union.'[27]

Now that we were leaving the European Union, 'developing trade links with the Commonwealth countries has never been more important', it added. After years of neglect, the Commonwealth (with a population of 2.3 billion) now accounted for only 9 per cent of the UK's exports, compared to about 44 per cent for the EU.

To this end, it would organise a major events programme and promote better contacts through British diplomatic posts and chambers overseas. That is not to say that Birmingham was not already active. GBCC chief executive Paul Faulkner had recently joined West Midlands mayor Andy Street on a trade mission to Toronto. A Birmingham delegation was due to make a visit to the Auto Expo Components event in New Delhi the following February.

Fortunately, the Midlands was, by and large, well-placed to take advantage of overseas opportunities. Aside from the difficult days after the financial crash in 2008, the area had reversed its fortunes after the dark days of the 1980s. By 2017, it had the fastest-growing economy outside London, seeing more start-ups than anywhere else apart from the capital, and accounting for 22 per cent of England's total exports. In addition to its traditional expertise in automotive equipment clustered around household names such as Jaguar Land Rover, it also had key strengths in other forms of advanced manufacturing – in food and environment technologies, for instance – as well as in financial services, life sciences, creative industries and digital, and education.[28]

It was also the second-largest region overall in terms of overseas students outside the EU studying at its educational institutions, with a quarter of students studying in Birmingham from the Commonwealth.

Even before the GBCC initiative, though, the Commonwealth was already playing a bigger role in the Birmingham story. India had become a major investor in the city, and the Birmingham Commonwealth Association had been launched in 2014 to strengthen partnerships such as this. The association proclaimed three areas of focus: trade and business, links between Commonwealth academic establishments, and increased engagement with Birmingham communities hailing from the Commonwealth.[29]

The initiative would have earned the full support, no doubt, of Joseph Chamberlain, who had died exactly 100 years before. The wheel of history had turned again.

൭൭

A couple of weeks after the launch of the Greater Birmingham Commonwealth Chamber of Commerce, I was in town. My mother had passed away the previous year. My father had gone a long time before. I felt a need to go back to see the old place again. See the grimy city where I was born and grew up. Perhaps even rekindle some childhood memories.

On the first day of tramping around I had ended up in the Gas Street Basin, the hub of the old canal network, in the icy stranglehold of a midwinter's day; and, as the early night descended, I had lost myself in the soft incandescence of all the lights coming on – the lamps on the crumbling warehouse walls at the side of the water, and the bright smudge of Broad Street up on the bridge that hung over the Main Line canal.

Had it ended there, that might have been that, I suppose. A sense of sadness about all those faraway years of my youth amid the wintry lights of my hometown.

But on my second day of wandering around the city centre, the news came through. Birmingham would be hosting the Commonwealth Games in 2022. The twenty-second Commonwealth Games, as it happened.

And as a result, my curiosity was awoken. I had listened to my father's tales of West Africa and Australia during my childhood; I had been surrounded by my mother's books, *A Passage to India* among her favourites; and later on, I had travelled myself. Working in Singapore, wending my way around India, Sri Lanka and Malaysia.

It was nothing really. Others had done far greater things, and in a city of 180 different languages many people in Birmingham had far closer ties overseas than I could ever profess.

But, in my own mind, I could see a connection. In my own limited way, I *was* also a link between Birmingham and the wider world.

൭൭

So, not long afterwards, I got a few books out of the library, sat down at my computer and started to write. And that was the beginning of this book.

NOTES

1   Ronald Wilcox, 'Viewpoint', *Birmingham Chamber of Commerce Journal*, January 1958, vol. 57, no. 661, p.4.

2   W.J. Williams, 'European Free Trade', *Birmingham Chamber of Commerce Journal*, January 1958, vol. 57, no. 661, p.33.

3   Ronald Wilcox, 'Viewpoint', *Birmingham and West Midlands Chambers of Commerce Journal*, September 1962, vol. 61, no. 717.

4   Ibid.

5   Advertisement, Woodcocks of Melbourne, *Midlands Industry and Commerce*, June 1970, vol. 70, no. 810, p.437.

6   Advertisement, National and Grindlays Bank, *Birmingham and West Midlands Chambers of Commerce Journal*, May 1963, vol. 62, no. 725, p.427.

7   Advertisement, Bank of Montreal, *Midlands Industry and Commerce*, February 1966, vol. 65, no. 758, p.128.

8   Ronald Wilcox, 'Prime Minister told of Midlands Problems', *Midlands Industry and Commerce*, October 1971, vol. 71, no. 826, p.698.

9   Ibid., pp.710–712.

10 Ibid., p.714.

11 Martin Kitchen, *The British Empire and Commonwealth: A Short History* (Basingstoke and London: Macmillan Press, 1996), p.147.

12 Ibid.

13 Ibid., p.145.

14 Ibid., p.148.

15 The Commonwealth of Nations, Singapore Declaration 1971. thecommonwealth.org/declaration-commonwealth-principles.

16 Martin Kitchen, *The British Empire and Commonwealth: A Short History*, p.144.

17 Ronald Wilcox, 'Prime Minister starts the building of the NEC', *Midlands Industry and Commerce*, March 1973, vol. 73, no. 843, p.117.

18 In 1970, the UK's GDP was US$1.21 trillion. In 2019, it was US$2.83 trillion.

19 William Dalrymple wrote about a love affair in the early nineteenth century between an East India Company man and a Hyderabadi noblewoman in the 2002 history book *White Mughals*; former *Newsnight* anchor Jeremy Paxman fronted a history of the British Empire in the BBC TV series called *Empire* in 2012; Judi Dench starred in the 2017 film *Victoria and Abdul* about the relationship between Queen Victoria and her Indian Muslim servant Abdul Karim. This is just to give a few examples.

20 The full details of this return to a focus on trade and investment can be found on the Commonwealth website – https://thecommonwealth.org/promoting-shared-prosperity-edinburgh-commonwealth-economic-declaration

21 More information on the Commonwealth Development Corporation's history can be found at www.cdcgroup.com. More information on Joseph Chamberlain's overseas investment programme, meanwhile, can be found in this book's chapter on West Africa.

22   Simon Wilcox, 'Destination UK', *Orient*, magazine of British Chamber of Commerce in Singapore, Winter 2000, Mita (P) 344/03/2000, p.6.

23   Various history books tell the history of Singapore, but for brief but trustworthy insights travel guides such as the *Footprint Singapore Handbook* can be invaluable.

24   This story of transformation is told by modern Singapore's charismatic founding father Lee Kuan Yew in *From Third World to First: Singapore and the Asian Economic Boom* (Singapore: Harper Business, 2011).

25   The Commonwealth economy overtook the Eurozone back in 2013, according to one of these articles, www.telegraph.co.uk/news/newstopics/eureferendum/12193101/Brexit-will-allow-Britain-to-embrace-the-Commonwealth.html.

26   Boris Johnson MP speech, 9 May 2016. Available online at www.conservativehome.com/parliament/2016/05/boris-johnsons-speech-on-the-eu-referendum-full-text.html.

27   Press statement, 'Birmingham to launch Commonwealth Chamber', Greater Birmingham Chambers of Commerce, 5 December 2017, www.greaterbirminghamchambers.com/latest-news/news-listing.

28   More information can be found at www.midlandsengine.org. The organisation's internationalisation strategy report of February 2019 provides an interesting read.

29   More information can be found at www.b-ca.org.

POSTSCRIPT

If there is one saying that best summed up 2020, then a much-quoted aphorism from the Russian revolutionary, Lenin, was probably it. 'There are decades where nothing happens; and there are weeks where decades happen,' he once wrote. A year or so after I had started writing *From Gas Street to the Ganges,* the world, and Birmingham with it, was suddenly plunged, seemingly out of the blue, into a deadly pandemic.

Now, as I was writing the last few chapters, I wondered whether it was ever going to be a book with a happy ending. I had always intended it to be. That, after all, was the very nature of the work – an exploration, and then ultimately a celebration, of Birmingham's historical links with the Commonwealth in the run-up to one of the world's great sporting spectacles. The good news was that the local authorities were pressing ahead with preparations for the event. On the flip side, the Midlands had been badly hit by the coronavirus with thousands of serious cases; and more 'lockdowns' of society, like the one the region had first experienced with the rest of the country in the spring, loomed on the horizon.

Everyone's world had been turned upside down. In so much as people could look forward to the future, they looked forward to returning to some sort of job security, and renewing old acquaintances. In other words, just picking up the threads of normality again after all the disruption.

I, too, wanted all that. At the same time, I was also wondering how I was going to find a finale for my book. Originally, I imagined myself attending a festival of some kind, finding out how Birmingham's diverse communities were preparing for the Games. Perhaps they would be contributing in their different ways to the six-month arts festival that would be running before, during and after the Games. At the beginning of 2020, I was ready, poised with pen and paper, to join in with the Sikh Vaisakhi celebration in Handsworth Park in April, pay a visit to one of the Birmingham mosques at their annual open day in June, and throw myself into the Mela festival in Victoria Park, Smethwick, in July: all to see what I could find out about plans for a much greater multicultural celebration two years on. I was ready to talk bhangra, raga and reggae; ready to exchange views over rice and peas; ready to chat and drink chai.

But everything had been cancelled. Festivals had been postponed. Impromptu face-to-face discussions were off the agenda as people looked out nervously from behind makeshift face masks.

History had definitely taken a turn for the worse.

But there was something that I had been pondering ever since I had sat down in my study at home to write this book, glancing out from time to time on the changing colours of the acer tree in the front garden. That the end of my book would probably lie in its beginnings. As I had been writing each chapter, I had often reflected on that winter's afternoon back in 2017 when I had visited the canal junction that had inspired the book's title; and there probably lay the key.

The Gas Street Basin had looked eerily beautiful when I had paid it a visit on that bitterly cold day just before Christmas. Surrounding it was all the paraphernalia of a modern city – the harsh cubes and squares of phosphorus lighting in the late afternoon darkness that made up all the new shopping malls and hotels. But down at the water's edge the lights flickering on seemed to lose their definition. Here, they were more of a half glow: reflections of rusty Victorian warehouse brick shimmering underneath the barges tied up at the mooring, the soft lamps hanging over the door of a local gin bar, a flush of smoky orange on the wall of the old Regency Wharf that just managed to pick out the words inscribed on it: 'Food, Drink, Cheer'.

In its heyday, the wharf would have taken in cereal grain for use in the nearby malt house, hence the words, and much more besides: from the coal of the Staffordshire and Derbyshire pits feeding the nearby foundries to copper and iron from North Wales and the North supplying the metalworking industries of 'the city of a thousand trades'.

There was little hint of that heavy industrial past now. These days, the brightly painted barges moored up at the wharf were used for leisure trips.

Nevertheless, it was the Gas Street Basin, and the extensive network of canals that emanated from it, that would, in their own way, subsequently transport me through Birmingham's rich and varied past. As if travelling on my own narrow boat – my hand on the tiller and a pot of coffee constantly on the go in the cabin below – I had chugged my way through the tunnel underneath Broad Street at the north end of the basin, and then onwards, through flights of locks, underneath arches into the heart of things: the derelict factories that once housed great industries like the Chance Bros Glassworks, the dreaming towers of King Edward's school that had inspired travellers and academics, the dreary brick walls of meeting houses and Methodist halls that had inspired the city's free thinkers.

Yes, canals had always pointed the way. From the Broad Street Bridge and then northwards for a hundred metres to the Old Turn Junction where a signpost sitting on an odd little island in the middle of the waterway ushers you either to the left onto the Birmingham Main Line canal leading to the Soho Foundry of Matthew Boulton and James Watt, or to the right, up the Birmingham & Fazeley Canal and into old Gun Quarter that was once involved in a great evil – the transatlantic slave trade – before Quakers and Unitarians reset the dial for Birmingham, making it one of the leading lights in the campaign for abolition.

If a sense of divine providence drove early Protestants to colonise the New World – that it was somehow they who were God's chosen people and other races and peoples did not benefit from this special type of guardianship – this was not the case for Quakers and other nonconformist sects that followed. For Quakers, the 'light of God' was to be found in every person, and that meant everyone, including people of other races. For their part, Unitarians believed in the oneness of God and the underlying unity and connectedness of humanity. Crucially, both denominations believed that it was important to strive for a better world in the here and now, and were thus both heavily involved in the anti-slavery movement – the biggest human rights campaign of the age.

It was no surprise then, that Josiah Wedgwood was moulding his famous earthenware anti-slavery medallion or, later on, that the army of anti-slavery activists that made up the Female Society for Birmingham consisted of so many women of a Christian nonconformist bent – Mary Lloyd and Sophia Sturge were Quakers, while Lucy Townsend was the daughter of an evangelical minister.

Neither was it a surprise when nonconformists living in spitting distance of the Worcester and Birmingham Canal heading out of Birmingham in a south-westerly direction took up the mantle. When Quaker Joseph Sturge of Wheeleys Road in Edgbaston was instrumental in getting the exploitative Caribbean apprenticeship scheme of the 1830s abolished; when Unitarian Helen Caddick left the Midlands in 1889 clutching a Thomas Cook ticket for the Holy Land and never looked back; or when the Unitarian with an orchid in his buttonhole, Joseph Chamberlain, despite his Boer War antics, established the important principle of investing in under-developed countries that would eventually lead to the founding of the Commonwealth Development Corporation, the mission of which was 'to do good without losing money'.[1]

As for the Birmingham MP's dreams of a commercial union between Britain and all the countries orbiting around her in a great realm 'of sentiment' (see Chapter Five), the answer to that one probably came from fellow Birmingham luminary Charles Freer Andrews, who joined Gandhi's fight to free India from Britain's imperial grip, desiring only a 'friendship between India and Britain as equals'.

What Chamberlain and C.F. Andrews still shared in common, though, was that they were both, in their own ways, products of the same city of dissenting creeds. Chamberlain nurtured orchids and a radical vision of Empire. Andrews became a 'rebel' church minister working among poor communities in India, Fiji and South Africa. Both hailed from a city peppered with nonconformist places of worship – from the Church of the Messiah on Broad Street or the Quaker Meeting House on the corner of George Street to the whole welter of chapels and Methodist halls in Cannon Street, Carrs Lane and so forth – which made Birmingham a melting pot for different religions and political ideas.

If you were looking for aristocracy or feudal splendour or high church, Birmingham was not the place for you, but if you were looking for thinking outside the box and a simple sense of humanity it quite possibly was.

๑๑

Or if you were looking for a job. As Birmingham emerged from the ruins of the Second World War, its canal banks began to hum again with industry. From all the Black Country foundries on the New Main Line Cut and the Longbridge Works out near the Worcester & Birmingham Canal, to the likes of Metro Cammell, BSA Motorbikes and Typhoo opening up the throttle back at the centre of city's canal network, the city of a thousand trades was booming again, supplying people from all over the world 'from the Tagus to the Ganges' with the goods they needed, as the poet John Freeth would have had it.

What the eighteenth-century poet probably would not have anticipated, though, was that all this industry within the Midlands canal navigations was now about to bring the world back to Birmingham, as people from the Commonwealth arrived, searching for work. Bringing the Ganges, as it were, back to the Gas Street Basin.

As Sikhs and Hindus from Gujarat and the Punjab, Muslims from Mirpur in Pakistan and from Sylhet in Bangladesh, and African-Caribbeans settled in

From industrial innovator to multicultural powerhouse, Birmingham's journey has taken it all the way from the Gas Street Basin to the River Ganges and back. (*Above:* photograph by Madrugada Verde, Shutterstock.com) (*Below:* Commonwealth Secretariat photo)

during the ensuing decades, they brought a new vitality to the Midlands city: not only in their industriousness, but also in their cultures and religions (as we have seen in Chapters Three and Four).

Now, alongside Birmingham's old churches and chapels, there was the Birmingham Central Mosque on the Belgrave Middleway, the Guru Nanak Gurdwara serving Sikhs in Smethwick, and the Shree Geeta Bhawan at the heart of the Hindu community in Handsworth. Moreover, there was the Shri Venkateswara mandir in the Black Country, one of the largest Hindu temples in Europe, the duck-egg blue of the Ramgarhia Sikh temple in the Jewellery Quarter, the Jamia Masjid in Small Heath, and many more places of worship serving Birmingham's newcomers.

There are no grand palaces in Birmingham to speak of, still less the majestic boulevards or crescents that London, Bath or Edinburgh can boast. Broadly speaking, with the occasional exception here and there, it is a rather challenging place to love architecturally. The thing that no one can deny, however, is the city's dynamic intercultural character.

Perhaps this is a favourable harbinger for the future. As the local newspaper, the *Birmingham Mail*, said in a piece on 12 July 2017: 'The Commonwealth has already come to Birmingham – so the Games will be more than welcome.'[2]

෮

Birmingham's new communities gathered like all the city's earlier communities around the canals. The Sikhs near the New Main Line, the Muslims either side of the Grand Union, and African-Caribbeans just to the north of the Soho Loop.

Canals were always the key. Half-submerged, virtually subterranean; and yet these canals, it seemed to me, offered a particular vantage point from which to witness Birmingham's global history. Wherever there was a piece of important history, there always appeared to be a cut somewhere nearby, as if it was these lines of water that thread everything together, taking me on a journey through the past.

And if they could do this, perhaps they could finish the job too. Take me to the finishing line. It was just a hunch, an act of faith if you like, but in this drift of mind, I figured, a final design, a final pattern, might emerge.

There was one final branch of the Birmingham canal network that I now needed to follow. The first bit I knew well. The giddy descent of twelve locks pivoting away from the Old Turn Junction and down past the small leaded-light windows of old factories sitting right on the water's edge, and then through a string of low red-brick tunnels – underneath Newhall Street, Ludgate Hill and Snow Hill – until you pass under the wrought-iron Barker Bridge and arrive at Aston Top Lock. If you ignore the lock and swing right here, you will be on the Digbeth Cut, passing underneath the curiously named Love Lane Bridge and through the Curzon Tunnel until you emerge from the darkness and find yourself in the long, lost Typhoo Basin.

But now I wanted to take the other route through the Aston Locks, following the Birmingham & Fazeley Canal to the point where it meets the Tame Valley Canal, and where, if you look up, you will find the compellingly ugly Spaghetti Junction spiralling high above your head.

From there I would turn left and chug a couple of miles onwards, underneath College Road where my parents spent their early married life, past the Perry Reservoir, and on to the Perry Barr Locks. And here I would finally disembark, underneath the looming steelwork of the new stand taking shape at Birmingham's main athletics venue, Alexander Stadium. It is here that the opening ceremony of the Birmingham Commonwealth Games will be held on the evening of Thursday, 28 July 2022.

Over the following twelve days, approximately 6,500 athletes and team officials from seventy-two nations and territories across the Commonwealth will come together to compete across nineteen sports. All the athletics will be held at the Alexander Stadium, while other events will be held at venues all across Birmingham and the West Midlands.

The 1982 Commonwealth Games hosted by Brisbane featured 1,583 athletes from forty-six countries. The Birmingham Games will involve more than 6,000 athletes from seventy-two nations and territories. (Commonwealth Secretariat photo by Tony Duffy)

Notwithstanding the outbreak of the coronavirus pandemic in the early months of 2020, and the immense suffering that it was to cause, that ceremony at the Alexander Stadium would remain the focus of Birmingham organisations and communities throughout the year. The opening day had been shifted by twenty-four hours due to the significant impact that Covid-19 was having on the international sporting calendar, but otherwise it was full steam ahead on an event that was now seen as more essential to hold than ever.

Iain Reid, the chief executive officer of the Birmingham 2022 organising body, said as much at a virtual global trade conference organised by the Greater Birmingham Chambers of Commerce (GBCC) on 24 June 2020. The Games, he said, were 'a historical opportunity at a critical time'.[3]

In the wake of the pandemic by then – with a fair wind – it would be a historical opportunity for the Midlands to welcome visitors from all over the Commonwealth, for Midlands businesses to expand their horizons, and for the region to give the Games a distinctively 'Birmingham flavour'.[4]

A hint of what that flavour would be perhaps arrived with another online event that summer, which came about as a replacement for the Sports & Culture Festival 2020 at Edgbaston Stadium, hastily cancelled because of the pandemic.

This is My City 2020 Digital Festival held over the August Bank Holiday was a community event celebrating the diverse identity of Birmingham; and over three days it showcased live cooking demonstrations from Birmingham-based chefs, presentations on how sport could be used to bring different genders and races together in the city, and a selection of local films highlighting the Commonwealth migration stories that made up the fabric of the city; for instance, Saturday's film event featured Birmingham Cypriots sharing their experiences of coming to live in the city in the 1950s and '60s.

In addition to the various events and discussions, This is My City was an opportunity for local groups to promote themselves. These included the second Generation of Barbadians & Friends, which was founded in 1998 to bring families originally from Barbados but now living in Birmingham together; the Ghana Union Midlands supporting the local Ghanaian community; and the Handsworth-based Legacy West Midlands, which, in a district where 170 languages are spoken, is in the business of celebrating the heritage of post-migrant communities in Birmingham.

There was also LGK in the Community, which ever since 2014 has run a pop-up taverna in a back garden in the neighbourhood of Great Barr. It was set up by a Greek Cypriot in honour of his late father Lakis, who had originally opened the Greek kitchen in the garden only to lose his battle with small cell lung cancer in 2012. On occasional Saturday evenings throughout the year, people gather in the taverna – its traditional clay oven serving up the LGK signature dish of lamb kleftiko – to raise money for good causes.

There may be no grand palaces in Birmingham, no majestic avenues to speak of; but there are, as the This is My City festival illustrated, numerous groups and societies, based wherever they can, in small meeting halls, in the corners of offices or even in private houses. A loose network but all united by one thing: Birmingham. In fact, the festival's main backer was a community programme called United by Birmingham 2022, which, recognising that the city as 'a community of communities',[5] has been set up to help grassroots projects make the most of welcoming people to the Games. Out of huge diversity, creating something like 'a community of interest', as Joseph Chamberlain might have put it in another age, in another context.

The same could possibly be said for the Commonwealth itself during the challenging days of 2020. A huge network of differing initiatives and organisations, but broadly speaking, all pulling in the same direction. Outside the 'official' Commonwealth, historian Martin Kitchen talks about the presence now of a vital 'unofficial' Commonwealth, 'made up of a large number of non-government organisations (NGOs) concerned with every imaginable topic from forest to literature, scouting to town planning, Methodism to the press …',[6] and all this was very much in evidence during the early months of the pandemic. The Association of Commonwealth Universities, comprising more than 500 institutions in fifty countries, for instance, was mobilising its digital network to deliver online webinars and gatherings to students and academics unable to meet up in person. Youth organisations were getting involved in a webinar designed to involve more young people in the Caribbean in politics. Scientists across the Commonwealth were raising the alarm bells over the plight of the fast-disappearing mangrove forests around the world.

In fact, it might be argued that both the Commonwealth and Birmingham have become in their own ways and at their own speeds very visible symbols of the spirit of co-operation. That, at any rate, gradually became my opinion as I observed the long trek of both entities during the course of writing this book.

I might even venture a bit further: that this book has been a piece of work about journeys. Both Birmingham and the Commonwealth are very much products of the British Empire; yet both, it could be argued, have come a long way from the warmongering of the East India Company. In a long process of enlightenment,

Birmingham saw off the slavers and the worst excesses of post-war racism to become the multicultural city it is today – flawed, no doubt, but at least striving. The Commonwealth shrugged off the British imperial swagger of its early days and the incessant squabbling of the 1960s and '70s to become 'an instrument of genuine international co-operation'[7] – not an 'empire of sentiment', by any means, but possibly as close as you can get today to a club of friendly nations.

∞

Those are two journeys. The third one has been mine. The one that started in the Gas Street Basin on a cold winter's evening and then took me through all the twists and turns of Birmingham's long history with the Commonwealth.

I am coming to the end of it now, and as I write the last few lines of this book on an autumn evening in 2020, moonlight is peeping in shyly through my window blinds.

A hazy moon will be hovering now all over Birmingham, too, as the city lights flicker into life. The minaret at the Central Jamia Mosque will be bathed in a soft green hue, the home of the BBC Asian Network radio station at the Mailbox centre will be wrapped in radiant neon, while Millennium Point will be glimmering like a blue sapphire in the cold city air.

The Hindu temple in Tividale is bounded on all sides by canals – the often invisible threads that bind Birmingham together. (Kalki/Alamy Stock Photo)

∞

There will be a warm glow emanating from the Hen & Chickens Desi pub on Constitution Hill, and over on the Ladypool Road the sequins on the Pakistani bridalware in the window display of Meena Bazaar will be sparkling brightly. There will be a shaft of light in the library at King Edward's School in Edgbaston and there will be the night-time glare of the clock at the top of the 'Old Joe' tower at the University of Birmingham.

Up in the Black Country hills, however, the Sri Venkateswara Shrine will be struggling to glow in the grimy Tividale night. The building that draws its inspiration from a temple set in a tropical glade in southern India sits, after all, in the industrial Midlands, bounded on all sides by canal.

But to be in Birmingham is always to be bounded by a canal. They seep through the city in the dark gullies below the lights, never seen if not looked for, just a watery whisper between old industrial walls.

Nevertheless, they are the invisible threads that hold the city together. Connecting the dank, misty Typhoo Basin with the Al Faisal Balti House on Stoney Lane. Connecting the King Edward's visionary, Charlie Freer Andrews, who touched Gandhi's feet and yearned for Indo-British friendship, with Birmingham's modern Asian communities. Connecting Lucy Townsend of the Birmingham Female Society with Handsworth poet Benjamin Zephaniah.

Linking an industrial past with an industrious present. Nonconformity with diversity. The local with the global. Entwining an uncertain present with a brighter future.

Alexander Stadium is that brighter future. Just before the twelfth lock, I step off my canal barge and amble along the towpath. The moon hangs hazily high up in the night sky, and I know that I have reached the end of my journey.

Now, as I turn right onto a track just before the Perry Barr Lock Bridge, I will see it. I will see the light of a July night in 2022, when thousands will gather for the opening ceremony of the twenty-second Commonwealth Games.

This is the light on which we pin all our hopes. This is the light that will bring us all together again, and draw us closer in international friendship. This is the light. This is Birmingham. This is Birmingham 2022.

NOTES

1   For more information see the CDC website, www.cdcgroup.com/en/about.
2   Neil Elkes, 'The Commonwealth has already come to Birmingham – so the Games will be more than welcome', *Birmingham Mail*, 12 July 2017. Available online at www.birmingham-hammail.co.uk/news/midlands-news/one-ten-brummies-born-overseas-13320715.

3   Presentation by Iain Reid, chief executive officer of Birmingham 2022 Commonwealth Games at Global Trade Conference, 24 June 2020.

4   Comment by Paul Faulkner, chief executive of Greater Birmingham Chambers of Commerce in panel discussion, 'Sport and Regeneration post-Brexit' at Global Birmingham – Beyond Brexit Conference organised by Centre for Brexit Studies, Birmingham City University, 23 September 2020.

5   More information can be found at www.birmingham2022.com/united.

6   Martin Kitchen, *The British Empire and Commonwealth: A Short History* (Basingstoke and London: Macmillan Press, 1996), pp.176–77.

7   Kitchen, p.177.

FURTHER READING

Archer, E.G., *Gibraltar, Identity and Empire* (Abingdon, Oxfordshire: Routledge, 2006).

Artmonsky, Ruth, *P&O: A History* (Oxford: Shire Publications, 2012).

Artmonsky, Ruth; Cox, Susie, *P&O: Across the Oceans, Across the Years: a Pictorial Voyage* (Woodbridge: Antique Collectors' Club, 2012).

Bashir, Tesawar (ed.), *The Sampad Story: A Twenty Year Retrospective* (Birmingham: Sampad South Asian Arts, 2010).

Beddoes, Keith; Wheeler, Colin & Stephen, *Metro-Cammell: 150 Years of Craftsmanship* (Cheltenham: Runpast Publishing, 1999).

Bhatia, Gautam, *Laurie Baker, Life, Works, Writings* (London: Penguin, 1994).

Bloomfield, Jon, *Our City: Migrants and the Making of Modern Birmingham* (London: Unbound, 2019).

Bourne, Stephen, *The Motherland Calls: Britain's Black Servicemen and Women 1939–45* (Stroud: The History Press, 2012).

Bourne, Stephen, *Black Poppies: Britain's Black Community and the Great War* (Cheltenham: The History Press, 2019).

Carpenter, Humphrey, *J.R.R. Tolkien: A Biography* (London: HarperCollins, 2016).

Chance, Toby & Williams, Peter, *Lighthouses: The Race to Illuminate the World* (London: New Holland Publishers, 2008).

Choudhury, Yousef & Drake, Peter, *From Bangladesh to Birmingham* (2001).

Crosby, Travis L., *Joseph Chamberlain: A Most Radical Imperialist* (London, New York: I.B. Taurus & Co., 2018).

Fage, J.D., *To Africa and Back: Memoirs* (Birmingham: Centre for African Studies, University of Birmingham, 2002).

Ferguson, Niall, *Empire: How Britain Made the Modern World* (London: Penguin Books, 2004).

Grosvenor, Ian; McLean, Rita & Roberts, Sian (eds), *Making Connections: Birmingham Black International History* (Birmingham Futures Group, 2002).

Gupta, Uma Das (ed.), *Friendships of 'largeness and freedom': Andrews, Tagore and Gandhi: An Epistolary Account 1912–1940* (New Delhi: Oxford University Press, 2018).

Kitchen, Martin, *The British Empire and Commonwealth: A Short History* (Basingstoke and London: Macmillan Press, 1996).

Marshall, P.J. (ed.), *The Cambridge Illustrated History of the British Empire* (Cambridge: Cambridge University Press, 1996).

Metcalf, B.D. & Metcalf, T.R., *A Concise History of Modern India* (Cambridge: Cambridge University Press, 2006).

Munro, Andy, *Going for a Balti: The Story of Birmingham's Signature Dish* (Studley, Warwickshire: Brewin Books, 2015).

Olusoga, David, *Black and British: A Forgotten History* (London: Pan Books, 2017).

Peet, Graham & Purshouse, Emma (eds). *Black Country Sikhs: Life in in the Sikh and other Communities of the Black Country* (West Bromwich: Multistory, 2017).

Reekes, Andrew, *Two Titans, One City: Joseph Chamberlain and George Cadbury* (Alcester, Warwickshire: West Midlands History Ltd, 2017).

Schama, Simon, *A History of Britain* (London: BBC Worldwide Ltd, 2003).

Sharma, S.R., *Life and Works of C.F. Andrews* (Jaipur, India: Book Enclave, 2009).

Skipp, Victor, *The Making of Victorian Birmingham* (Studley, Warwickshire: Brewin Books, 1996).

Stein, Burton, *A History of India* (Chichester: Wiley-Blackwell, 2010).

Uglow, Jenny, *The Lunar Men: The Friends who Made the Future* (London: Faber & Faber, 2002).

Upton, Chris, *A History of Birmingham* (Stroud: Phillimore & Co./The History Press, 2011).

Ward, Roger, *The Chamberlains: Joseph, Austen and Neville 1836–1940* (Stroud: Fonthill Media, 2015).

Williams, Kenneth, *The story of Ty-phoo and the Birmingham Tea Industry* (London: Quiller Press, 1990).

COUNTRIES AND TERRITORIES OF THE COMMONWEALTH

Africa

Botswana, Cameroon, The Gambia, Ghana, Kenya, Eswatini, Lesotho, Malawi, Mauritius, Mozambique, Namibia, Nigeria, Rwanda, Seychelles, Sierra Leone, South Africa, St Helena, Uganda, Tanzania, Zambia

Asia

Bangladesh, Brunei Darussalam, India, Malaysia, Maldives, Pakistan, Seychelles, Singapore, Sri Lanka

Caribbean and Americas

Anguilla, Antigua and Barbuda, Bahamas, Barbados, Belize, Bermuda, British Virgin Islands, Canada, Cayman Islands, Dominica, Falkland Islands, Grenada, Guyana, Jamaica, Montserrat, Saint Lucia, St Kitts and Nevis, St Vincent and The Grenadines, Trinidad and Tobago, Turks & Caicos Islands

Europe

Cyprus, England, Gibraltar, Guernsey, Isle of Man, Jersey, Malta, Northern Ireland, Scotland, Wales

Pacific

Australia, Cook Islands, Fiji, Kiribati, Nauru, Niue, New Zealand, Norfolk Island, Papua New Guinea, Samoa, Solomon Islands, Tonga, Tuvalu, Vanuatu

INDEX